500 Baking
Recipes

igloobooks

igloobooks

Published in 2014
by Igloo Books Ltd
Cottage Farm
Sywell
NN6 0BJ
www.igloobooks.com

SHE001 0714
2 4 6 8 10 9 7 5 3 1
ISBN 978-1-78343-219-6

Food photography and recipe development: PhotoCuisine UK
Front and back cover images © PhotoCuisine UK

Printed and manufactured in China

CONTENTS

CAKES AND BAKES

Grape Clafoutis

1
SERVES 6

Cherry Clafoutis
2

- Substitute the grapes for whole pitted cherries for a more classic version of the clafoutis.

Shiny Fruit Clafoutis
3

- For a shiny more sumptuous finish, warm 4 tablespoons of apricot jam in a pan, add a little water if necessary to thin. Strain through a sieve, and using a pastry brush, glaze the tart for a professional patisserie-style finish.

Prune Clafoutis
4

- Substitute the grapes for pitted prunes.

PREPARATION TIME 20 MINUTES

COOKING TIME 35–40 MINUTES

INGREDIENTS

75 g / 2 ½ oz / ⅓ cup caster (superfine) sugar, plus 1 tbsp to serve
75 g / 2 ½ oz / ⅓ cup butter
300 ml / 10 ½ fl. oz / 1 ¼ cups whole milk
2 large eggs
50 g / 1 ¾ oz / ⅓ cup plain (all purpose) flour
2 tbsp ground almonds
1 lemon, zest finely grated
300 g / 10 ½ oz / 2 cups mixed seedless grapes

- Preheat the oven to 190⁰C (170⁰C fan) / 375F / gas 5.
- Melt the butter in a saucepan and cook over a low heat until it starts to smell nutty.
- Brush a little of the butter around the inside of a 20 cm round pie dish then add a spoonful of caster sugar and shake to coat.
- Whisk together the milk and eggs with the rest of the butter.
- Sift the flour into a mixing bowl with a pinch of salt and stir in the ground almonds, lemon zest and the rest of the sugar.
- Make a well in the middle of the dry ingredients and gradually whisk in the liquid, incorporating all the flour from round the outside until you have a lump-free batter.
- Arrange the grapes in the prepared pie dish, pour over the batter and transfer to the oven immediately.
- Bake the clafoutis for 35–45 minutes or until a skewer inserted in the centre comes out clean.
- Serve warm or at room temperature, sprinkled with 1 tbsp sugar.

Apple and Cinnamon Loaf Cake

5
SERVES 8

- Preheat the oven to 170°C (150°C fan) / 325F / gas 3 and line a large loaf tin with non-stick baking paper.
- Sieve the flour, cinnamon and baking powder into a mixing bowl and add the sugar, butter and eggs.
- Beat the mixture with an electric whisk for 4 minutes or until smooth and well whipped.
- Fold in the chopped apples and scrape the mixture into the loaf tin.
- Bake for 55 minutes or until a skewer inserted in the centre comes out clean.
- Transfer the cake to a wire rack and leave to cool completely. Serve dusted with icing sugar.

PREPARATION TIME 15 MINUTES

COOKING TIME 55 MINUTES

INGREDIENTS

300 g / 10 ½ oz / 2 cups self-raising flour
2 tsp ground cinnamon
2 tsp baking powder
250 g / 9 oz / 1 ½ cups light brown sugar
250 g / 9 oz / 1 ¼ cups butter, softened
5 large eggs
2 eating apples, cored and chopped
icing (confectioners') sugar, to dust

Pear and Cinnamon Loaf

6

- Use 2 pears instead of apples for a different texture and flavour. Conference pears or similar work well in this recipe.

Apple and Poppy Seed Cake

7
SERVES 8

- Preheat the oven to 170°C (150°C fan) / 325F / gas 3 and butter a 23 cm round baking dish.
- Sieve the flour and baking powder into a mixing bowl and add the brown sugar, butter, eggs and half the poppy seeds.
- Beat the mixture with an electric whisk for 4 minutes or until smooth and well whipped.
- Sprinkle the rest of the poppy seeds and the caster sugar over the base of the baking dish and arrange the apple slices on top.
- Spoon the cake mixture on top of the apple and bake for 45 minutes or until a skewer inserted in the centre comes out clean.
- Leave the cake to cool for 20 minutes before turning out onto a serving plate.

PREPARATION TIME 20 MINUTES

COOKING TIME 45 MINUTES

INGREDIENTS

300 g / 10 ½ oz / 2 cups self-raising flour
2 tsp baking powder
250 g / 9 oz / 1 ½ cups dark brown sugar
250 g / 9 oz / 1 ¼ cups butter, softened
5 large eggs
2 tbsp poppy seeds
1 tbsp caster (superfine) sugar
3 eating apples, cored and sliced

Pear and Almond Upside-down Cake

8

- Substitute the apples for sliced pears and sprinkle with 4 tbsp of flaked (slivered) almonds.

9

SERVES 8

Apple and Cider Loaf Cake

PREPARATION TIME 15 MINUTES

COOKING TIME 55 MINUTES

INGREDIENTS

300 g / 10 ½ oz / 2 cups self-raising
flour
2 tsp baking powder
250 g / 9 oz / 1 ½ cups light brown
sugar
250 g / 9 oz / 1 ¼ cups butter,
softened
4 large eggs
100 ml / 3 ½ fl. oz / ⅓ cup dry cider
2 eating apples, coarsely grated
1 eating apple, cored, quartered and
sliced

- Preheat the oven to 170°C (150°C fan) / 325F / gas 3 and line
  a large loaf tin with non-stick baking paper.
- Sieve the flour and baking powder into a mixing bowl and add the rest of the ingredients, except the sliced apple.
- Beat the mixture with an electric whisk for 4 minutes or until smooth and well whipped.
- Scrape the mixture into the loaf tin and arrange the apple slices in 2 rows on top, slightly overlapping. Bake for 55 minutes or until a skewer inserted in the centre comes out clean.
- Transfer the cake to a wire rack and leave to cool completely.

Pear and Perry Loaf Cake

10

- Use pears (varieties such as Conference lend themselves well to this recipe) and Perry instead of cider for a different take on this classic loaf cake.

11

SERVES 8

Banana and Walnut Loaf Cake

PREPARATION TIME 10 MINUTES

COOKING TIME 55 MINUTES

INGREDIENTS

3 very ripe bananas
110 g / 4 oz / ½ cup soft light brown
sugar
2 large eggs
120 ml / 4 fl. oz / ½ cup sunflower oil
225 g / 8 oz / 1 ½ cups plain
(all purpose) flour
1 tsp bicarbonate of (baking) soda
75 g / 2 ½ oz / ⅔ cup walnuts,
chopped

- Preheat the oven to 170°C (150°C fan) / 325F / gas 3 and line a long thin loaf tin with non-stick baking paper.
- Mash the bananas roughly with a fork then whisk in the sugar, eggs and oil.
- Sieve the flour and bicarbonate of soda into the bowl and add the chopped walnuts. Stir just enough to evenly mix all the ingredients together.
- Scrape the mixture into the loaf tin and bake for 55 minutes or until a skewer inserted in the centre comes out clean.
- Transfer the cake to a wire rack and leave to cool completely.

Banana and Hazelnut Loaf

12

- Use the same quantity of chopped hazelnuts (cob nuts) instead of the walnuts to help bring out the fruity notes of the banana in this delicious loaf cake.

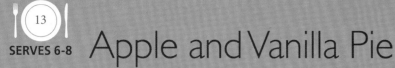

13
SERVES 6-8

Apple and Vanilla Pie

Apple and Nutmeg Pie

14

- For a more autumnal taste to this delicious pie use 1 teaspoon of freshly grated nutmeg instead of the vanilla pod.

Apple, Pear and Vanilla Pie

15

- Use half pear and half apple for a more fruity and delicious variation of this classic pie.

PREPARATION TIME 45 MINUTES

COOKING TIME 35–45 MINUTES

INGREDIENTS

125 g / 4 ½ oz / ½ cup caster (superfine) sugar
2 tbsp plain (all purpose) flour
1 vanilla pod, seeds only
900 g / 2 lb / 2 cups Bramley apples, peeled and chopped
1 egg, beaten

FOR THE PASTRY

300 g / 11 oz / 2 cups plain (all purpose) flour
150 g / 5 ½ oz / ⅔ cup butter, chilled

- Sieve the flour for the pastry into a mixing bowl. Dip the chilled butter in the flour then grate it into the bowl and mix evenly.
- Add enough cold water to bring it together into a pliable dough then chill for 30 minutes.
- Preheat the oven to 190°C (170 °C fan) / 355F / gas 5 and butter a 23 cm round pie tin.
- Mix the sugar, flour and vanilla seeds together then add the apples and mix together.
- Roll out half the pastry on a floured surface and use it to line the pie tin.
- Pack the apples into the pastry case and brush around the top of the pastry with beaten egg.
- Roll out the other half of the pastry and lay it over the apples. Press down round the outside to seal.
- Crimp the edges and trim away any excess pastry.
- Make a couple of holes in the top with a knife and brush with beaten egg then bake for 35–45 minutes – the pastry should be crisp and golden brown on top and starting to shrink away from the edge of the tin.

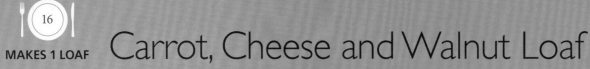

16

MAKES 1 LOAF

Carrot, Cheese and Walnut Loaf

Parsnip, Parmesan and Pine Nut Bread

17

- Use parsnip instead of carrot, Parmesan instead of Cheddar and coarsely chopped pine nuts instead of the walnuts.

Potato, Cheese and Walnut Bread

18

- Replace the carrot with the same weight of cold cooked potatoes, either mashed or finely chopped.

Carrot, Blue Cheese and Walnut Bread

19

- A good quality blue cheese, broken into small chunks, combined with the walnuts makes a delicious festive style savoury loaf cake.

PREPARATION TIME 2 HOURS 30 MINUTES

COOKING TIME 35–45 MINUTES

....

INGREDIENTS

400 g / 14 oz / 2 ⅔ cups strong white bread flour, plus extra for dusting
½ tsp easy blend dried yeast
1 tbsp caster (superfine) sugar
1 tsp fine sea salt
100 g / 3 ½ oz / ¾ cup carrot, grated
100 g / 3 ½ oz / 1 cup Cheddar cheese, grated
100 g / 3 ½ oz / ¾ cup walnuts, roughly chopped

- In a large bowl, mix together the flour, yeast, sugar and salt. Stir the grated carrot, cheese and walnuts into 280 ml of warm water.
- Stir it into the dry ingredients then knead the mixture on a lightly oiled surface with your hands for 10 minutes or until the dough is smooth and elastic.
- Leave the dough to rest in a lightly oiled bowl, covered with oiled cling film, for 1–2 hours.
- Punch the dough with your fist to knock out the air then knead it for 2 more minutes.
- Roll the dough with your hands into a fat sausage, then turn it 90⁰ and roll it tightly the other way. Tuck the ends under and transfer the dough to a large loaf tin, keeping the seam underneath.
- Cover the tin loosely with oiled cling film and leave to prove somewhere warm for 45 minutes.
- Preheat the oven to 220⁰C (200⁰C fan) / 325F / gas 7.
- Bake for 35–40 minutes or until the loaf sounds hollow when you tap it underneath. Transfer the bread to a wire rack and leave to cool completely before slicing.

Pineapple Upside-down Cake

20

SERVES 8

- Preheat the oven to 170°C (150°C fan) / 325F / gas 3 and butter a 23 cm round cake tin.
- Sieve the flour and baking powder into a mixing bowl and add sugar, butter and eggs.
- Beat the mixture with an electric whisk for 4 minutes or until smooth and well whipped.
- Spread the jam over the base of the cake tin and arrange the pineapple rings on top.
- Spoon in the cake mixture and bake for 35 minutes or until a skewer inserted in the centre comes out clean.
- Leave the cake to cool for 20 minutes before turning out onto a serving plate.

PREPARATION TIME 15 MINUTES

COOKING TIME 35 MINUTES

INGREDIENTS

300 g / 10 ½ oz / 2 cups self-raising flour
2 tsp baking powder
250 g / 9 oz / 1 ¼ cups caster (superfine) sugar
250 g / 9 oz / 1 ¼ cups butter, softened
5 large eggs
4 tbsp raspberry jam (jelly)
4 canned pineapple rings, drained

Banana Upside-down Cake

21

- Use 3 ripe bananas, sliced into ½ cm rounds, instead of the pineapple for a delicious fruity twist to this classic upside-down cake.

Chocolate Brownies

22

MAKES 9

- Preheat the oven to 170°C (150°C fan) / 325F / gas 3 and oil and line a 20 cm square cake tin.
- Melt the chocolate, cocoa and butter together in a saucepan, then leave to cool a little.
- Whisk the sugar and eggs together with an electric whisk for 3 minutes or until very light and creamy.
- Pour in the chocolate mixture and sieve over the flour, then fold everything together until evenly mixed.
- Scrape into the tin and bake for 35–40 minutes or until the outside is set, but the centre is still quite soft, as it will continue to cook as it cools.
- Leave the brownie to cool completely before cutting into 9 squares.

PREPARATION TIME 25 MINUTES

COOKING TIME 35–40 MINUTES

INGREDIENTS

110 g / 4 oz / ½ cup milk chocolate, chopped
85 g / 3 oz / ¾ cup unsweetened cocoa powder, sifted
225 g / 8 oz / 1 cup butter
450 g /15 oz / 2 ½ cups light brown sugar
4 large eggs
110 g / 4 oz / ⅔ cup self-raising flour

Double Chocolate Brownies

23

- Instead of using one type of chocolate use half milk or dark and half white for an extra sweet take on this delicious tray bake.

Chocolate Sponge Squares

24

MAKES 12

PREPARATION TIME 15 MINUTES

COOKING TIME 30–35 MINUTES

....

INGREDIENTS

150 g / 5 ½ oz / 1 cup self-raising flour
28 g / 1 oz / ¼ cup unsweetened cocoa powder
2 tsp baking powder
175 g / 6 oz / ¾ cup caster (superfine) sugar
175 g / 6 oz / ¾ cup butter, softened
3 eggs

TO DECORATE

12 silver or gold dragees or sugar-coated cake decorations

- Preheat the oven to 180°C (160°C fan) / 350F / gas 4 and grease and line a 30 cm x 23 cm cake tin.
- Put all of the cake ingredients in a large mixing bowl and whisk them together with an electric whisk for 4 minutes or until pale and well whipped.
- Scrape the mixture into the tin and level the top with a spatula.
- Bake for 30–35 minutes. The cake is ready when a toothpick inserted in the centre comes out clean.
- Transfer the cake to a wire rack to cool completely before cutting into 12 squares and topping each one with a silver dragee.

Chocolate and Coffee Squares **25**

- Add 2 tablespoons of espresso or very strong coffee to the batter mix for a more grown up take on this delicious cake.

Chestnut Bread with Pine Nuts and Raisins

26

MAKES 1 LOAF

PREPARATION TIME 2 HOURS 30 MINUTES

COOKING TIME 35–40 MINUTES

....

INGREDIENTS

200 g / 7 oz / 1 ⅓ cups chestnut flour
200 g / 7 oz / 1 ⅓ cups strong white bread flour, plus extra for dusting
½ tsp easy blend dried yeast
1 tbsp caster (superfine) sugar
1 tsp fine sea salt
2 tbsp olive oil
100 g / 3 ½ oz / ¾ cup pine nuts
100 g / 3 ½ oz / ½ cup raisins
2 tbsp runny honey

- In a large bowl, mix together the flours, yeast, sugar and salt. Stir the oil, pine nuts and raisins into 280 ml of warm water and stir it into the dry ingredients.
- Knead the mixture on a lightly oiled surface for 10 minutes or until the dough is smooth and elastic.
- Leave the dough to rest in a lightly oiled bowl, covered with oiled cling film, for 1–2 hours or until doubled in size.
- Transfer the dough to an oiled roasting tin and push it out with your fingers to fill the bottom.
- Cover again with oiled cling film and leave to prove for 1 hour or until doubled in size.
- Meanwhile, preheat the oven to 220°C (200°C fan) / 425F / gas 7.
- Bake for 35–40 minutes or until the loaf sounds hollow when you tap it underneath. Transfer the bread to a wire rack and brush with honey; then leave to cool.

Chestnut Bread with Cranberry and Almond **27**

- Use chopped dried cranberries instead of raisins and chopped almonds instead of the pine nuts.

28
SERVES 8

Rhubarb and Chestnut Loaf Cake

- Preheat the oven to 170°C (150°C fan) / 325F / gas 3 and line a large loaf tin with non-stick baking paper.
- Sieve the flours and baking powder into a mixing bowl and add the sugar, butter and eggs.
- Beat the mixture with an electric whisk for 4 minutes or until smooth and well whipped then fold in the rhubarb.
- Scrape the mixture into the loaf tin and bake for 55 minutes or until a skewer inserted in the centre comes out clean.
- Transfer the cake to a wire rack and leave to cool completely.

PREPARATION TIME 10 MINUTES

COOKING TIME 55 MINUTES

INGREDIENTS

200 g / 7 oz / 1 ⅓ cups self-raising flour
100 g / 3 ½ oz / ⅔ cup chestnut flour
2 tsp baking powder
250 g / 9 oz / 1 ½ cups light brown sugar
250 g / 9 oz / 1 ¼ cups butter, softened
5 large eggs
2 sticks rhubarb, chopped

Rhubarb, Chestnut and Chocolate Loaf Cake

29

- Add 2 tbsp of chocolate chips to the mix, at the same time as you add the rhubarb.

30
SERVES 8

Chocolate and Cherry Summer Pudding

- Put the cherries in a bowl with the sugar and kirsch and leave to macerate for 2 hours. Line a pudding basin with cling film.
- Put the cherries in a sieve and collect the juice.
- Dip the bread in the cherry juice and use it to line the pudding basin, saving one slice for the lid.
- Bring the cream to a simmer then pour it over the chocolate and stir gently to emulsify.
- Fold the cherries into the chocolate ganache and spoon it into the pudding basin.
- Top with the last slice of soaked bread then cover the basin with cling film.
- Put a small board on top of the pudding basin and weigh it down with a can, then leave it to chill in the fridge for at least 4 hours.
- Invert the pudding onto a plate and peel away the film.

PREPARATION TIME 15 MINUTES

INGREDIENTS

300 g / 10 ½ oz / 2 cups cherries, stoned and halved
4 tbsp caster (superfine) sugar
1 tbsp kirsch
6 slices white bread, crusts removed
250 ml / 9 fl. oz / 1 cup double (heavy) cream
250 g / 9 oz / 1 ½ cups dark chocolate (minimum 60 % cocoa solids), chopped

White Chocolate and Raspberry Summer Pudding

31

- Use white chocolate instead of dark, replace the cherries with the same weight of raspberries, and soak them in framboise liqueur instead of kirsch.

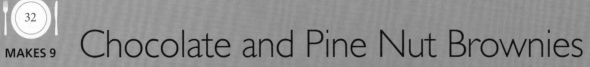

32
MAKES 9

Chocolate and Pine Nut Brownies

Chocolate and Hazelnut Brownies

33

- Hazelnuts (cob nuts) make a great alternative to pine nuts and give this decadent brownie an extra nutty quality. Roughly chop them before using.

Chocolate and Fudge Brownies

34

- If you fancy a change from chocolate and nuts then use chocolate and mini fudge pieces. These little sweet nuggets give a delicious extra chewy texture to the brownie.

PREPARATION TIME 25 MINUTES

COOKING TIME 35–40 MINUTES

INGREDIENTS

110 g / 4 oz / ½ cups milk chocolate, chopped
85 g / 3 oz / ¾ cup unsweetened cocoa powder, sifted
225 g / 8 oz / 1 cup butter
450 g / 15 oz / 2 ½ cups light brown sugar
4 large eggs
110 g / 4 oz / ⅔ cup self-raising flour
85 g / 3 oz / ⅔ cup pine nuts

- Preheat the oven to 170°C (150°C fan) / 325F / gas 3 and oil and line a 20 cm square cake tin.
- Melt the chocolate, cocoa and butter together in a saucepan, then leave to cool a little.
- Whisk the sugar and eggs together with an electric whisk for 3 minutes or until very light and creamy.
- Pour in the chocolate mixture and sieve over the flour, then fold everything together with the pine nuts until evenly mixed.
- Scrape into the tin and bake for 35–40 minutes or until the outside is set, but the centre is still quite soft, as it will continue to cook as it cools.
- Leave the brownie to cool completely before cutting into 9 squares.

Mini Chocolate Orange Loaf Cakes

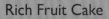
35
MAKES 12

- Preheat the oven to 180°C (160°C fan) / 350F / gas 4 and line 12 mini loaf cake tins with cases.
- Beat the egg in a jug with the oil and the orange juice and zest until well mixed.
- Mix the flour, cocoa, baking powder, sugar, hazelnuts and chocolate in a bowl, then pour in the egg mixture and stir just enough to combine.
- Divide the mixture between the paper cases, then bake in the oven for 20–25 minutes.
- Test with a wooden toothpick, if it comes out clean, the cakes are done.
- Transfer the cakes to a wire rack and leave to cool completely.

PREPARATION TIME 25 MINUTES

COOKING TIME 20–25 MINUTES

INGREDIENTS

1 large egg
120 ml / 4 fl. oz / ½ cup sunflower oil
120 ml / 4 fl. oz / ½ cup orange juice
1 tbsp orange zest, finely grated
375 g / 12 ½ oz / 2 ½ cups self-raising flour, sifted
55 g / 2 oz / ½ cup unsweetened cocoa powder, sifted
1 tsp baking powder
200 g / 7 oz / ¾ cup caster (superfine) sugar
75 g / 2 ½ oz / ⅔ cup hazelnuts (cob nuts), chopped
110 g / 4 oz / ½ cup dark chocolate (minimum 60% cocoa solids), chopped

Chocolate, Coffee and Hazelnut Mini Loaf Cakes

36

- For a richer tasting mini loaf cake use 120 ml / 4 fl.oz strong coffee instead of the orange juice.

Light Fruit Cake

37
SERVES 8

- Preheat the oven to 180°C (160°C fan) / 355F / gas 4 and line a loaf tin with non-stick baking paper.
- Sieve the flour into a mixing bowl and rub in the butter until it resembles fine breadcrumbs then stir in the sugar, dried fruit, cherries and lemon zest.
- Lightly beat the egg with the milk and stir it into the dry ingredients until just combined.
- Scrape the mixture into the loaf tin and bake for 55 minutes or until a skewer inserted into the centre comes out clean.
- Transfer the cake to a wire rack and leave to cool completely.

PREPARATION TIME 15 MINUTES

COOKING TIME 55 MINUTES

INGREDIENTS

225 g / 8 oz / 1 ½ cups self-raising flour
100 g / 3 ½ oz / ½ cup butter, cubed
100 g / 3 ½ oz / ½ cup caster (superfine) sugar
100 g / 3 ½ oz / ⅔ cup mixed dried fruit
8 glacé cherries, quartered
1 tsp grated lemon zest
1 large egg
75 ml / 2 ½ fl. oz / ⅓ cup whole milk

Rich Fruit Cake

38

- Using dark muscovado sugar and adding a tablespoon of brandy to the basic mixture, will give this cake a richer, fruitier flavour.

39

SERVES 8-10

Coconut Cake with Redcurrant Compote

PREPARATION TIME 20 MINUTES

COOKING TIME 45–55 MINUTES

INGREDIENTS

225 g / 8 oz / 1 cup butter, softened
225 g / 8 oz / 1 cup caster (superfine) sugar
4 large eggs, beaten
225 g / 4 ½ oz / 1 ½ cups self-raising flour
100 g / 3 ½ oz / 1 cup desiccated coconut

FOR THE COMPOTE

100 g / 3 ½ oz / ⅔ cup redcurrants
4 tbsp caster (superfine) sugar

- Preheat the oven to 180⁰C (160⁰ C fan) / 355F / gas 4 and grease and line a 23 cm round cake tin with greaseproof paper.
- Cream the butter and sugar together then gradually whisk in the eggs, beating well after each addition.
- Fold in the flour and coconut then scrape the mixture into the tin.
- Bake the cake for 45–55 minutes or until a skewer inserted in the centre comes out clean.
- Meanwhile, put the redcurrants in a small saucepan with the sugar. Cover and cook gently for 5 minutes then remove the lid, give it a stir and cook for a few more minutes until the redcurrants start to burst and the juices thicken.
- Leave the cake to cool for 20 minutes before serving warm with the compote spooned over the top.

Coconut Cake with Gooseberry Compote

40

- Use tart gooseberries instead of the redcurrants. Check the tartness and add an extra tbsp of sugar to taste if necessary.

41

MAKES 12

Flower Cupcakes

PREPARATION TIME 20 MINUTES

COOKING TIME 15–20 MINUTES

INGREDIENTS

110 g / 4 oz / ⅔ cup self-raising flour, sifted
110 g / 4 oz / ½ cup caster (superfine) sugar
110 g / 4 oz / ½ cup butter, softened
2 large eggs
1 tsp vanilla extract

TO DECORATE

110 g / 4 oz / ½ butter, softened
225 g / 8 oz / 2 ¼ cups icing (confectioner's) sugar
2 tbsp milk
a few drops of food dye
sugar flowers to decorate

- Preheat the oven to 190⁰C (170⁰C fan) / 375F / gas 5 and line a 12-hole cupcake tin with paper cases.
- Combine the flour, sugar, butter, eggs and vanilla extract in a bowl and whisk together until smooth.
- Divide the mixture between the paper cases, then bake for 15–20 minutes.
- Test with a wooden toothpick, if it comes out clean, the cakes are done.
- Transfer the cakes to a wire rack and leave to cool.
- To make the buttercream, beat the butter with a wooden spoon until light and fluffy then beat in the icing sugar a quarter at a time. Use a whisk to incorporate the milk then whisk until smooth.
- Divide the buttercream into separate bowls and stir in the food colourings of your choice.
- Spread the buttercream onto the cakes and decorate each one with a sugar flower.

Flower Essence Cupcakes

42

- For extra depth of flavour you could add a few drops of flower essence such as rose to your buttercream before piping.

Fresh Fruit Sponge Pudding

43
SERVES 6

Dried Fruit Sponge Pudding

 44

- Substitute the fresh fruit with 4 dried apricots and 55 g / 1 oz / ⅓ each of raisins and prunes. Soak in hot water for 5 minutes then quarter the apricots and prunes before using.

Brandy and Fruit Sponge Pudding

45

- Add 3 tablespoons of brandy to the dried fruit sponge mixture before baking.

PREPARATION TIME 15 MINUTES

COOKING TIME 30–35 MINUTES

INGREDIENTS

110 g / 4 oz / ⅔ cup self-raising flour, sifted
110 g / 4 oz / ½ cup caster (superfine) sugar
110 g / 4 oz / ½ cup butter, softened
2 large eggs
1 tsp vanilla extract
2 plums, cut into eighths
55 g / 1 oz / ⅓ cup raspberries
55 g / 1 oz / ⅓ cup seedless black grapes

- Preheat the oven to 190°C (170°C fan) / 375F / gas 5 and butter a small baking dish.
- Combine the flour, sugar, butter, eggs and vanilla extract in a bowl and whisk together for 2 minutes or until smooth.
- Arrange half of the fruit in the baking dish and spoon in the cake mixture.
- Top with the rest of the fruit then bake for 30–35 minutes.
- Test with a wooden toothpick, if it comes out clean, the cake is done.
- Serve warm with custard or cream.

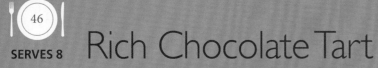

46

SERVES 8

Rich Chocolate Tart

Rich Chocolate and Rum Tart

47

- After adding the butter to the ganache mixture, drizzle in 2 tablespoons of rum for deeper, richer tart.

Rich Chocolate and Gold Leaf Tart

48

- Once the tart is finished and set add a little gold leaf to the ganache topping for decadent look and finish.

PREPARATION TIME 25 MINUTES

COOKING TIME 15–20 MINUTES

INGREDIENTS

250 ml / 9 fl. oz / 1 cup double cream
250 g / 9 oz / 1 ½ cups dark chocolate (minimum 60 % cocoa solids), chopped
55 g / 2 oz / ¼ cup butter, softened

FOR THE PASTRY

100 g / 3 ½ oz / ½ cup butter, cubed
200 g / 7 oz / 1 ⅓ cup plain (all purpose) flour
55 g / 2 oz / ¼ cup caster (superfine) sugar
1 egg, beaten

- Preheat the oven to 200⁰C (180⁰C fan) / 390F / gas 6.
- To make the pastry, rub the butter into the flour and sugar and add the egg with just enough cold water to bind.
- Wrap the dough in cling film and chill for 30 minutes then roll out on a floured surface.
- Use the pastry to line a 23 cm loose-bottomed tart tin and trim the edges.
- Prick the pastry with a fork, line with cling film and fill with baking beans or rice.
- Bake for 10 minutes then remove the cling film and baking beans and cook for another 8 minutes to crisp.
- Heat the cream to simmering point then pour it over the chocolate and stir until smooth.
- Add the butter and blend it in with a stick blender.
- Pour the ganache into the pastry case and level the top with a palette knife.
- Leave the ganache to cool and set for at least 2 hours before cutting and serving.

Grape and Mascarpone Tart

49 SERVES 8

- Preheat the oven to 200°C (180°C fan) / 390F / gas 6.
- To make the pastry, rub the butter into the flour and add just enough cold water to bind.
- Chill for 30 minutes then roll out on a floured surface. Use the pastry to line a regular tart tin.
- Prick the pastry with a fork, line with cling film and fill with baking beans or rice.
- Bake for 10 minutes then remove the cling film and baking beans.
- Brush the inside of the pastry case with beaten egg and cook for another 8 minutes to crisp.
- Whisk the mascarpone cheese with the icing sugar and vanilla extract until smooth.
- When the pastry case has cooled to room temperature, spoon in the filling and level the top.
- Cut the grapes in half and arrange in alternating lines.

Summer Berry and Mascarpone Tart
50

- Use a mix of summer berries such as strawberries, raspberries and blueberries for a colourful topping to this delicious tart.

PREPARATION TIME 20 MINUTES

COOKING TIME 15–20 MINUTES

INGREDIENTS

450 g / 1 lb / 2 cups mascarpone cheese
100 g / 3 ½ oz / 1 cup icing (confectioners') sugar
1 tsp vanilla extract
a small bunch red seedless grapes
a small bunch green seedless grapes

FOR THE PASTRY
200 g / 7 oz / 1 ⅓ cups plain (all purpose) flour
100 g / 3 ½ oz / ½ cup butter, cubed
1 egg, beaten

Custard Tarts with Marsala Sultanas

51 MAKES 12

- Bring the Masala almost to a simmer then take the pan off the heat and pour it over the sultanas. Cover and leave to macerate overnight.
- Preheat the oven to 200°C (180°C fan) / 390F / gas 6.
- To make the pastry, rub the butter into the flour and add just enough cold water to bind.
- Chill for 30 minutes then roll out on a floured surface. Cut out 12 circles with a pastry cutter, rerolling the trimmings as necessary, and use them to line a 12-hole cupcake tin.
- Whisk the custard ingredients together in a jug and three quarter fill the pastry cases.
- Bake the tarts for 15–20 minutes or until the custard has set and the pastry is crisp.
- Serve warm or at room temperature with a sprinkling of icing sugar and the sultanas spooned over.

Custard Tarts with Sweet Sherry Sultanas
52

- If you find Marsala difficult to find or not to your taste, a sweet sherry will work just as well in these delicious tarts.

PREPARATION TIME 45 MINUTES

COOKING TIME 15–20 MINUTES

INGREDIENTS

100 ml / 3 ½ fl. oz / ½ cup Marsala
150 g / 5 ½ oz / ¾ cup golden sultanas
icing (confectioners') sugar to dust

FOR THE PASTRY
200 g / 7 oz / 1 ⅓ cups plain (all purpose) flour
100 g / 3 ½ oz / ½ cup butter, cubed

FOR THE CUSTARD
2 large egg yolks
55 g / 2 oz / ¼ cup caster (superfine) sugar
1 tsp vanilla extract
2 tsp cornflour (cornstarch)
225 ml / 8 fl. oz / ¾ cup double (heavy) cream

53 MAKES 12 Lemon Madeleines

PREPARATION TIME
1 HOUR 30 MINUTES

COOKING TIME 10–15 MINUTES

INGREDIENTS

110 g / 4 oz / ½ cup butter
55 g / 2 oz / ⅓ cup plain (all purpose) flour
1 lemon, zest finely grated
55 g / 2 oz / ½ cup ground almonds
110 g / 4 oz / 1 cup icing (confectioners') sugar
3 large egg whites

- Heat the butter until it foams and starts to smell nutty then leave to cool.
- Combine the flour, lemon zest, ground almonds and icing sugar in a bowl and whisk in the egg whites.
- Pour the cooled butter into the bowl and whisk into the mixture until evenly mixed.
- Leave the cake mixture to rest in the fridge for an hour.
- Preheat the oven to 170°C (150°C fan) / 325F / gas 3 and oil and flour a 12-hole Madeleine mould.
- Spoon the mixture into the moulds, then transfer the tin to the oven and bake for 10–15 minutes.
- Test with a wooden toothpick, if it comes out clean, the cakes are done.
- Transfer the cakes to a wire rack to cool for 5 minutes before serving.

Orange Madeleines 54

- Swap the zest of the lemon for the zest of half a large navel orange for a different take on this classic recipe.

55 SERVES 10 Chocolate and Almond Marble Loaf

PREPARATION TIME 25 MINUTES

COOKING TIME 45–50 MINUTES

INGREDIENTS

100 g / 3 ½ oz / ⅔ cup self-raising flour
1 tsp baking powder
50 g / 1 ¾ oz / ½ cup ground almonds
150 g / 5 ½ oz / ⅔ cup caster (superfine) sugar
150 g / 5 ½ oz / ⅔ cup butter, softened
3 large eggs
2 tbsp cocoa powder
4 tbsp flaked (slivered) almonds

- Preheat the oven to 180°C (160°C fan), 355F, gas 4 and grease and line a loaf tin with greaseproof paper.
- Sieve the flour and baking powder into a mixing bowl then add the ground almonds, sugar, butter and eggs and whisk with an electric whisk for 4 minutes or until pale and well whipped.
- Divide the mixture into 2 bowls. Mix the cocoa powder with 2 tbsp hot water until smooth and stir it into one of the bowls.
- Spoon the mixtures into the tin, alternating between chocolate and plain, then draw a knife down the centre to marble.
- Sprinkle with flaked almonds and bake for 45–50 minutes. The cake is ready when a toothpick inserted in the centre comes out clean.
- Transfer the cake to a wire rack to cool completely.

Chocolate and Pistachio Marble Loaf Cake 56

- Grind the pistachios up until they resemble the rough texture of the ground almonds and use 4 tbsp of chopped pistachios to top the cake before baking.

57
SERVES 8

Green Tea and Raspberry Loaf Cake

- Preheat the oven to 170°C (150°C fan) / 340F / gas 3 and line a large loaf tin with non-stick baking paper.
- Sieve the flour, matcha and baking powder into a mixing bowl and add the sugar, butter and eggs.
- Beat the mixture with an electric whisk for 4 minutes or until smooth and well whipped.
- Fold in the raspberries and scrape the mixture into the loaf tin.
- Bake for 55 minutes or until a skewer inserted in the centre comes out clean.
- Transfer the cake to a wire rack and leave to cool completely.

PREPARATION TIME 15 MINUTES

COOKING TIME 55 MINUTES

....

INGREDIENTS

300 g / 10 ½ oz / 2 cups self-raising flour
2 tbsp matcha green tea powder
2 tsp baking powder
250 g / 9 oz / 1 ¼ cups caster (superfine) sugar
250 g / 9 oz / 1 ¼ cups butter, softened
5 large eggs
75 g / 2 ½ oz / ½ cup raspberries

Green Tea and Cherry Loaf Cake
58
- Use 75 g / 2 ½ oz / ½ cup fresh pitted cherries instead of the raspberries for a slightly firmer fruit texture to the loaf cake.

59
SERVES 8

Chocolate Orange Loaf Cake

- Preheat the oven to 180°C (160°C fan) / 355F / gas 4 and grease and line a small loaf tin with greaseproof paper.
- Cream together the butter, sugar and orange zest until well whipped then gradually whisk in the eggs, beating well after each addition.
- Sift over and fold in the flour and cocoa powder.
- Scrape the mixture into the tin and bake for 45 minutes or until a skewer inserted in the centre comes out clean.
- Turn the loaf out onto a wire rack and leave to cool completely before decorating with candied peel.

PREPARATION TIME 15 MINUTES

COOKING TIME 45 MINUTES

....

INGREDIENTS

225 g / 8 oz / 1 cup butter, softened
225 g / 8 oz / 1 cup caster (superfine) sugar
1 orange, zest finely grated
4 large eggs, beaten
225 g / 8 oz / 1 ½ cups self-raising flour
1 tbsp unsweetened cocoa powder
55 g / 1 oz / ⅓ cup candied orange peel

Chocolate, Coffee and Orange Cake
60
- After incorporating the eggs add 2 tablespoons of strong coffee or espresso to the cake mixture for a richer fuller flavoured cake.

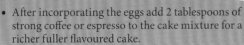

Peach Cake with Lemon Thyme Sugar

61

SERVES 8

PREPARATION TIME 25 MINUTES

COOKING TIME 55 MINUTES

....

INGREDIENTS

225 g / 8 oz / 1 ½ cups self-raising flour
100 g / 3 ½ oz / ½ cup butter, cubed
100 g / 3 ½ oz / ½ cup caster (superfine) sugar
1 large egg
75 ml / 2 ½ fl. oz / ⅓ cup whole milk
4 peaches, halved and stoned

FOR THE LEMON THYME SUGAR

1 tbsp lemon thyme leaves
60 g / 2 oz / ¼ cup caster (superfine) sugar

- Preheat the oven to 180°C (160°C fan) / 355F / gas 4 and butter a round baking dish.
- First make the lemon thyme sugar. Bruise the thyme leaves with a mortar and pestle then add half the sugar and pound again. Stir in the rest of the sugar and set aside.
- Sieve the flour into a mixing bowl and rub in the butter until it resembles fine breadcrumbs then stir in the sugar.
- Lightly beat the egg with the milk and stir it into the dry ingredients until just combined.
- Scrape the mixture into the baking dish and level the surface then press in the peach halves, cut side up.
- Bake the cake for 55 minutes or until a skewer inserted in the centre comes out clean.
- Transfer the cake to a wire rack and sprinkle with the lemon thyme sugar then leave to cool completely.

Peach Cake with Lavender Sugar   **62**

- Use edible lavender flowers for a more aromatic but delicious cake. Follow recipe above using 1 tablespoon of lavender instead of the lemon thyme.

Golden Syrup Cake

63

SERVES 8

PREPARATION TIME 15 MINUTES

COOKING TIME 30 MINUTES

....

INGREDIENTS

110 g / 4 oz / ⅔ cup self-raising flour, sifted
110 g / 4 oz / ½ cup soft brown sugar
110 g / 4 oz / ½ cup butter, softened
2 large eggs
1 tsp vanilla extract
225 g / 8 oz / ⅔ cup golden syrup

- Preheat the oven to 190°C (170°C fan) / 375F / gas 5 and butter a shallow baking dish.
- Combine the flour, sugar, butter, eggs and vanilla extract in a bowl and whisk together for 2 minutes or until smooth.
- Spoon the golden syrup into the baking dish and level the surface and spoon the cake mixture on top.
- Bake the cake for 30 minutes then leave to cool in the dish for 10 minutes.
- Wearing oven gloves, put a large plate on top of the dish then turn them both over in one smooth movement to unmould the cake.
- Serve warm with cream or ice cream.

Black Treacle Cake   **64**

- For a deeper, richer flavour use 175 g / 6 oz / ½ cup golden syrup and 50 g / 2 fl. oz / ¼ cup of black treacle.

Coffee and Almond Sponge

65

SERVES 10

Chocolate and Hazelnut Cake

66

- Use 2 tablespoons of cocoa powder instead of the coffee and swap the almonds for finely chopped hazelnuts (cob nuts) for a deliciously decadent cake.

Green Tea and Almond Cake

67

- Use the same quantity of Matcha green tea as you would espresso coffee for a delicate and delicious cake.

PREPARATION TIME 30 MINUTES

COOKING TIME 35–40 MINUTES

INGREDIENTS

200 g / 7 oz / 1 ⅓ cups self-raising flour
200 g / 7 oz / ¾ cup caster (superfine) sugar
200 g / 7 oz / ¾ cup butter
4 eggs
1 tsp baking powder
1 tbsp instant espresso powder

TO DECORATE

200 g / 7 oz / ¾ cup butter, softened
400 g / 14 oz / 4 cups icing (confectioners') sugar
1 tbsp instant espresso powder
100 g / 3 ½ oz / 1 ⅓ cups flaked (slivered) almonds, toasted
6 chocolate coated coffee beans

- Preheat the oven to 180°C (160°C fan) / 355F / gas 4 and grease and line 2 x 20 cm round loose-bottomed cake tins.
- Put all of the cake ingredients in a large mixing bowl and whisk them together with an electric whisk for 4 minutes or until pale and well whipped.
- Divide the mixture between the 2 tins and bake for 35–40 minutes. The cakes are ready when a toothpick inserted in the centre comes out clean.
- Transfer the cakes to a wire rack to cool completely.
- To make the buttercream, whisk the butter with an electric whisk then gradually add the icing sugar and espresso powder. Whisk until smooth and well whipped. If the mixture is too stiff add a tablespoon of warm water.
- Use half of the buttercream to sandwich the 2 cakes together and spread the rest over the top and sides with a palette knife. Draw lines across the top of the cake with the back of a fork.
- Press the almonds onto the side of the cake with your hands and decorate the top with coffee beans.

Clementine Upside-down Cake

68

SERVES 8

PREPARATION TIME 20 MINUTES

COOKING TIME 35 MINUTES

....

INGREDIENTS

300 g / 10 ½ oz / 2 cups self-raising
flour
2 tsp baking powder
250 g / 9 oz / 1 ¼ cups caster
(superfine) sugar
250 g / 9 oz / 1 ¼ cups butter,
softened
5 large eggs
4 tbsp golden syrup
4 clementines, thinly sliced

- Preheat the oven to 170°C (150°C fan) / 325F / gas 3 and butter a 23 cm round cake tin.
- Sieve the flour and baking powder into a mixing bowl and add sugar, butter and eggs.
- Beat the mixture with an electric whisk for 4 minutes or until smooth and well whipped.
- Spread the golden syrup over the base of the cake tin and arrange the clementine slices on top and up the sides of the tin.
- Spoon in the cake mixture and bake for 35 minutes or until a skewer inserted in the centre comes out clean.
- Leave the cake to cool for 20 minutes before turning out onto a serving plate.

Lemon Upside-down Cake

69

- This cake works well with very thinly sliced lemons. Use 2 unwaxed lemons cut very thinly and lightly coat in 2 tablespoons of sugar and follow as per recipe above.

70

MAKES 12

Marmalade Sponge Squares

PREPARATION TIME 25 MINUTES

COOKING TIME 30–35 MINUTES

....

INGREDIENTS

175 g / 6 oz / 1 ¼ cups self-raising
flour
2 tsp baking powder
175 g / 6 oz / ¾ cup caster (superfine)
sugar
175 g / 6 oz / ¾ cup butter
3 eggs
4 tbsp marmalade

TO DECORATE
1–2 tsp orange juice
100 g / 3 ½ oz / 1 cup icing
(confectioners') sugar
orange rind and leaves

- Preheat the oven to 180°C (160°C fan), 355F, gas 4 and grease and line a 30 cm x 23 cm cake tin.
- Put all of the cake ingredients in a large mixing bowl and whisk them together with an electric whisk for 4 minutes or until pale and well whipped.
- Scrape the mixture into the tin and level the top with a spatula.
- Bake for 30–35 minutes. The cake is ready when a toothpick inserted in the centre comes out clean.
- Transfer the cake to a wire rack to cool completely.
- Stir the orange juice into the icing sugar drop by drop until you reach a spreadable consistency.
- Spread the icing over the cake and cut into squares then decorate with the orange rind and leaves.

Apricot Sponge Squares

71

- Swap the marmalade for apricot jam for a sweeter less tart sponge cake.

72
SERVES 10

Orange Drizzle Cake

- Preheat the oven to 180°C (160°C fan) / 350F / gas 4 and grease and 20 cm round cake tin.
- Put all of the cake ingredients in a large mixing bowl and whisk them together with an electric whisk for 4 minutes or until pale and well whipped.
- Scrape the mixture into the tin and level the top with a spatula.
- Bake for 35–40 minutes. The cake is ready when a toothpick inserted in the centre comes out clean.
- While the cake is cooking, stir the caster sugar with the orange juice until dissolved.
- When the cake comes out of the oven, spoon the orange drizzle all over the surface and leave it to cool in the tin.

Lemon Drizzle Cake 73
- For a sharper but delicious tasting cake swap the orange juice and zest for lemon.

PREPARATION TIME 20 MINUTES

COOKING TIME 35–40 MINUTES

INGREDIENTS

150 g / 5 ½ oz / 1 cup self-raising flour
150 g / 5 ½ oz / ⅔ cup caster (superfine) sugar
150 g / 5 ½ oz / ⅔ cup butter, softened
3 eggs
1 tsp baking powder
1 tbsp orange zest
2 tbsp orange juice

FOR THE DRIZZLE
100 g / 3 ½ oz / ½ cup caster (superfine) sugar
50 ml / 1 ¾ fl. oz / ¼ cup orange juice

74
SERVES 8

Orange and Cinnamon Treacle Tart

- To make the pastry, rub the butter into the flour and add just enough cold water to bind.
- Chill for 30 minutes.
- Meanwhile, put the sugar in a saucepan with 200 ml water and stir over a low heat until dissolved. Add the orange slices then simmer for 25 minutes.
- Preheat the oven to 200°C (180°C fan) / 390F / gas 6.
- Roll out the pastry on a floured surface and use it to line a rectangular tart tin.
- Heat the golden syrup with the orange zest and juice until runny then stir in the breadcrumbs and cinnamon.
- Spoon the filling into the pastry case and top with the candied orange slices.
- Bake for 25–30 minutes or until the pastry is cooked through underneath.

Orange and Mixed Spice Tart 75
- For a more spicy taste to this festive tart add 1 teaspoon of mixed spice instead of the cinnamon.

PREPARATION TIME 45 MINUTES

COOKING TIME 50–55 MINUTES

INGREDIENTS

350 g / 12 ½ oz / 1 cup golden syrup
1 orange, zest and juice
150 g / 5 ½ oz / 2 cups white breadcrumbs
1 tsp ground cinnamon

FOR THE PASTRY
200 g / 7 oz / 1 ⅓ cups plain (all purpose) flour
100 g / 3 ½ oz / ½ cup butter, cubed

FOR THE CANDIED ORANGE SLICES
400 g / 14 oz / 1 ¾ cups caster (superfine) sugar
2 oranges, sliced

76
MAKES 12
Chocolate and Pistachio Cupcakes

PREPARATION TIME 20 MINUTES

COOKING TIME 15–20 MINUTES

INGREDIENTS

110 g / 4 oz / ⅔ cup self-raising flour, sifted
28 g / 1 oz cocoa powder
110 g / 4 oz / ½ cup caster (superfine) sugar
110 g / 4 oz / ½ cup butter, softened
2 large eggs
1 tsp almond essence

TO DECORATE

225 g / 8 oz / 2 ¼ cups icing (confectioners') sugar
½ tsp almond essence
3 tbsp pistachio nuts, chopped

- Preheat the oven to 190°C (170°C fan) / 375F / gas 5 and line a 12-hole cupcake tin with paper cases.
- Combine the flour, cocoa, sugar, butter, eggs and almond essence in a bowl and whisk together for 2 minutes or until smooth.
- Divide the mixture between the paper cases, then transfer the tin to the oven and bake for 15–20 minutes.
- Test with a wooden toothpick, if it comes out clean, the cakes are done.
- Transfer the cakes to a wire rack and leave to cool completely before peeling off the papers.
- To make the icing, sieve the icing sugar into a bowl and add the almond essence. Stir in enough hot water, drop by drop, to form a spreadable icing and spoon it over the cakes.
- Sprinkle with chopped pistachios and leave the icing to set.

77
SERVES 8
Lemon and Lime Tart

PREPARATION TIME 55 MINUTES

COOKING TIME 45–50 MINUTES

INGREDIENTS

2 lemons, juiced
4 limes, juiced
175 g / 6 oz / ¾ cup caster (superfine) sugar
2 tsp cornflour (cornstarch)
4 large eggs, beaten
225 g / 8 oz / ¾ cup double (heavy) cream

FOR THE PASTRY

100 g / 3 ½ oz / ½ cup butter, cubed
100 g / 3 ½ oz / ⅔ cup plain (all purpose) flour
100 g / 3 ½ oz / ⅔ cup wholemeal flour
55 g / 2 oz / ¼ cup caster (superfine) sugar
1 egg, beaten

TO DECORATE

1 lemon, zest finely pared
1 lime, zest finely pared

- Preheat the oven to 200°C (180°C fan) / 390F / gas 6.
- To make the pastry, rub the butter into the flours and sugar then add the egg with just enough cold water to bind.
- Wrap the dough in cling film and chill for 30 minutes then roll out on a floured surface.
- Use the pastry to line a 24 cm loose-bottomed tart tin and trim the edges.
- Prick the pastry with a fork, line with cling film and fill with baking beans or rice.
- Bake for 10 minutes then remove the cling film and baking beans and cook for another 8 minutes to crisp.
- Reduce the oven temperature to 170°C (150°C fan) / 340F / gas 3.
- Stir the lemon and lime juices into the caster sugar and cornflour to dissolve, then whisk in the eggs and cream.
- Strain the mixture into the pastry case and bake for 25–30 minutes or until just set in the centre.
- Leave to cool completely before decorating with the lemon and lime zest.

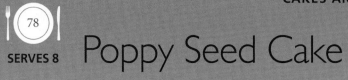

78
SERVES 8

Poppy Seed Cake

- Preheat the oven to 180°C (160°C fan) / 355F / gas 4 and line a 18 cm round cake tin with non-stick baking paper.
- Sieve the flour into a mixing bowl and rub in the butter until it resembles fine breadcrumbs then stir in the sugar and poppy seeds.
- Lightly beat the egg with the milk and stir it into the dry ingredients until just combined.
- Scrape the mixture into the tin and bake for 55 minutes or until a skewer inserted in the centre comes out clean.
- Transfer the cake to a wire rack and leave to cool completely.

PREPARATION TIME 15 MINUTES

COOKING TIME 55 MINUTES

INGREDIENTS

225 g / 8 oz / 1 ½ cups self raising flour
100 g / 3 ½ oz / ½ cup butter, cubed
100 g / 3 ½ oz / ½ cup caster (superfine) sugar
2 tbsp poppy seeds
1 large egg
75 ml / 3 ½ fl. oz / ⅓ cup whole milk

79
SERVES 10

Pumpkin Pie

PREPARATION TIME 25 MINUTES

COOKING TIME
1 HOUR 10 MINUTES

INGREDIENTS

600 g / 1 lb 5 oz / 1 ½ cups pumpkin or butternut squash, peeled, deseeded and cubed
2 large eggs

150 ml / 5 ½ fl. oz / ⅔ cup maple syrup
150 ml / 5 ½ fl. oz / ⅔ cup evaporated milk
1 tsp mixed spice
1 pastry case, sweet

- Preheat the oven to 200°C (180°C fan) / 390F / gas 6.
- Put the pumpkin in a roasting tin and cover with foil then bake for 30 minutes.
- Drain the pumpkin of any excess liquid then puree it in a food processor.
- Add the eggs, maple syrup, evaporated milk and spice and pulse until smoothly combined.
- Reduce the oven temperature to 180°C (160°C fan) / 355F / gas 4.
- Pour the pumpkin mixture into the pastry case and bake for 30–40 minutes or until just set in the centre.
- Leave to cool completely before slicing.

80
SERVES 6

Pear and Almond Sponge

PREPARATION TIME 15 MINUTES

COOKING TIME 30–35 MINUTES

INGREDIENTS

85 g / 3 oz / ½ cup self-raising flour, sifted
28 g / 1 oz / ¼ cup ground almonds
110 g / 4 oz / ½ cup caster (superfine) sugar

110 g / 4 oz / ½ cup butter, softened
2 large eggs
½ tsp almond essence
2 pears, peeled, cored and diced
icing (confectioners') sugar to dust

- Preheat the oven to 190°C (170°C fan) / 375F / gas 5 and grease and line a 20 cm round cake tin.
- Combine the flour, ground almonds, sugar, butter, eggs and almond essence in a bowl and whisk together for 2 minutes or until smooth.
- Fold in the chopped pears and spoon into the prepared tin then bake for 30–35 minutes.
- Test with a wooden toothpick, if it comes out clean, the cake is done.
- Transfer the cake to a wire rack and leave to cool completely before dusting with icing sugar.

81 MAKES 6

Plum Tartlets

PREPARATION TIME 20 MINUTES

COOKING TIME 25–35 MINUTES

INGREDIENTS

110 g / 4 oz / ½ cup butter, cubed and chilled
110 g / 4 oz / ⅔ cup plain (all purpose) flour
110 g / 4 oz / ⅔ cup stoneground wholemeal flour
450 g / 1 lb / 1 cup plums, halved and stoned
450 g / 1 lb / 1 ¼ cup plum jam (jelly)

- Preheat the oven to 200°C (180°C fan) / 400F / gas 6.
- Rub the butter into the flours until the mixture resembles fine breadcrumbs.
- Stir in just enough cold water to bring the pastry together into a pliable dough.
- Roll out the pastry on a floured surface and cut out 6 circles then use them to line 6 tartlet tins.
- Arrange the halved plums in the pastry cases and spoon over the jam.
- Bake for 25–35 minutes or until the pastry is crisp and the jam has melted around the plums.

Apricot Tartlets
82

- Use apricots instead of plums and apricot jam instead of plum jam for a golden delicious tartlet.

83 MAKES 12

Raspberry Sponge Squares

PREPARATION TIME 20 MINUTES

COOKING TIME 30–35 MINUTES

INGREDIENTS

175 g / 6 oz / 1 ¼ cups self-raising flour
2 tsp baking powder
175 g / 6 oz / ¾ cup caster (superfine) sugar
175 g / 6 oz / ¾ cup butter, softened
3 eggs
200 g / 7 oz / 1 ⅓ cups raspberries
icing (confectioners') sugar to dust

- Preheat the oven to 180°C (160°C fan) / 350F / gas 4 and grease and line a 20 cm square cake tin.
- Put the flour, baking powder, sugar, butter and eggs in a mixing bowl and whisk them together with an electric whisk for 4 minutes or until pale and well whipped.
- Arrange the raspberries in the bottom of the cake tin and spoon over the cake mixture.
- Bake for 30–35 minutes. The cake is ready when a toothpick inserted in the centre comes out clean.
- Transfer the cake to a wire rack to cool completely before dusting with icing sugar and cutting into squares.

Strawberry Sponge Squares
84

- Use 200 g / 7 oz / 1 ⅓ of fresh strawberries for a summer twist to this sponge classic.

85
MAKES 6

Redcurrant Tartlets

- Preheat the oven to 200°C (180°C fan) / 400F / gas 6.
- Rub the butter into the flour until the mixture resembles fine breadcrumbs.
- Stir in just enough cold water to bring the pastry together into a pliable dough.
- Roll out the pastry on a floured surface and cut out 6 circles then use them to line 6 tartlet tins.
- Divide the redcurrant jelly between the pastry cases and bake for 20–25 minutes or until the pastry is crisp.
- Arrange the redcurrants on top while the tarts are still warm then leave to cool. Dust with icing sugar before serving.

PREPARATION TIME 20 MINUTES

COOKING TIME 20–25 MINUTES

INGREDIENTS

110 g / 4 oz / ½ cup butter, cubed and chilled
225 g / 8 oz / 1 ½ cups plain (all purpose) flour
300 g / 10 ½ oz / ¾ cup redcurrant jelly
300 g / 10 ½ oz / 2 cups redcurrants
icing (confectioners') sugar to dust

Blackcurrant Tartlets
86
- For a darker but equally delicious looking and tasting tart use blackcurrants instead of redcurrants.

87
SERVES 8

Rhubarb Frangipane Tart

- Preheat the oven to 200°C (180°C fan) / 390F / gas 6.
- To make the pastry, rub the butter into the flour until the mixture resembles fine breadcrumbs.
- Stir in the sugar and add enough cold water to bring the pastry together into a pliable dough.
- Chill the dough for 30 minutes then roll out on a floured surface. Use the pastry to line a 24cm round loose-bottomed cake tin.
- Prick the pastry with a fork, line with greaseproof paper and fill with baking beans or rice.
- Bake for 10 minutes then remove the paper and baking beans. Return to the oven for 8 minutes to crisp.
- Mix together the remaining ingredients and spoon the mixture into the pastry case.
- Bake the tart for 25 minutes or until the frangipane is cooked through.

PREPARATION TIME 50 MINUTES

COOKING TIME 35–45 MINUTES

INGREDIENTS

150 g / 5 ½ oz / 1 ½ cups ground almonds
150 g / 5 ½ oz / ⅔ cup butter, softened
150 g / 5 ½ oz / ⅔ cup caster (superfine) sugar
2 large eggs
2 tbsp plain (all purpose) flour
3 sticks rhubarb, chopped

FOR THE PASTRY
200 g / 7 oz / 1 ⅓ cup plain (all purpose) flour
100 g / 3 ½ oz / ½ cup butter, cubed
50 g / 1 ¾ oz / ¼ cup caster (superfine) sugar

Raspberry Frangipane Tart
88
- For a sweeter tasting tart use 175 g / 6 oz / 1 ¼ cups of fresh raspberries in this delicious tasting recipe.

89 | SERVES 8

Rhubarb and Custard Tart

Rhubarb, Nutmeg and Custard Tart

90

- Add ½ teaspoon of grated nutmeg to the custard recipe for a slightly spiced tasting tart.

Rhubarb and Raisin Custard Tart

91

- To add a little sweetness to this tart add 4 tablespoons of raisins to the custard base mix.

PREPARATION TIME 50 MINUTES

COOKING TIME 45–55 MINUTES

INGREDIENTS

3 sticks rhubarb, chopped
4 tbsp caster (superfine) sugar
icing (confectioners') sugar to dust

FOR THE PASTRY
200 g / 7 oz / 1 ⅓ cups plain (all purpose) flour
100 g / 3 ½ oz / ½ cup butter, cubed

FOR THE CUSTARD
4 large egg yolks
75 g / 2 ½ oz / ⅓ cup caster (superfine) sugar
1 tsp vanilla extract
2 tsp cornflour (cornstarch)
450 ml / 16 fl. oz / 1 ¾ cups whole milk

- Preheat the oven to 200⁰C (180⁰C fan) / 390F / gas 6.
- Put the rhubarb in a roasting tin and sprinkle with sugar then bake for 20 minutes or until tender.
- Meanwhile, make the pastry. Rub the butter into the flour and add just enough cold water to bind.
- Chill for 30 minutes then roll out on a floured surface. Use the pastry to line a rectangular tart tin.
- Prick the pastry with a fork, line with cling film and fill with baking beans or rice.
- Bake for 10 minutes then remove the cling film and baking beans and cook for another 8 minutes to crisp.
- Reduce the oven temperature to 170⁰C (150⁰C fan) / 340F / gas 3.
- Whisk together the custard ingredients and pour into the pastry case. Arrange the rhubarb on top.
- Bake the tart for 25–35 minutes or until the custard is just set in the centre.
- Leave to cool completely before dusting with icing sugar.

Summer Fruit Meringue Roulade

92

SERVES 8

- Preheat the oven to 180°C (160°C fan) / 355F / gas 4 and line a Swiss roll tin with non-stick baking paper.
- Whisk the egg whites with the cream of tartar until stiff then whisk in the caster sugar a tablespoon at a time until stiff and glossy.
- Spread it onto the Swiss roll tray in an even layer with a palette knife and bake for 15 minutes.
- Leave to cool completely.
- Whip the double cream until it just holds its shape.
- Sprinkle a large sheet of greaseproof paper with icing sugar and turn the meringue out onto it.
- Spread the meringue with cream and sprinkle over the berries then roll it up, using the greaseproof paper to help you.
- Dust with more icing sugar before serving.

PREPARATION TIME 30 MINUTES

COOKING TIME 15 MINUTES

INGREDIENTS

4 large egg whites
a pinch cream of tartar
200 g / 7 oz / ¾ cup caster (superfine) sugar
300 ml / 10 ½ fl. oz / 1 ¼ cups double (heavy) cream
200 g / 7 oz / 1 ⅓ cups mixed berries
icing (confectioners') sugar for dusting

Tropical Fruit Meringue Roulade

93

- Use 200 g / 7 oz / 1 cup of mixed tropical fruit such as mango, pineapple and banana instead of the berries for a colourful and exotic tasting roulade.

Rose and Mint Cheesecake

94

SERVES 10-12

- Preheat the oven to 180°C (160°C fan) / 355F / gas 4.
- Whisk together the filling ingredients until smooth.
- Place the pastry case into a baking tin and spoon in the filling mixture. Level the top with a palette knife.
- Bake the cheesecake for 40–50 minutes or until the centre is only just set.
- Leave to cool completely in the tin.
- Brush the rose petals and mint leaves with a thin layer of egg white and dip them in the caster sugar. Leave to dry on a wire rack for 2 hours.
- Decorate the tart with the leaves and petals and serve.

PREPARATION TIME 30 MINUTES

COOKING TIME 40–50 MINUTES

INGREDIENTS

1 square 30 cm pastry case

FOR THE FILLING
600 g / 1 lb 5 oz / 2 ¾ cups cream cheese
250 ml / 9 fl. oz / 1 cup whole milk
175 g / 6 oz / ¾ cup caster (superfine) sugar
2 large eggs
1 egg yolk
2 tbsp plain (all purpose) flour
2 tsp rose water
2 tbsp rose petal jam
1 tbsp mint leaves, finely shredded

TO DECORATE
12 fresh rose petals
8 fresh mint leaves
1 egg white, beaten
3 tbsp caster (superfine) sugar

Rose and Apricot Cheesecake

95

- For a fruity yet floral tasting cheesecake use 3 dried apricots very finely diced in the filling mix instead of the fresh mint leaves.

96 | MAKES 6

Cranberry Sponges

PREPARATION TIME 20 MINUTES

COOKING TIME 20–25 MINUTES

INGREDIENTS

175 g / 6 oz / 1 ¼ cups self-raising flour
2 tsp baking powder
175 g / 6 oz / ¾ cup caster (superfine) sugar
175 g / 6 oz / ¾ cup butter
3 eggs
200 g / 7 oz / 1 ⅓ cups cranberries

- Preheat the oven to 180°C (160°C fan) / 350F / gas 4 and grease and line 6 individual cake tins.
- Put the flour, baking powder, sugar, butter and eggs in a mixing bowl and whisk them together with an electric whisk for 4 minutes or until pale and well whipped.
- Fold in the cranberries and divide the mixture between the tins.
- Bake for 20–25 minutes. The cakes are ready when a toothpick inserted in the centre comes out clean.
- Transfer the cakes to a wire rack to cool completely.

Sour Cherry Sponges | 97

- Sour cherries work well in this recipe if you don't want to use the cranberries. Use the same quantities indicated in the recipe above just remember to chop the cherries up a little.

98 | MAKES 12

Apricot Cupcakes

PREPARATION TIME 15 MINUTES

COOKING TIME 15–20 MINUTES

INGREDIENTS

110 g / 4 oz / ⅔ cup self-raising flour, sifted
110 g / 4 oz / ½ cup caster (superfine) sugar
110 g / 4 oz / ½ cup butter, softened
2 large eggs
1 tsp vanilla extract
12 canned apricot halves, drained

- Preheat the oven to 190°C (170°C fan) / 375F / gas 5 and line a 12-hole cupcake tin with paper cases.
- Combine the flour, sugar, butter, eggs and vanilla extract in a bowl and whisk together for 2 minutes or until smooth.
- Divide the mixture between the paper cases and press an apricot half into each one.
- Transfer the tin to the oven and bake for 15–20 minutes.
- Test with a wooden toothpick, if it comes out clean, the cakes are done.
- Transfer the cakes to a wire rack and leave to cool completely.

Peach Cupcakes | 99

- Use canned peaches cut into quarters for slightly sweeter but equally delicious tasting cupcakes.

Treacle Tart

100
SERVES 8

Treacle and Ginger Tart **101**
- Adding 2 teaspoons of ground ginger to this delicious classic will add a little warmth to every mouthful.

Treacle and Lime Tart **102**
- Add the zest of 2 limes to the tart filling mixture for a fresher more tropical taste.

PREPARATION TIME 25 MINUTES

COOKING TIME 25–30 MINUTES

....

INGREDIENTS

250 g / 9 oz / ¾ cup puff pastry
350 g / 12 ½ oz / 1 cup golden syrup
2 lemons, zest and juice
110 g / 3 ½ oz / 1 ⅓ cups fresh white breadcrumbs

- Preheat the oven to 200°C (180°C fan) / 390F / gas 6.
- Roll out the pastry on a floured surface and use it to line a round tart tin. Trim the edges and reserve any off-cuts.
- Heat the golden syrup with the lemon zest and juice until runny then stir in the breadcrumbs.
- Spoon the filling into the pastry case and level the top.
- Roll out the pastry off-cuts and cut them into thin strips. Twist each strip and lay it across the tart in a lattice pattern, securing the ends with a dab of water.
- Bake for 25–30 minutes or until the pastry is cooked through underneath.

103

**MAKES 1 LARGE
OR 2 SMALL**

Tea Leaf Pound Cake

Lavender Pound Cake

104

- Use edible lavender flowers instead of the tea leaves for a more aromatic cake.

Lemon and Stem Ginger Pound Cake

105

- Swap the tea leaves for finely chopped stem ginger and add the zest of one unwaxed lemon to the cake batter mix.

PREPARATION TIME 20 MINUTES

COOKING TIME 45–55 MINUTES

INGREDIENTS

55 g / 2 oz / ⅓ cup good quality tea leaves
450 g / 1 lb / 2 cups butter, softened
450 g / 1 lb / 2 cups caster (superfine) sugar
8 large eggs, beaten
450 g / 1 lb / 3 cups self-raising flour
2 tbsp granulated sugar

- Preheat the oven to 180°C (160°C fan) / 355F / gas 4 and grease and line a 4 lb loaf tin, or 2 x 2 lb loaf tins, with greaseproof paper.
- Soak the tea leaves in warm water for 5 minutes.
- Cream the butter and caster sugar together until well whipped then gradually whisk in the eggs, beating well after each addition.
- Fold in the flour and half of the tea leaves then scrape the mixture into the tin.
- Bake the cake for 45–55 minutes or until a skewer inserted in the centre comes out clean.
- Turn the loaf out onto a wire rack and leave to cool.
- Meanwhile, dry the rest of the tea leaves with kitchen paper and mix them with the granulated sugar. Sprinkle in a line along the top of the cake.

Blackcurrant and Redcurrant Tartlets

106
MAKES 6

- Preheat the oven to 200⁰C (180⁰C fan) / 390F / gas 6.
- To make the pastry, rub the butter into the flour and sugar then add the egg with just enough cold water to bind.
- Wrap the dough in cling film and chill for 30 minutes then roll out on a floured surface.
- Use the pastry to line 6 tartlet tins and trim the edges.
- Prick the pastry with a fork, line with cling film and fill with baking beans or rice.
- Bake for 10 minutes then remove the cling film and baking beans and cook for another 8 minutes to crisp.
- Mix the blackcurrants and redcurrants with the redcurrant jelly and spoon the mixture into the tartlet cases. Return them to the oven for 10 minutes.
- Leave the tartlets to cool for 10 minutes before dusting with icing sugar and serving with the passion fruit sorbet.

PREPARATION TIME 45 MINUTES

COOKING TIME 25–30 MINUTES

INGREDIENTS

200 g / 7 oz / 1 ⅓ cups blackcurrants
200 g / 7 oz / 1 ⅓ cups redcurrants
100 g / 3 ½ oz / ⅓ cup redcurrant jelly
100 g / 3 ½ oz / ½ cup butter, cubed
200 g / 7 oz / 1 ⅓ cups plain (all purpose) flour
55 g / 2 oz / ¼ cup caster (superfine) sugar
1 egg, beaten
icing (confectioners') sugar to dust
6 scoops passion fruit sorbet

Kumquat Tartlets

107

- Swap the currents for chopped kumquats and use marmalade instead of redcurrant jelly to bind for a sharp tasting tartlet. Serve with vanilla ice cream if desired.

Chocolate Layer Cake

108
SERVES 10-12

- Preheat the oven to 180⁰C (160⁰C fan) / 355F / gas 4 and grease and line 3 x 20 cm round cake tins.
- Whisk together all of the cake ingredients with an electric whisk for 4 minutes or until well whipped.
- Divide the mixture between the tins and bake for 30–35 minutes.
- The cakes are ready when a toothpick inserted in the centre comes out clean.
- Transfer the cakes to a wire rack to cool completely.
- Bring the cream almost to a simmer then pour it over the chopped chocolate and stir until smooth.
- Add the butter and blend it in with a stick blender.
- When the ganache has cooled to a spreadable consistency, use it to sandwich the cakes together, finishing with a thick layer on top.

PREPARATION TIME 30 MINUTES

COOKING TIME 30–35 MINUTES

INGREDIENTS

225 g / 8 oz / 1 ½ cups self-raising flour
55 g / 2 oz / ½ cup unsweetened cocoa powder
3 tsp baking powder
225 g / 8 oz / 1 cup caster (superfine) sugar
225 g / 8 oz / 1 cup butter
4 large eggs

FOR THE GANACHE

300 ml / 10 ½ fl. oz / 1 ¼ cups double (heavy) cream
300 g / 10 ½ oz / 1 ⅔ cups dark chocolate (minimum 60 % cocoa solids), chopped
75 g / 2 ½ oz / ⅓ cup butter, cubed

Mocha Layer Cake

109

- Add 2 tablespoons of espresso to the cake batter mix for a mocha sponge. As an optional extra add 1 tablespoon of camp coffee extract to the ganache topping.

110

SERVES 8-10

Gluten-free Coconut Cake

PREPARATION TIME 15 MINUTES

COOKING TIME 45–55 MINUTES

....

INGREDIENTS

225 g / 8 oz / 1 cup butter, softened
225 g / 8 oz / 1 cup caster (superfine) sugar
1 vanilla pod, seeds only
4 large eggs, beaten
225 g/ 4 ½ oz / 1 ½ cups rice flour
1 tsp baking powder
100 g / 3 ½ oz / 1 cup desiccated coconut

- Preheat the oven to 180°C (160°C fan) / 355F / gas 4 and grease and line a 23 cm round cake tin with greaseproof paper.
- Cream the butter, sugar and vanilla seeds together until well whipped then gradually whisk in the eggs, beating well after each addition.
- Fold in the flour, baking powder and coconut then scrape the mixture into the tin.
- Bake the cake for 45–55 minutes or until a skewer inserted in the centre comes out clean.

Gluten-free Almond Cake   111

- Substitute the desiccated coconut for ground almonds and decorate with flaked (slivered) almonds if desired.

112

MAKES 6

Fig and Almond Tartlets

PREPARATION TIME 45 MINUTES

COOKING TIME 35 MINUTES

....

INGREDIENTS

150 g / 5 ½ oz / 1 ½ cups ground almonds
150 g / 5 ½ oz / ⅔ cup butter, softened
150 g / 5 ½ oz / ⅔ cup caster (superfine) sugar
2 large eggs
2 tbsp plain (all purpose) flour
3 fresh figs, chopped
2 tbsp flaked (slivered) almonds

FOR THE PASTRY

200 g / 7 oz / 1 ⅓ cups plain (all purpose) flour
100 g / 3 ½ oz / ½ cup butter, cubed
50 g / 1 ¾ oz / ¼ cup caster (superfine) sugar

- Preheat the oven to 200°C (180°C fan) / 390F / gas 6.
- To make the pastry, rub the butter into the flour until the mixture resembles fine breadcrumbs.
- Stir in the sugar and add enough cold water to bring the pastry together into a pliable dough.
- Chill the dough for 30 minutes then roll out on a floured surface. Use the pastry to line 6 tartlet cases.
- Prick the pastry with a fork, line with greaseproof paper and fill with baking beans or rice.
- Bake for 10 minutes then remove the paper and beans.
- Return to the oven for 8 minutes to crisp.
- Whisk together the almonds, butter, sugar, eggs and flour until smoothly whipped and fold in the figs.
- Spoon the mixture into the pastry cases, sprinkle with flaked almonds and bake for 15 minutes or until the filling is cooked through.

Pear and Almond Tarts   113

- Substitute the figs for 4 canned pears roughly chopped for a different fruity tasting tart.

114
MAKES 9
Summer Berry Chocolate Brownies

- Preheat the oven to 170°C (150°C fan) / 325F / gas 3 and oil and line a 20 cm square cake tin.
- Melt the chocolate, cocoa and butter together in a saucepan, then leave to cool a little.
- Whisk the sugar and eggs together with an electric whisk for 3 minutes or until very light and creamy.
- Pour in the chocolate mixture and sieve over the flour. Reserve some of the berries for decoration and add the rest to the bowl, then fold everything together until evenly mixed.
- Scrape into the tin and bake for 35–40 minutes or until the outside is set, but the centre is still quite soft, as it will continue to cook as it cools.
- Leave the brownie to cool completely before cutting into 9 squares.

PREPARATION TIME 25 MINUTES

COOKING TIME 35–40 MINUTES

INGREDIENTS

110 g / 4 oz / ½ cup dark chocolate
(minimum 60 % cocoa solids),
chopped
85 g / 3 oz / ¾ cup unsweetened
cocoa powder, sifted
225 g / 8 oz / 1 cup butter
450 g /15 oz / 2 ½ cups light brown
sugar
4 large eggs
110 g / 4 oz / ⅔ cup self-raising flour
175 g / 6 oz / 1 ¼ cups mixed berries

Winter Berry
Chocolate Brownies

115

- Swap summer berries such as raspberries and strawberries for winter favourites such as blackberry, loganberry and blueberry.

116
SERVES 8-10
Chocolate and Pecan Bundt Cake

- Preheat the oven to 180°C (160°C fan) / 355F / gas 4 and butter a bundt tin.
- Cream the butter and sugar together until well whipped then gradually whisk in the eggs, beating well after each addition.
- Fold in the flour, ground pecans and chocolate chunks then scrape the mixture into the tin.
- Bake the cake for 45 minutes or until a skewer inserted in the centre comes out clean.
- Turn the cake out onto a wire rack and leave to cool.
- Melt the chocolate, butter and syrup together over a low heat, stirring regularly, then spoon it over the cake. Sprinkle with chopped pecan nuts.

PREPARATION TIME 25 MINUTES

COOKING TIME 45 MINUTES

INGREDIENTS

225 g / 8 oz / 1 cup butter, softened
225 g / 8 oz / 1 cup caster (superfine)
sugar
4 large eggs, beaten
125 g/ 4 ½ oz / ¾ cup self-raising
flour
100 g / 3 ½ oz / 1 cup ground pecan
nuts
100 g / 3 ½ oz / ½ cup dark chocolate
(minimum 60 % cocoa solids),
chopped

TO DECORATE

100 g / 3 ½ oz / ½ cup dark chocolate
(minimum 60 % cocoa solids),
chopped
28 g / 1 oz butter
2 tbsp golden syrup
55 g / 2 oz / ½ cup pecan nuts,
chopped

Chocolate and Pistachio
Bundt Cake

117

- Instead of pecans use chopped pistachios for a more colourful take on this traditional round cake.

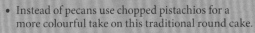

118

SERVES 8

Apple Crumble Tart

PREPARATION TIME 55 MINUTES

COOKING TIME 35–40 MINUTES

INGREDIENTS

450 g / 1 lb / 1 cup Bramley apples, peeled and chopped
50 g / 1 ¾ oz / ¼ cup caster (superfine) sugar
1 tbsp cornflour (cornstarch)

FOR THE PASTRY
200 g / 7 oz / 1 ⅓ cups plain (all purpose) flour
100 g / 3 ½ oz / ½ cup butter, cubed and chilled

FOR THE CRUMBLE
150 g / 5 oz / ⅔ cup butter
100 g / 3 ½ oz / ⅔ cup plain (all purpose) flour
50 g / 1 ¾ oz / ½ cup ground almonds
75 g / 2 ½ oz / ½ cup light brown sugar

- Preheat the oven to 200°C (180°C fan) / 390F / gas 6.
- First make the pastry. Sieve the flour into a mixing bowl then rub in the butter until the mixture resembles fine breadcrumbs.
- Stir in just enough cold water to bring the pastry together into a pliable dough then chill for 30 minutes.
- Mix the chopped apples with the sugar and cornflour.
- Roll out the pastry on a floured surface and use it to line a 23 cm round pie dish. Spoon in the apples and level the top.
- To make the crumble topping, rub the butter into the flour then stir in the almonds and sugar.
- Take handfuls of the topping and squeeze it into a clump, then crumble it over the apple.
- Bake the tart for 35–40 minutes until the crumble is golden brown. Leave to cool for 20 minutes before cutting.

Apple, Pear and Raisin Crumble Tart

119

- Use half apple and half pear for your fruit filling and add 4 tablespoons of raisins to the crumble mixture.

120

MAKES 6

Wholemeal Apple Tartlets

PREPARATION TIME 25 MINUTES

COOKING TIME 25–35 MINUTES

INGREDIENTS

110 g / 4 oz / ½ cup butter, cubed and chilled
110 g / 4 oz / ⅔ cup stoneground wholemeal flour
110 g / 4 oz / ⅔ cup plain (all purpose) flour
3 apples, peeled and halved
6 tbsp apricot jam (jelly)

- Preheat the oven to 200°C (180°C fan) / 390F / gas 6.
- Rub the butter into the flours until the mixture resembles fine breadcrumbs.
- Stir in just enough cold water to bring the pastry together into a pliable dough.
- Roll out the pastry on a floured surface and cut out 6 circles then use them to line 6 tartlet tins.
- Slice each apple half and fan them out inside the pastry cases. Spoon a tablespoon of apricot jam on top of each one.
- Bake for 25–35 minutes or until the pastry is crisp and the jam has melted around the apples.

Wholemeal Pineapple Tartlets

121

- Use one small pineapple peeled, cored and sliced instead of the apples for a tropical tasting tartlet.

122

MAKES 6

Apple, Walnut and Honey Tartlets

Apple, Maple Syrup and Walnut Tartlets

123

- Using maple syrup instead of honey to glaze the tartlets gives a richer flavour to these delicious treats.

Peach, Pistachio and Lavender Honey Tartlets

124

- Use 4 peaches instead of apples to fill your tartlets. Use chopped pistachios with lavender honey for a fragrant colourful glaze.

PREPARATION TIME 30 MINUTES

COOKING TIME 30 MINUTES

INGREDIENTS

225 g / 8 oz / ¾ cup puff pastry
150 g / 5 ½ oz / 1 ½ cups ground walnuts
150 g / 5 ½ oz / ⅔ cup butter, softened
150 g / 5 ½ oz / ⅔ cup caster (superfine) sugar
2 large eggs
2 tbsp plain (all purpose) flour
4 eating apples, cored and sliced
4 tbsp runny honey
2 tbsp chopped walnuts

- Preheat the oven to 200°C (180°C fan) / 390F / gas 6.
- Roll out the pastry on a floured surface and use it to line 6 round loose-bottomed tartlet cases.
- Prick the pastry with a fork, line with greaseproof paper and fill with baking beans or rice.
- Bake for 10 minutes then remove the paper and baking beans.
- Whisk together the ground walnuts, butter, sugar, eggs and flour until smoothly whipped and spoon the mixture into the pastry case.
- Arrange the apple slices on top and bake for 20 minutes or until the frangipane is cooked through and the pastry is crisp underneath.
- Heat the honey until very liquid and stir in the walnuts then drizzle it over the hot tarts.
- Serve warm with clotted cream or ice cream.

Blackcurrant Tart

Fresh Raspberry and Lemon Curd Tart

126

- Use 4 tablespoons of lemon curd at the base of the tart case and top with fresh raspberries for a sweet tangy tart. Dust with a little icing sugar to finish.

Strawberries and Cream Tart

127

- Use 4 tablespoons of lightly whipped double cream at the base of the tart and top with chopped fresh strawberries.

PREPARATION TIME 45 MINUTES

COOKING TIME 40 MINUTES

INGREDIENTS

400 g / 14 oz / 2 ⅔ cups fresh blackcurrants
200 g / 7 oz / ¾ cup caster (superfine) sugar

FOR THE PASTRY
200 g / 7 oz / ⅓ cup plain (all purpose) flour
100 g / 3 ½ oz / ½ cup butter, cubed
50 g / 1 ¾ oz / ¼ cup caster (superfine) sugar
1 large egg, beaten

- Preheat the oven to 200°C (180°C fan) / 390F / gas 6.
- To make the pastry, rub the butter into the flour until the mixture resembles fine breadcrumbs.
- Stir in the sugar and add enough cold water to bring the pastry together into a pliable dough.
- Chill for 30 minutes then roll out on a floured surface.
- Use the pastry to line a 24 cm round loose-bottomed tart case and trim the edges, leaving a 1cm overhang to allow for shrinkage.
- Prick the pastry all over with a fork, line with cling film and fill with baking beans or rice.
- Bake the case for 10 minutes then remove the cling film and baking beans.
- Brush the inside with egg and return to the oven for 8 minutes or until golden and crisp.
- Meanwhile, put the blackcurrants in a large saucepan with 100ml water and bring to a simmer.
- Cook for 10 minutes until the skins have softened then add the sugar and stir well to dissolve.
- Boil for 8 minutes then pour the mixture into the pastry case and leave to cool and thicken.

128
MAKES 6

Blueberry Tartlets

- To make the pastry, rub the butter into the flour and add just enough cold water to bind. Chill for 30 minutes.
- Preheat the oven to 200°C (180°C fan) / 390F / gas 6.
- Roll out the pastry on a floured surface and use it to line 6 tartlet cases, rerolling the trimmings as necessary.
- Prick the pastry with a fork, line with cling film and fill with baking beans or rice. Bake for 10 minutes then remove the cling film and baking beans.
- Brush the inside of the pastry cases with beaten egg and cook for another 8 minutes to crisp.
- Whisk the custard ingredients together in a jug and fill the pastry cases until three quarters full.
- Bake the tarts for 15–20 minutes or until the custard has set.
- Leave the tartlets to cool completely before topping with the blueberries.

Summer Berry Tartlets

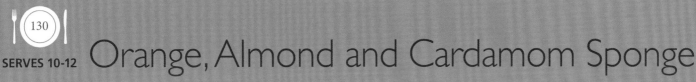

129

- Use a mix of fresh summer berries such as strawberries and raspberries for a bright colourful topping.

PREPARATION TIME 55 MINUTES

COOKING TIME 35–40 MINUTES

INGREDIENTS

200 g / 7 oz / 1 ⅓ blueberries

FOR THE PASTRY
200 g / 7 oz / 1 ⅓ plain (all purpose) flour
100 g / 3 ½ oz / ½ cup butter, cubed
1 egg, beaten

FOR THE CUSTARD
2 large egg yolks
55 g / 2 oz / ¼ cup caster (superfine) sugar
1 tsp vanilla extract
2 tsp cornflour (cornstarch)
225 ml / 8 fl. oz / 1 cup whole milk

130
SERVES 10-12

Orange, Almond and Cardamom Sponge

- Preheat the oven to 180°C (160°C fan) / 355F / gas 4 and grease and line a deep 20 cm round cake tin.
- Whisk together all of the cake ingredients with an electric whisk for 4 minutes or until well whipped.
- Scrape the mixture into the tin and bake for 45–50 minutes. The cake is ready when a toothpick inserted in the centre comes out clean.
- Transfer the cake to a wire rack to cool completely before cutting in half horizontally.
- To make the crème patisserie, whisk together the egg yolks, sugar, vanilla extract and cornflour.
- Heat the milk and cardamom almost to a simmer then strain it through a sieve and gradually whisk it into the egg mixture.
- Scrape the custard back into the saucepan and cook over a medium heat until it thickens, stirring constantly.
- Pour it into a bowl and leave to cool to room temperature.
- Beat the crème patisserie until smooth and use it to sandwich the cake back together. Dust with icing sugar before serving.

PREPARATION TIME 30 MINUTES

COOKING TIME 45–50 MINUTES

INGREDIENTS

150 g / 6 oz / 1 cup wholemeal flour
1 tsp baking powder
28 g / 1 oz / ¼ cup ground almonds
28 g / 1 oz / ¼ cup blanched almonds, finely chopped
2 tsp baking powder
175 g / 6 oz / ¾ cup caster (superfine) sugar
175 g / 6 oz / ¾ cup butter, softened
3 large eggs
1 orange, zest finely grated

FOR THE FILLING
4 large egg yolks
75 g / 2 ½ oz / ⅓ cup caster (superfine) sugar
1 tsp vanilla extract
2 tsp cornflour (cornstarch)
450 ml / 16 fl. oz / 1 ¾ cups milk
4 cardamom pods, crushed
icing (confectioners') sugar to dust

131 · MAKES 12
Chocolate and Cherry Cupcakes

PREPARATION TIME 25 MINUTES

COOKING TIME 15–20 MINUTES

....

INGREDIENTS

100 g / 3 ½ oz / ⅔ cup self-raising flour, sifted
28g / 1 oz / ¼ cup unsweetened cocoa powder, sifted
100 g / 3 ½ oz / ½ cup caster (superfine) sugar
100 g / 3 ½ oz / ½ cup butter, softened
3 large eggs
75 g / 2 ½ oz / ⅓ cup glacé cherries, chopped

TO DECORATE

225 ml / 8 fl. oz / 1 cup double (heavy) cream
2 tbsp icing (confectioners') sugar
½ tsp vanilla extract
12 glacé cherries
chocolate shavings

- Preheat the oven to 190°C (170°C fan) / 375F / gas 5 and line a 12-hole cupcake tin with paper cases.
- Combine the flour, cocoa, sugar, butter and eggs in a bowl and whisk together for 2 minutes or until smooth. Fold in the chopped cherries.
- Divide the mixture between the paper cases, then transfer to the oven and bake for 15–20 minutes.
- Test with a wooden toothpick, if it comes out clean, the cakes are done.
- Transfer the cakes to a wire rack and leave to cool.
- Whip the cream with the icing sugar and vanilla until thick then spoon it into a piping bag fitted with a large star nozzle.
- Pipe a rosette of cream on top of each cake then top each one with a cherry and a sprinkle of chocolate shavings.

Chocolate and Cranberry Cupcakes · 132

- For a more tart tasting cupcake use chopped dried cranberries in the cake mixture and use chopped cranberries to top.

133 · MAKES 12
Black Sesame and Orange Cupcakes

PREPARATION TIME 25 MINUTES

COOKING TIME 15–20 MINUTES

....

INGREDIENTS

100 g / 3 ½ oz / ⅔ cup self-raising flour, sifted
100 g / 3 ½ oz / ½ cup caster (superfine) sugar
100 g / 3 ½ oz / cup butter, softened
3 large eggs
1 orange, zest finely grated
2 tbsp black sesame seeds

- Preheat the oven to 190°C (170°C fan) / 375F / gas 5 and oil 12 silicone cupcake cases.
- Combine the flour, sugar, butter and eggs in a bowl and whisk together for 2 minutes or until smooth. Fold in the orange zest and sesame seeds.
- Divide the mixture between the cupcake cases, then transfer to the oven and bake for 15–20 minutes.
- Test with a wooden toothpick, if it comes out clean, the cakes are done.
- Transfer the cakes to a wire rack and leave to cool completely.

Lemon and Poppy Seed Cupcakes · 134

- Use the zest of 2 lemons instead of the orange and swap the black sesame for poppy seeds for a more classic take on this cupcake.

MAKES 24

Blackberry Mini Muffins

Blackberry and Orange Mini Muffins 136

- By using the zest of one orange and adding it to the cupcake mixture you will have an even more fruity tasting cake.

Lemon and Blueberry Mini Muffins 137

- Use the zest of one lemon and substitute the blackberries for blueberries for a delicious tasting mini muffin.

Chocolate and Blackberry Muffins 138

- Melt a bar of dark chocolate and drizzle over the top before serving.

PREPARATION TIME 25 MINUTES

COOKING TIME 15–20 MINUTES

INGREDIENTS

1 large egg
120 ml / 4 fl. oz / ½ cup sunflower oil
120 ml / 4 fl. oz / ½ cup milk
375 g / 12 ½ oz / 2 ½ cups self-raising flour, sifted
1 tsp baking powder
200 g / 7 oz / ¾ cup caster (superfine) sugar
200 g / 7 oz / 1 ⅓ cups blackberries

- Preheat the oven to 180°C (160°C fan) / 350F / gas 4 and line a 24-hole mini muffin tin with paper cases.
- Beat the egg in a jug with the oil and milk until well mixed.
- Mix the flour, baking powder and sugar in a bowl.
- Pour in the egg mixture and stir just enough to combine then fold in the blackberries.
- Divide the mixture between the paper cases and bake for 15–20 minutes.
- Test with a wooden toothpick, if it comes out clean, the cakes are done.
- Transfer the muffins to a wire rack and leave to cool completely.

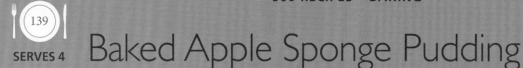

139

SERVES 4

Baked Apple Sponge Pudding

Festive Apple and Mincemeat Sponge Pudding

140

- Use mincemeat instead of plum jam to fill the apples and sprinkle with a little cinnamon before baking.

Baked Pear and Walnut Sponge Pudding

141

- Change the apples for pears and stuff with 4 tablespoons of chopped walnuts bound with a little honey for a nutty taste and texture.

PREPARATION TIME 15 MINUTES

COOKING TIME 30–35 MINUTES

INGREDIENTS

110 g / 4 oz / ⅔ cup self-raising flour, sifted
110 g / 4 oz / ½ cup caster (superfine) sugar
110 g / 4 oz / ½ cup butter, softened
2 large eggs
1 tsp vanilla extract
4 Bramley apples, peeled and cored
4 tbsp plum jam

- Preheat the oven to 190°C (170°C fan) / 375F / gas 5 and butter a small baking dish.
- Combine the flour, sugar, butter, eggs and vanilla extract in a bowl and whisk together for 2 minutes or until smooth.
- Spoon the cake mixture into the baking dish and level the top.
- Stuff the apples with the plum jam and push them into the cake mixture.
- Bake the pudding for 30–35 minutes.
- Test with a wooden toothpick, if it comes out clean, the cake is done.
- Serve warm with custard or cream.

142
SERVES 8

Wholemeal Banana Loaf Cake

- Preheat the oven to 170°C (150°C fan) / 325F / gas 3 and line a long thin loaf tin with non-stick baking paper.
- Mash the bananas roughly with a fork then whisk in the sugar, eggs and oil.
- Sieve the flour and baking powder into the bowl and stir just enough to evenly mix all the ingredients together.
- Scrape the mixture into the loaf tin and bake for 55 minutes or until a skewer inserted comes out clean.
- Transfer the cake to a wire rack and leave to cool completely.

PREPARATION TIME 10 MINUTES

COOKING TIME 55 MINUTES

INGREDIENTS

3 very ripe bananas
110 g / 4 oz / ½ cup soft light brown sugar
2 large eggs
120 ml / 4 fl. oz / ½ cup sunflower oil
225 g / 8 oz / 1 ½ cups stoneground wholemeal flour
2 tsp baking powder

Chocolate and Banana Wholemeal Loaf Cake

143

- Add 55 g / 2 oz / ⅓ cup of dark chocolate chips to the mixture for a decadent taste.

144
SERVES 8-10

Carrot and Walnut Cake

- Preheat the oven to 190°C (170°C fan) / 375F / gas 5 and line 2 x 20 cm round cake tins with greaseproof paper.
- Whisk the sugar, eggs and oil together until thick.
- Fold in the flour, baking powder and cinnamon, followed by the orange zest, carrots and walnuts.
- Divide the mixture between the tins and bake for 30–35 minutes.
- Transfer the cakes to a wire rack and leave to cool.
- To make the icing, beat the cream cheese and butter together with a wooden spoon until light and fluffy then beat in the icing sugar a quarter at a time.
- Add the vanilla extract then use a whisk to whip the mixture until smooth and light.
- Use a third of the icing to sandwich the cakes together and spread the rest over the top and sides.

PREPARATION TIME 25 MINUTES

COOKING TIME 30–35 MINUTES

INGREDIENTS

175 g / 6 oz / 1 cup soft light brown sugar
2 large eggs
150 ml / 5 fl. oz / ⅔ cup sunflower oil
175 g / 6 oz / 1 ¼ cups stoneground wholemeal flour
3 tsp baking powder
2 tsp ground cinnamon
1 orange, zest finely grated
200 g / 7 oz / 1 ⅔ cups carrots, washed and coarsely grated
100 g / 3 ½ oz / ¾ cup walnuts, chopped

FOR THE ICING
225 g / 8 oz / 1 cup cream cheese
110 g / 4 oz / ½ cup butter, softened
275 g / 10 oz / 2 ½ cups icing (confectioners') sugar
1 tsp vanilla extract

Carrot and Hazelnut Cake

145

- For those who can find walnuts a little strong in flavour, the milder nutty flavour of hazelnuts (cob nuts) roughly chopped works well in this recipe.

146

SERVES 8

Chocolate and Marmalade Swiss Roll

Chocolate and Apricot Swiss Roll

147

- Swap the marmalade for a good quality apricot jam. If you prefer a more fruity swiss roll, stir 2 coarsely chopped dried apricots into the jam.

Milk Chocolate and Marmalade Swiss Roll

148

- Use milk chocolate instead of dark for a less bitter more creamy tasting swiss roll.

PREPARATION TIME 45 MINUTES

COOKING TIME 15–20 MINUTES

INGREDIENTS

100 g / 3 ½ oz / ⅔ cup self-raising flour
28 g / 1 oz / ¼ cup unsweetened cocoa powder
1 tsp baking powder
100 g / 3 ½ oz / ½ cup caster (superfine) sugar
100 g / 3 ½ oz / ½ cup butter, softened
2 large eggs

TO DECORATE

200 g / 7 oz / ⅔ cup marmalade
100 g / 3 ½ oz / ½ cup dark chocolate (minimum 60 % cocoa solids)

- Preheat the oven to 180°C (160°C fan) / 355F / gas 4 and grease and line a Swiss roll tin.
- Put all of the cake ingredients in a large mixing bowl and whisk them together with an electric whisk for 4 minutes or until pale and well whipped.
- Spoon the mixture into the tin and spread into an even layer with a palette knife.
- Bake for 15–20 minutes or until springy to the touch.
- Turn the cake out onto a sheet of greaseproof paper and peel off the lining paper. Spread the cake with marmalade and roll up whilst warm, using the greaseproof paper to help you.
- Leave the cake to cool.
- Melt the chocolate in a microwave or bain-marie then leave it to cool and thicken a little.
- Drizzle the chocolate all over the cake, spreading it round the sides with a palette knife.

149
MAKES 9

Chocolate and Pecan Brownies

- Preheat the oven to 170⁰C (150⁰C fan) / 340F / gas 3 and oil and line a 20 cm square cake tin.
- Melt the chocolate, cocoa and butter together in a saucepan, then leave to cool a little.
- Whisk the sugar and eggs together with an electric whisk for 3 minutes or until very light and creamy.
- Pour in the chocolate mixture and sieve over the flour, then fold everything together with the pecans until evenly mixed.
- Scrape into the tin and bake for 35–40 minutes or until the outside is set, but the centre is still quite soft, as it will continue to cook as it cools.
- Leave the brownie to cool for 10 minutes then cut into squares and serve warm with the ginger ice cream.

Chocolate and Walnut Brownies
150
- Walnuts work well in this recipe, swap the same quantity of pecans for these sharper tasting nuts.

PREPARATION TIME 25 MINUTES

COOKING TIME 35–40 MINUTES

INGREDIENTS

110 g / 4 oz / ½ cup dark chocolate, chopped
85 g / 3 oz / ¾ cup unsweetened cocoa powder, sifted
225 g / 8 oz / 1 cup butter
450 g / 15 oz / 2 ½ cups light brown sugar
4 large eggs
110 g / 4 oz / ⅔ cup self-raising flour
110 g / 4 oz / ¾ cup pecan nuts, chopped

TO SERVE
ginger ice cream

151
SERVES 8

Dark and White Chocolate Layer Cake

- Preheat the oven to 180⁰C (160⁰C fan) / 325F / gas 4 and grease and line 2 Swiss roll tins.
- Put all of the chocolate cake ingredients in a large mixing bowl and whisk them together with an electric whisk for 4 minutes or until pale and well whipped.
- Spoon the mixture into one of the tins and spread into an even layer with a palette knife.
- Bake for 15–20 minutes or until springy to the touch.
- Make the plain cake layer in the same way.
- To make the ganache, chop the chocolates and transfer to 2 seperate bowls.
- Heat the cream until it starts to simmer, then pour half over the white chocolate and half over the dark. Stir until cooled and thickened.
- Cut the 2 cakes into thirds and sandwich alternate layers together with the chocolate ganaches.

Dark and White Chocolate Layer Cake with Rum
152
- Add 1–2 tablespoons of rum into the white chocolate ganache for a richer tasting cake.

PREPARATION TIME 45 MINUTES

COOKING TIME 15–20 MINUTES

INGREDIENTS

FOR THE CHOCOLATE LAYER
100 g / 3 ½ oz / ⅔ cup self-raising flour
28 g / 1 oz / ¼ cup cocoa powder
1 tsp baking powder
100 g / 3 ½ oz / ½ cup caster (superfine) sugar
100 g / 3 ½ oz / ½ cup butter, softened
2 large eggs

FOR THE PLAIN CAKE LAYER
100 g / 3 ½ oz / ⅔ cup self-raising flour
1 tsp baking powder
100 g / 3 ½ oz / ½ cup caster (superfine) sugar
100 g / 3 ½ oz / ½ cup butter, softened
2 large eggs

FOR THE GANACHE
225 g / 8 oz / 1 ⅓ cup white chocolate
225g / 8 oz / 1 ⅓ cup dark chocolate
225 ml / 8 fl. oz / 1 cup double cream

153

SERVES 8-10

Chocolate-covered Coconut Loaf Cake

PREPARATION TIME 15 MINUTES

COOKING TIME 45–55 MINUTES

INGREDIENTS

225 g / 8 oz / 1 cup butter, softened
225 g / 8 oz / 1 cup caster (superfine) sugar
4 large eggs, beaten
225 g / 4 ½ oz / 1 ½ cups self-raising flour
100 g / 3 ½ oz / 1 cup desiccated coconut
200 g / 7 oz / 1 ¼ cups dark chocolate (minimum 60 % cocoa solids)

- Preheat the oven to 180°C (160°C fan) / 355F / gas 4 and grease and line a loaf tin with greaseproof paper.
- Cream the butter and sugar together until well whipped then gradually whisk in the eggs, beating well after each addition.
- Fold in the flour and coconut then scrape the mixture into the tin.
- Bake the cake for 45–55 minutes or until a skewer inserted in the centre comes out clean.
- Transfer the cake to a wire rack and leave to cool completely.
- Melt the chocolate in a microwave or bain-marie then pour it over the cake and smooth the sides with a palette knife. Leave to set before serving.

154

MAKES 9

Chocolate and Sponge Biscuit Brownies

PREPARATION TIME 25 MINUTES

COOKING TIME 35–40 MINUTES

INGREDIENTS

110 g / 4 oz / ½ cup milk chocolate, chopped
85 g / 3 oz / ¾ cup cocoa powder, sifted
225 g / 8 oz / 1 cup butter
450 g / 15 oz / 2 ½ cups light brown sugar
4 large eggs
110 g / 4 oz / ⅔ cup self-raising flour
8 sponge finger biscuits, broken into pieces

- Preheat the oven to 170°C (150°C fan) / 340F / gas 3 and oil and line a 20 cm square cake tin.
- Melt the chocolate, cocoa and butter together in a saucepan, then leave to cool a little.
- Whisk the sugar and eggs together with an electric whisk for 3 minutes or until very light and creamy.
- Pour in the chocolate mixture and sieve over the flour, then fold everything together with the sponge finger biscuits until evenly mixed.
- Scrape into the tin and bake for 35–40 minutes or until a skewer inserted comes out clean.
- Leave the brownie to cool completely before cutting into 9 squares.

155
SERVES 8

Chocolate and Mandarin Cake

- Preheat the oven to 170°C (150°C fan) / 325F / gas 3 and butter a 23 cm round cake tin.
- Sieve the flour, cocoa and baking powder into a mixing bowl and add sugar, butter and eggs.
- Beat the mixture with an electric whisk for 4 minutes or until smooth and well whipped.
- Arrange the mandarin segments in the bottom of the tin and spoon the cake mixture on top.
- Bake for 35 minutes or until a skewer inserted comes out clean.
- Leave the cake to cool for 20 minutes before turning out onto a serving plate.

PREPARATION TIME 15 MINUTES

COOKING TIME 35 MINUTES

INGREDIENTS

300 g / 10 ½ oz / 2 cups self-raising flour
28 g / 1 oz / ¼ cup unsweetened cocoa powder
2 tsp baking powder
250 g / 9 oz / 1 ¼ cup caster (superfine) sugar
250 g / 9 oz / 1 ¼ cup butter, softened
5 large eggs
1 can mandarin segments in syrup, drained

Chocolate and Apricot Tart

156
SERVES 8-10

PREPARATION TIME 25 MINUTES

COOKING TIME 15–20 MINUTES

INGREDIENTS

250 ml / 9 fl. oz / 1 cup double (heavy) cream
250 g / 9 oz / 1 ⅓ cups dark chocolate, chopped
55 g / 2 oz / ¼ cup butter, softened
100 g / 3 ½ oz / ½ cup dried apricots, chopped
100 g / 3 ½ oz / ½ cup butter, cubed
200 g / 7 oz / 1 ⅓ cups plain (all purpose) flour
55 g / 2 oz / ¼ cups caster sugar
1 egg, beaten
cocoa powder for dusting
2 dried apricots, halved
1 physalis
gold leaf

- Preheat the oven to 200°C (180°C fan) / 390F / gas 6.
- To make the pastry, rub the cubed butter into the flour and sugar and add the egg with just enough cold water to bind.
- Wrap the dough in cling film and chill for 30 minutes then roll out on a floured surface. Use the pastry to line a 23 cm loose-bottomed tart tin and trim the edges.
- Prick the pastry with a fork, line with cling film and fill with baking beans or rice. Bake for 10 minutes then remove the cling film and baking beans and cook for another 8 minutes to crisp.
- Heat the cream to a simmer then pour it over the chocolate and stir until smooth.
- Add the soft butter and blend. Sprinkle the chopped apricots over the pastry base and pour the ganache on top.
- Leave the ganache to cool for 2 hours. Dust the top of the tart with cocoa and arrange the apricots and physalis on top.
- Apply the gold leaf with a dry brush.

Chocolate and Pine Nut Loaf

157
SERVES 8

PREPARATION TIME 15 MINUTES

COOKING TIME 45–50 MINUTES

INGREDIENTS

100 g / 3 ½ oz / ⅔ cup self-raising flour
1 tsp baking powder
2 tbsp cocoa powder
50 g / 1 ¾ oz / ½ cup ground almonds
150 g / 5 ½ oz / ⅔ cup caster (superfine) sugar
150 g / 5 ½ oz / ⅔ cup butter, softened
3 large eggs
100 g / 3 ½ oz / ¾ cup pine nuts

- Preheat the oven to 180°C (160°C fan) / 355F / gas 4 and line a loaf tin with greaseproof paper.
- Sieve the flour, baking powder and cocoa into a mixing bowl then add the ground almonds, sugar, butter and eggs and whisk with an electric whisk for 4 minutes or until pale and well whipped.
- Fold in the pine nuts and spoon into the tin, then bake for 45–50 minutes.
- The cake is ready when a toothpick inserted in the centre comes out clean.
- Transfer the cake to a wire rack and leave to cool completely.

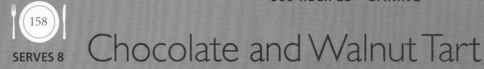

Chocolate and Walnut Tart

Chocolate and Pistachio Tart

159

- You can swap the walnuts for pistachios in this rich, delicious tasting tart.

Chocolate and Stem Ginger Tart

160

- Use 60 g / 2 oz / ¼ cup of finely chopped stem ginger instead of the nuts for a warm tasting, rich tart.

PREPARATION TIME 25 MINUTES

COOKING TIME 15–20 MINUTES

....

INGREDIENTS

250 ml / 9 fl. oz / 1 cup double (heavy) cream
250 g / 9 oz / 1 ⅓ cups dark chocolate (minimum 60 % cocoa solids), chopped
55 g / 2 oz / ¼ cup butter, softened
150 g / 5 ½ oz / 1 ¼ cups caramelised walnuts, chopped to serve

FOR THE PASTRY

100 g / 3 ½ oz / ½ cup butter, cubed
200 g / 7 oz / 1 ⅓ cups plain (all purpose) flour
55 g / 2 oz / ¼ cup light brown sugar
1 egg, beaten

- Preheat the oven to 200°C (180°C fan) / 390F / gas 6.
- To make the pastry, rub the butter into the flour and sugar and add the egg with just enough cold water to bind.
- Wrap the dough in cling film and chill for 30 minutes then roll out on a floured surface.
- Use the pastry to line a 23 cm loose-bottomed tart tin and trim the edges.
- Prick the pastry with a fork, line with cling film and fill with baking beans or rice.
- Bake for 10 minutes then remove the cling film and baking beans and cook for another 8 minutes to crisp.
- Heat the cream to simmering point then pour it over the chocolate and stir until smooth.
- Add the butter and blend it in with a stick blender.
- Scatter the walnuts over the bottom of the pastry case then pour in the ganache and level the top with a palette knife.
- Leave the ganache to cool and set for at least 2 hours before cutting and serving, scattered with caramelised walnuts.

Wholemeal Chocolate Muffins

161 MAKES 12

- Preheat the oven to 180°C (160°C fan) / 355F / gas 4 and line a 12-hole muffin tin with paper cases.
- Beat the egg in a jug with the oil and milk until well mixed.
- Mix the flours, cocoa, baking powder, sugar and chocolate in a bowl.
- Pour in the egg mixture and stir just enough to combine.
- Divide the mixture between the paper cases and bake for 20–25 minutes.
- Test with a wooden toothpick, if it comes out clean, the cakes are done.
- Transfer the muffins to a wire rack and leave to cool completely.

PREPARATION TIME 25 MINUTES

COOKING TIME 20–25 MINUTES

INGREDIENTS

1 large egg
120 ml / 4 fl. oz / ½ cup sunflower oil
120 ml / 4 fl. oz / ½ cup milk
200 g / 7 oz / 1 ⅓ cups self-raising flour, sifted
175 g / 6 oz / 1 ¼ cups stoneground wholemeal flour
2 tbsp cocoa powder
2 tsp baking powder
200 g / 7 oz / ¾ cup caster (superfine) sugar
150 g / 5 ½ oz / ¾ cup dark chocolate (minimum 60% cocoa solids), grated

Wholemeal, Chestnut and Chocolate Muffins

162

- Swap out half the wholemeal flour and use half chestnut flour for a nuttier tasting chocolate muffin.

Chocolate Truffle Loaf Cake

163 SERVES 8-10

- Preheat the oven to 180°C (160°C fan) / 355F / gas 4 and grease and line a large loaf tin with greaseproof paper.
- Put all of the ingredients in a bowl and whisk together until smooth.
- Scrape the mixture into the loaf tin and level the top with a palette knife.
- Put the tin in a large roasting tin pour around enough boiling water to come half way up the side of the loaf tin.
- Bake the cake for 40–50 minutes or until the centre is only just set.
- Leave to cool completely in the tin then refrigerate for 2 hours before turning out and dusting with cocoa.

PREPARATION TIME 15 MINUTES

COOKING TIME 40–50 MINUTES

INGREDIENTS

600 g / 1 lb 5 oz / 2 ¾ cups cream cheese
150 ml / 5 fl. oz / ⅔ cup soured cream
175 g / 6 oz / ¾ cup caster (superfine) sugar
2 large eggs
1 egg yolk
2 tbsp plain (all purpose) flour
2 tbsp cocoa powder, plus extra for dusting
200 g / 7 oz / 1 cup dark chocolate (minimum 60 % cocoa solids), melted

Chocolate and Mint Truffle Loaf Cake

164

- Add 2 teaspoons of peppermint essence to the truffle mix for a subtle mint flavour.

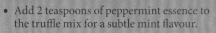

165

MAKES 9

Chocolate and Date Squares

PREPARATION TIME 15 MINUTES

COOKING TIME 30–35 MINUTES

INGREDIENTS

150 g / 6 oz / 1 cup self-raising flour
28 g / 1 oz / ¼ cup unsweetened
cocoa powder
2 tsp baking powder
175 g / 6 oz / ¾ cup caster (superfine)
sugar
175 g / 6 oz / ¾ cup butter, softened
3 eggs
100 g / 3 ½ oz / ½ cup dates, stoned
and chopped

- Preheat the oven to 180°C (160°C fan) / 355F / gas 4 and grease and line a square cake tin.
- Put all of the cake ingredients, except the dates, in a large mixing bowl and whisk them together with an electric whisk for 4 minutes or until pale and well whipped. Fold in the dates.
- Scrape the mixture into the tin and level the top with a spatula.
- Bake for 30–35 minutes. The cake is ready when a toothpick inserted in the centre comes out clean.
- Transfer the cake to a wire rack to cool completely before cutting into squares.

166

Chocolate, Raisin and Sultana Squares

- Instead of the dates use half raisins and half sultanas for a different twist to this chocolate cake.

167

SERVES 8-10

Raspberry and Coconut Cake

PREPARATION TIME 20 MINUTES

COOKING TIME 45–55 MINUTES

INGREDIENTS

225 g / 8 oz / 1 cup butter, softened
225 g / 8 oz / 1 cup caster (superfine)
sugar
4 large eggs, beaten
225 g/ 4 ½ oz / 1 ½ cups self-raising
flour
100 g / 3 ½ oz / 1 cup desiccated
coconut
150 g / 5 ½ oz / 1 cup raspberries
3 tbsp toasted coconut flakes

- Preheat the oven to 180°C (160°C fan) / 355F / gas 4 and grease and line a 23 cm round cake tin with greaseproof paper.
- Cream the butter and sugar together until well whipped then gradually whisk in the eggs, beating well after each addition.
- Fold in the flour, desiccated coconut and raspberries then scrape the mixture into the tin. Sprinkle over the coconut flakes.
- Bake the cake for 45–55 minutes or until a skewer inserted in the centre comes out clean.
- Transfer the cake to a wire rack and leave to cool.

168

Blueberry and Coconut Cake

- Out of season you can use blueberries instead of raspberries which are equally delicious in this coconut cake.

169

SERVES 8

Coconut, Pineapple and Kiwi Loaf Cake

Coconut, Mango and Banana Loaf Cake

170

- Chop 2 bananas and substitute them for the pineapple in the filling mix. Dice half a mango into 1 cm chunks to decorate.

Coconut, Pineapple and Chocolate Loaf Cake

171

- When decorating the cake gently melt 150 g/ 6 oz / ¾ cup of dark chocolate and drizzle over the cake with a sprinkle of desiccated ccoconut.

PREPARATION TIME 30 MINUTES

COOKING TIME 45–50 MINUTES

....

INGREDIENTS

150 g / 6 oz / 1 cup plain (all purpose) flour
28 g / 1 oz / ¼ cup desiccated coconut
2 tsp baking powder
175 g / 6 oz / ¾ cup caster (superfine) sugar
175 g / 6 oz / ¾ cup butter, softened
3 large eggs

FOR THE CRÈME PATISSERIE

4 large egg yolks
75 g / 2 ½ oz / ⅓ cup caster (superfine) sugar
1 tsp vanilla extract
2 tsp cornflour (cornstarch)
450 ml / 16 fl. oz / 1 ¾ cups whole milk
1 can pineapple chunks, drained

TO DECORATE

2 tbsp desiccated coconut, toasted
1 kiwi, sliced

- Preheat the oven to 180⁰C (160⁰ C fan) / 355F / gas 4 and grease and line a loaf tin with greaseproof paper.
- Whisk together all of the cake ingredients with an electric whisk for 4 minutes or until well whipped.
- Scrape the mixture into the tin and bake for 45–50 minutes.
- The cake is ready when a toothpick inserted in the centre comes out clean.
- Transfer the cake to a wire rack to cool completely before cutting in half horizontally.
- To make the crème patisserie, whisk together the egg yolks, sugar, vanilla extract and cornflour.
- Heat the milk almost to a simmer then strain it through a sieve and gradually whisk it into the egg mixture.
- Scrape the custard back into the saucepan and cook over a medium heat until it thickens, stirring constantly.
- Pour it into a bowl and stir in the pineapple then leave it to cool to room temperature.
- Beat the crème patisserie until smooth and use it to sandwich the cake back together.
- Sprinkle the cake with toasted coconut and arrange the kiwi slices on top.

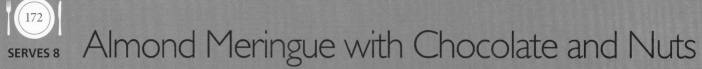

172

SERVES 8

Almond Meringue with Chocolate and Nuts

Fruit and Nut Meringue with Chocolate

173

- Swap the hazelnuts (cob nuts) for a mix of raisins and sultanas for a tasty fruit and nut taste. Combined with the chocolate this meringue is truly delicious.

Almond Meringue with Coffee and Chocolate

174

- Add 2 tablespoons of espresso to the ganache mixture for a sharper tasting filling.

Almond Meringue with Fruit

175

- Try changing the nuts for the same quantity of dried fruit instead.

PREPARATION TIME 35 MINUTES

COOKING TIME 15 MINUTES

....

INGREDIENTS

4 large egg whites
a pinch cream of tartar
200 g / 7 oz / ¾ cup caster (superfine) sugar
200 g / 7 oz / 2 cups ground almonds

FOR THE GANACHE
200 ml / 7 fl. oz / ¾ cup double cream
200 g / 7 oz / 1 ¼ cups dark chocolate (minimum 60 % cocoa solids), chopped

FOR THE CARAMELISED NUTS
100 g / 3 ½ oz / ½ cup caster (superfine) sugar
75 g / 2 ½ oz / ⅔ cup pistachio nuts
75 g / 2 ½ oz / ⅔ cup blanched almonds
75 g / 2 ½ oz / ⅔ cup toasted hazelnuts (cob nuts), chopped

- Preheat the oven to 180°C (160°C fan) / 355F / gas 4 and line a Swiss roll tin with non-stick baking paper.
- Whisk the egg whites with the cream of tartar until stiff then whisk in the caster sugar a tablespoon at a time.
- Fold in the ground almonds then spread the mixture onto the Swiss roll tray in an even layer.
- Bake for 15 minutes then leave to cool completely.
- Bring the cream to simmering point then pour it over the chocolate. Stir until smooth then leave to cool and thicken to a pipeable consistency.
- Put the sugar in a heavy-bottomed saucepan and heat gently, without stirring, until it starts to melt round the edges. Continue to cook, swirling the pan occasionally, until the sugar has all dissolved and the caramel is golden.
- Spread the nuts out on a baking tray lined with a non-stick baking mat and drizzle the caramel all over the top. Leave to cool then break it up with your fingers.
- Pipe the ganache on top of the meringue and sprinkle with the caramelised nuts.

Apple Crumble One Crust Pie

176

SERVES 8

- Preheat the oven to 200°C (180°C fan), 390F, gas 6.
- First make the pastry. Sieve the flour into a mixing bowl then rub in the butter until the mixture resembles fine breadcrumbs.
- Stir in just enough cold water to bring the pastry together into a pliable dough then chill for 30 minutes.
- Mix the chopped apple with the sugar and cornflour.
- Roll out the pastry on a floured surface into a large circle. Prick it with a fork and transfer to a tray.
- Spoon the apples into a pile in the middle.
- To make the crumble topping, rub the butter into the flour then stir in the almonds and brown sugar.
- Take handfuls of the topping and squeeze it into a clump, then crumble it over the apples.
- Fold up the pastry edges and pinch to secure. Bake the tart for 35 – 40 minutes until golden brown.

Apricot Crumble One Crust Pie

177

- This crumble works well with fresh apricots, instead of the apples. Be sure to halve and stone the apricots before using in the above recipe as you would the apples.

PREPARATION TIME 50 MINUTES

COOKING TIME 35–40 MINUTES

INGREDIENTS

450 g / 1 lb / 1 ¼ cups Bramley apples, peeled and chopped
50 g / 1 ¾ oz / ¼ cup caster (superfine) sugar
1 tbsp cornflour (cornstarch)

FOR THE PASTRY
200 g / 7 oz / 1 ⅓ cups plain (all purpose) flour
100 g / 3 ½ oz / ½ cup butter, cubed and chilled

FOR THE CRUMBLE
150 g / 5 oz / ⅔ cup butter
100 g / 3 ½ oz / ⅔ cup plain (all purpose) flour
50 g / 1 ¾ oz / ½ cup ground almonds
75 g / 2 ½ oz / ½ cup light brown sugar

Mini Apricot Loaf Cakes

178

MAKES 12

- Preheat the oven to 190°C (170°C fan) / 375F / gas 5 and oil a 12-hole silicone mini loaf cake mould.
- Combine the flour, sugar, butter, eggs and vanilla in a bowl and whisk together for 2 minutes or until smooth. Fold in the chopped apricots.
- Divide the mixture between the moulds, then transfer the mould to the oven and bake for 15–20 minutes.
- Test with a wooden toothpick, if it comes out clean, the cakes are done.
- Transfer the cakes to a wire rack and leave to cool completely.

Date Mini Loaf Cakes

179

- For a richer slightly darker looking loaf cake use chopped dates instead of the apricots.

PREPARATION TIME 15 MINUTES

COOKING TIME 15–20 MINUTES

INGREDIENTS

110 g / 4 oz / ⅔ cup self-raising flour, sifted
110 g / 4 oz / ½ cup caster (superfine) sugar
110 g / 4 oz / ½ cup butter, softened
2 large eggs
1 tsp vanilla extract
75 g / 2 ½ oz / ⅓ cup dried apricots, chopped

180

MAKES 12

Fig and Honey Muffins

PREPARATION TIME 15 MINUTES

COOKING TIME 20–25 MINUTES

....

INGREDIENTS

1 large egg
120 ml / 4 fl. oz / ½ cup sunflower oil
120 ml / 4 fl. oz / ½ cup milk
100 g / 3 ½ oz / ⅓ cup runny honey
375 g / 12 ½ oz / 2 ½ cups self-raising flour, sifted
1 tsp baking powder
100 g / 3 ½ oz / ½ cup caster (superfine) sugar
4 fresh figs, chopped

- Preheat the oven to 180°C (160°C fan) / 350F / gas 4 and line a 12-hole muffin tin with paper cake cases.
- Beat the egg in a jug with the oil, milk and honey until well mixed.
- Mix the flour, baking powder, and sugar in a bowl.
- Pour in the egg mixture and stir just enough to combine then fold in the figs.
- Divide the mixture between the paper cases and bake for 20–25 minutes.
- Test with a wooden toothpick, if it comes out clean, the cakes are done.
- Transfer the muffins to a wire rack and leave to cool completely.

Date and Maple Syrup Muffins

181

- Use 6 chopped dates and maple syrup instead of the honey for a delicious, rich tasting muffin.

182

MAKES 12

Orange Flower Financiers

PREPARATION TIME 30 MINUTES

COOKING TIME 10–15 MINUTES

....

INGREDIENTS

110 g / 4 oz / ½ cup butter
55 g / 2 oz / ⅓ cup plain (all purpose) flour
55 g / 2 oz / ½ cup ground almonds
110 g / 4 oz / 1 cup icing (confectioners') sugar
3 large egg whites
1 tsp orange flower water

- Preheat the oven to 170°C (150°C fan) / 325F / gas 3 and oil and flour a 12-hole financier mould.
- Heat the butter until it foams and starts to smell nutty then leave to cool.
- Combine the flour, ground almonds and icing sugar in a bowl and whisk in the egg whites and orange flower water.
- Pour the cooled butter through a sieve into the bowl and whisk into the mixture until evenly mixed.
- Spoon the mixture into the moulds, then transfer the tin to the oven and bake for 10–15 minutes.
- Test with a wooden toothpick, if it comes out clean, the cakes are done.
- Transfer the cakes to a wire rack to cool for 5 minutes before serving.

Rose Water Financiers

183

- These delicious financiers work well with rose water for a delicate floral taste – use 1 teaspoon.

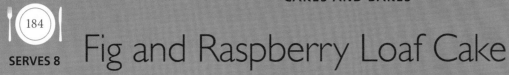

184
SERVES 8

Fig and Raspberry Loaf Cake

Fig and Date Loaf
185
- For a denser but equally tasty loaf use roughly chopped dates instead of the raspberries.

Fig, Raspberry and Vanilla Loaf
186
- Take 1 vanilla pod, split and scrape the seeds into the batter mix for a fuller tasting loaf cake.

PREPARATION TIME 15 MINUTES

COOKING TIME 55 MINUTES

INGREDIENTS

300 g / 10 ½ oz / 2 cups self-raising flour
2 tsp baking powder
250 g / 9 oz / 1 ¼ cups caster (superfine) sugar
250 g / 9 oz / 1 ¼ cups butter, softened
5 large eggs
75 g / 2 ½ oz / ½ cup raspberries
4 fresh figs, sliced

- Preheat the oven to 170°C (150°C fan) / 340F / gas 3 and line a loaf tin with greaseproof paper.
- Sieve the flour and baking powder into a mixing bowl and add the sugar, butter and eggs.
- Beat the mixture with an electric whisk for 4 minutes or until smooth and well whipped.
- Fold in the raspberries and figs and scrape the mixture into the loaf tin.
- Bake for 55 minutes or until a skewer inserted in the centre comes out clean.
- Transfer the cake to a wire rack and leave to cool completely.

Sweet Cinnamon Nut Bread

(187) MAKES 1

Cinnamon and Chocolate Bread

(188)

- Instead of the hazelnuts sprinkle dark chocolate chips onto the bread 10 minutes before the end of the baking time.

Mixed Spice Nut Bread

(189)

- For a more festive flavour to this delicious bread use mixed spice instead of cinnamon.

PREPARATION TIME
4 HOURS 45 MINUTES

COOKING TIME 25-35 MINUTES

....

INGREDIENTS

250 g / 9 oz / 1 ¼ cups butter, cubed
200 g / 7 oz / 1 ⅓ cups strong white bread flour
200 g / 7 oz / 1 ⅓ cups stoneground wholemeal flour
2 ½ tsp easy blend dried yeast
4 tbsp caster (superfine) sugar
1 tsp fine sea salt
4 large eggs, plus 3 extra yolks
100 g / 3 ½ oz / ½ cup soft brown sugar
3 tsp ground cinnamon
75 g / 2 ½ oz / ⅔ cup hazelnuts (cob nuts), chopped

- Rub half the butter into the flours then stir in the yeast, sugar and salt. Beat the whole eggs and yolks together and stir into the dry ingredients.
- Knead the very soft dough on a lightly oiled surface with 2 plastic scrapers for 10 minutes or until smooth and elastic.
- Leave the dough to rest in a lightly oiled bowl, covered with oiled cling film, for 2 hours or until doubled in size.
- Roll out the dough as big as possible on a floured surface.
- Cream the rest of the butter with the brown sugar and cinnamon and spread ¾ of it over the dough.
- Roll the dough up tightly and transfer to a greased baking tray.
- Cover with oiled cling film and leave to prove for 2 hours or until doubled in size.
- Meanwhile, preheat the oven to 220⁰C (200⁰C fan) / 430F / gas 7.
- Brush the top of the loaf with the reserved cinnamon mixture and make a few slashes across with a knife.
- Sprinkle with hazelnuts and bake for 25–35 minutes or until golden brown.

190

SERVES 8

Light Orange and Fruit Cake

- Preheat the oven to 180°C (160°C fan) / 355F / gas 4 and line a loaf tin with non-stick baking paper.
- Sieve the flour into a mixing bowl and rub in the butter until it resembles fine breadcrumbs then stir in the sugar, sultanas, candied peel, cherries and orange zest.
- Lightly beat the egg with the milk and stir it into the dry ingredients until just combined.
- Scrape the mixture into the loaf tin and bake for 55 minutes or until a skewer inserted in the centre comes out clean.
- Transfer the cake to a wire rack and leave to cool completely.

PREPARATION TIME 15 MINUTES

COOKING TIME 55 MINUTES

INGREDIENTS

225 g / 8 oz / 1 ½ cups self raising flour
100 g / 3 ½ oz / ½ cup butter, cubed
100 g / 3 ½ oz / ½ cup caster (superfine) sugar
100 g / 3 ½ oz / ½ cup sultanas
150 g / 5 ½ oz / ¾ cup candied orange peel, chopped
100 g / 3 ½ oz / ½ cup glacé cherries, halved
1 orange, zest finely grated
1 large egg
75 ml / 2 ½ fl. oz / ⅓ cup whole milk

Light Orange and Whisky Fruit Cake

191

- After baking, pierce the warm cake with a skewer and drizzle with 2 tablespoons of whisky. Leave to absorb as it cools.

192

MAKES 12

Banana Party Cupcakes

- Preheat the oven to 190°C (170°C fan) / 375F / gas 5 and line a 12-hole cupcake tin with paper cases.
- Combine the flour, sugar, butter, eggs and banana in a bowl and whisk together for 2 minutes or until smooth.
- Divide the mixture between the paper cases, then transfer the tin to the oven and bake for 15–20 minutes.
- Test with a wooden toothpick, if it comes out clean, the cakes are done.
- Transfer the cakes to a wire rack and leave to cool completely.
- To make the icing, mix the icing sugar with the banana syrup and food colouring, adding a few drops of water if the icing is too stiff.
- Spoon the icing over the cakes and sprinkle each one with hundreds and thousands or sugar stars.

PREPARATION TIME 30 MINUTES

COOKING TIME 15–20 MINUTES

INGREDIENTS

110 g / 4 oz / ⅔ cup self-raising flour, sifted
110 g / 4 oz / ½ cup caster (superfine) sugar
110 g / 4 oz / ½ cup butter, softened
2 large eggs
1 banana, chopped
225 g / 8 oz / 2 ¼ cups icing (confectioners') sugar
1 tbsp banana flavoured syrup
a few drops yellow food dye
hundreds and thousands and sugar stars

Banana and Chocolate Cupcakes

193

- Stir through 55 g / 2 oz / ⅓ cup of chocolate chips into the cake batter mixture.

194

SERVES 8

Apple and Rosemary Tarte Tatin

PREPARATION TIME 25 MINUTES

COOKING TIME 20–25 MINUTES

....

INGREDIENTS

2 tbsp butter
2 tbsp dark brown sugar
6 small apples, peeled, cored and halved
2 tbsp rosemary leaves
250 g / 9 oz / ¾ cup all-butter puff pastry
2 tbsp flaked (slivered) almonds

- Preheat the oven to 220°C (200°C fan) / 430F / gas 7.
- Heat the butter and sugar in an ovenproof frying pan and add the apples and rosemary. Cook over a very low heat for 5 minutes, turning occasionally, until they start to colour and soften.
- Arrange the apples, cut side up and leave to cool a little.
- Roll out the pastry on a floured surface and cut out a circle slightly larger than the frying pan.
- Lay the pastry over the apples and tuck in the edges, then pierce a couple of times with a sharp knife. Transfer the pan to the oven and bake for 25 minutes or until the pastry is golden brown and cooked through.
- Using oven gloves, put a large plate on top of the frying pan and turn them both over in one smooth movement to unmould the tart.
- Scatter over the flaked (slivered) almonds and serve immediately.

195

MAKES 12

Vanilla Sponge Rings

PREPARATION TIME 30 MINUTES

COOKING TIME 10–15 MINUTES

....

INGREDIENTS

110 g / 4 oz / ½ cup butter
55 g / 2 oz / ⅓ cup plain (all purpose) flour
55 g / 2 oz / ½ cup ground almonds
110 g / 4 oz / 1 cup icing (confectioners') sugar
3 large egg whites
1 vanilla pod, seeds only

- Preheat the oven to 170°C (150°C fan) / 325F / gas 3 and oil and flour 12 mini ring moulds.
- Heat the butter until it foams and starts to smell nutty then leave to cool.
- Combine the flour, ground almonds and icing sugar in a bowl and whisk in the egg whites and vanilla seeds.
- Pour the cooled butter through a sieve into the bowl and whisk into the mixture until evenly mixed.
- Spoon the mixture into the moulds, then transfer to the oven and bake for 10–15 minutes.
- Test with a wooden toothpick, if it comes out clean, the cakes are done.
- Transfer the cakes to a wire rack to cool for 5 minutes before serving.

Chocolate and Walnut Sponge Squares

196 MAKES 12

- Preheat the oven to 180°C (160°C fan) / 355F / gas 4 and grease and line a 30 cm x 23 cm cake tin.
- Put all of the ingredients except the walnuts in a large mixing bowl and whisk them together with an electric whisk for 4 minutes or until pale and well whipped.
- Scrape the mixture into the tin and level the top with a spatula then sprinkle over the walnuts.
- Bake for 30–35 minutes. The cake is ready when a toothpick inserted in the centre comes out clean.
- Transfer the cake to a wire rack to cool completely before cutting into 12 squares and dusting with cocoa.

PREPARATION TIME 15 MINUTES

COOKING TIME 30–35 MINUTES

INGREDIENTS

150 g / 6 oz / 1 cup self-raising flour
28 g / 1 oz / ¼ cup unsweetened cocoa powder, plus extra for dusting
2 tsp baking powder
175 g / 6 oz / ¾ cup caster (superfine) sugar
175 g / 6 oz / ¾ cup butter, softened
3 eggs
100 g / 3 ½ oz / ⅓ cup walnuts, chopped

Hazelnut Madeleines

197 MAKES 12

PREPARATION TIME
1 HOUR 30 MINUTES

COOKING TIME 10–15 MINUTES

INGREDIENTS

110 g / 4 oz / ½ cup butter
55 g / 2 oz / ⅓ cup plain (all purpose) flour
55 g / 2 oz / ½ cup ground hazelnuts (cob nuts)
110 g / 4 oz / 1 cup icing (confectioners') sugar
3 large egg whites

- Heat the butter until it foams and starts to smell nutty then leave to cool.
- Combine the flour, ground hazelnuts and icing sugar in a bowl and whisk in the egg whites.
- Pour the cooled butter through a sieve into the bowl and whisk into the mixture until evenly mixed.
- Leave the cake mixture to rest in the fridge for an hour.
- Preheat the oven to 170°C (150°C fan) / 325F / gas 3 and oil and flour a 12-hole Madeleine mould.
- Spoon the mixture into the moulds, then transfer the tin to the oven and bake for 10–15 minutes.
- Test with a wooden toothpick, if it comes out clean, the cakes are done.
- Transfer the cakes to a wire rack to cool for 5 minutes before serving.

Bundt Cake

198 SERVES 8-10

PREPARATION TIME 15 MINUTES

COOKING TIME 45 MINUTES

INGREDIENTS

225 g / 8 oz / 1 cup butter, softened
225 g / 8 oz / 1 cup caster (superfine) sugar
4 large eggs, beaten
125 g / 4 ½ oz / ¾ cup self-raising flour

- Preheat the oven to 180°C (160°C fan) / 355F / gas 4 and butter a bundt tin.
- Cream the butter and sugar together until well whipped then gradually whisk in the eggs, beating well after each addition.
- Fold in the flour then scrape the mixture into the tin.
- Bake the cake for 45 minutes or until a skewer inserted in the centre comes out clean.
- Turn the cake out onto a wire rack and leave to cool.

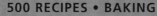

199

SERVES 8

Kiwi and Custard Tart

PREPARATION TIME I HOUR

COOKING TIME 25 MINUTES

⋯⋯⋯⋯⋯⋯⋯⋯⋯⋯⋯⋯

INGREDIENTS

6 kiwi fruit, peeled and sliced

FOR THE PASTRY
200 g / 7 oz / 1 ⅓ cups plain (all purpose) flour
100 g / 3 ½ oz / ½ cup butter, cubed

FOR THE CUSTARD
4 large egg yolks
75 g / 2 ½ oz / ⅓ cup caster (superfine) sugar
1 tsp vanilla extract
2 tsp cornflour (cornstarch)
450 ml / 16 fl. oz / 1 ¾ cups whole milk

- Preheat the oven to 200°C (180°C fan) / 390F / gas 6.
- Rub the butter into the flour and add just enough cold water to bind.
- Chill for 30 minutes then roll out on a floured surface. Use the pastry to line a 23 cm round loose-bottomed tart tin.
- Prick the pastry with a fork, line with cling film and fill with baking beans or rice.
- Bake for 10 minutes then remove the cling film and baking beans and cook for another 8 minutes to crisp.
- Reduce the oven temperature to 170°C (150°C fan) / 340F / gas 3.
- Whisk the custard ingredients together in a saucepan then stir over a low heat for 5 minutes until thickened.
- Pour the custard into the pastry case and leave to cool before arranging the kiwi fruit on top.

Mango and Custard Tart

200

- Substitute the kiwi fruit for 2 mangos and slice thinly, arranging in a fan like shape around the tart.

201

SERVES 8

Lemon and Poppy Seed Loaf Cake

PREPARATION TIME I5 MINUTES

COOKING TIME 35–40 MINUTES

⋯⋯⋯⋯⋯⋯⋯⋯⋯⋯⋯⋯

INGREDIENTS

150 g / 5 ½ oz / 1 cup self-raising flour
150 g / 5 ½ oz / ⅔ cup caster (superfine) sugar
150 g / 5 ½ oz / ⅔ cup butter, softened
3 eggs
1 tsp baking powder
1 tbsp lemon zest
2 tbsp lemon juice
2 tbsp poppy seeds

TO DECORATE
candied lemon peel, thinly sliced

- Preheat the oven to 180°C (160°C fan) / 355F / gas 4 and grease and line a small loaf tin.
- Put all of the cake ingredients in a large mixing bowl and whisk them together with an electric whisk for 4 minutes or until pale and well whipped.
- Scrape the mixture into the tin and level the top with a spatula.
- Bake for 35–40 minutes. The cake is ready when a toothpick inserted in the centre comes out clean.
- Transfer the cake to a wire rack to cool completely before garnishing with the candied lemon peel.

St Clements Loaf

202

- Mix 1 tablespoon of orange with the lemon juice and add 1 tablespoon of orange zest to the recipe. Use candied orange and lemon peel to decorate for a less acidic tasting topping.

Candied Lemon Sponge Squares

203

MAKES 12

- Blanch the lemon slices in boiling water for 5 minutes then drain well.
- Put the sugar in a saucepan with 200 ml water and stir over a low heat until dissolved. Bring to the boil and simmer then add the lemon slices and simmer for 10 minutes.
- Remove from the pan with a slotted spoon and leave to drip dry on a wire rack.
- Preheat the oven to 180⁰C (160⁰C fan) / 355F / gas 4 and grease and line a 30 cm x 23 cm cake tin.
- Put all of the cake ingredients in a large mixing bowl and whisk them together with an electric whisk for 4 minutes or until pale and well whipped.
- Scrape the mixture into the tin and level the top with a spatula then arrange 9 of the lemon slices on top.
- Bake for 30–35 minutes until springy to the touch.

Candied Orange Sponge Squares

204

- For a slight twist on this delicious cake use orange slices instead of lemon.

PREPARATION TIME 30 MINUTES

COOKING TIME 40–50 MINUTES

INGREDIENTS

175 g / 6 oz / 1 ¼ cups self-raising flour
2 tsp baking powder
175 g / 6 oz / ¾ cups caster (superfine) sugar
175 g / 6 oz / ¾ cup butter, softened
3 eggs
1 lemon, juice and zest

FOR THE CANDIED LEMON SLICES

2 lemons, thinly sliced
400 g / 14 oz / 1 ¾ cups caster (superfine) sugar

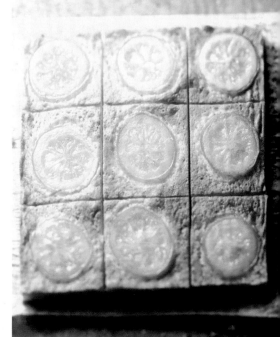

Iced Lemon Loaf Cake

205

SERVES 10

- Preheat the oven to 180⁰C (160⁰C fan) / 355F / gas 4 and grease and line a small loaf tin.
- Put all of the cake ingredients in a large mixing bowl and whisk them together with an electric whisk for 4 minutes or until pale and well whipped.
- Scrape the mixture into the tin and level the top with a spatula.
- Bake for 35–40 minutes. The cake is ready when a toothpick inserted in the centre comes out clean.
- Transfer the cake to a wire rack to cool completely.
- Sieve the icing sugar and stir in just enough lemon juice to produce a pourable icing.
- Pour the icing all over the cake and allow it to drip down the sides. Garnish with twisted lemon slices.

Iced Lemon and Lavender Loaf Cake

206

- Add 2 tablespoons of edible lavender flowers to the cake batter mix and sprinkle some extra onto the icing for decoration.

PREPARATION TIME 20 MINUTES

COOKING TIME 35–40 MINUTES

INGREDIENTS

150 g / 5 ½ oz / 1 cup self-raising flour
150 g / 5 ½ oz / ⅔ cup caster (superfine) sugar
150 g / 5 ½ oz / ⅔ cup butter, softened
3 eggs
1 tsp baking powder
1 tbsp lemon zest
2 tbsp lemon juice

TO DECORATE

200 g / 7 oz / 2 cups icing (confectioners') sugar
1–2 tbsp lemon juice
lemon slices

207

SERVES 8

Candied Lemon and Ginger Loaf Cake

PREPARATION TIME 30 MINUTES

COOKING TIME 50–55 MINUTES

....

INGREDIENTS

175 g / 6 oz / 1 ¼ cups self-raising flour
2 tsp baking powder
175 g / 6 oz / ¾ cup caster (superfine) sugar
175 g / 6 oz / ¾ cup butter, softened
3 eggs
1 lemon, juice and zest
100 g / 3 ½ oz / ½ cup crystallised ginger, finely chopped

FOR THE CANDIED LEMONS
3 lemons, quartered and thinly sliced
400 g / 14 oz / 1 ¾ cups caster (superfine) sugar

- Blanch the lemon slices in boiling water for 5 minutes then drain well. Put the sugar in a saucepan with 200 ml water and stir over a low heat until dissolved.
- Bring to the boil and simmer for 5 minutes then add the lemon slices and simmer for 10 minutes.
- Remove from the pan with a slotted spoon and leave to drip dry on a wire rack.
- Preheat the oven to 180°C (160°C fan) / 355F / gas 4 and grease and line a loaf tin.
- Put all of the cake ingredients in a large mixing bowl and whisk them together with an electric whisk for 4 minutes or until pale and well whipped. Fold in the candied lemon pieces.
- Scrape the mixture into the tin and level the top with a spatula then bake for 30–35 minutes.
- Transfer the cake to a wire rack to cool completely.

Candied Orange and Ginger Loaf Cake

208

- Use the zest and juice of 1 orange in place of the lemon in the cake mix. For the candied orange use 2 oranges, cut into six and thinly sliced.

209

SERVES 8

Wholemeal Raisin Loaf Cake

PREPARATION TIME 15 MINUTES

COOKING TIME 35–40 MINUTES

....

INGREDIENTS

100 g / 3 ½ oz / ⅔ cup stoneground wholemeal flour
50 g / 1 ¾ oz / ⅓ cup self-raising flour
150 g / 5 ½ oz / ⅔ cup caster (superfine) sugar
150 g / 5 ½ oz / ⅔ cup butter, softened
3 eggs
2 tsp baking powder
150 g / 5 ½ oz / ¾ cup raisins

- Preheat the oven to 180°C (160°C fan) / 355F / gas 4 and grease and line a small loaf tin.
- Put all of the cake ingredients in a large mixing bowl and whisk them together with an electric whisk for 4 minutes or until pale and well whipped.
- Scrape the mixture into the tin and level the top with a spatula.
- Bake for 35–40 minutes. The cake is ready when a toothpick inserted in the centre comes out clean.
- Transfer the cake to a wire rack to cool completely.

Wholemeal Date Loaf Cake

210

- Use finely chopped dates instead of the raisins for a denser, richer cake.

Chocolate Coated Sponge Cake

211
SERVES 12

White Chocolate Coated Sponge Cake **212**

- Using white chocolate instead of the dark and milk will give a sweeter taste to this delicious cake.

Chocolate and Coconut Coated Sponge Cake **213**

- Follow the recipe above but sprinkle a few tablespoons of desiccated coconut onto the chocolate before it sets.

PREPARATION TIME 10 MINUTES

COOKING TIME 45–50 MINUTES

....

INGREDIENTS

150 g / 5 ½ oz / 1 cup self-raising flour
150 g / 5 ½ oz / ⅔ cup caster (superfine) sugar
150 g / 5 ½ oz / ⅔ cup butter, softened
3 eggs
1 tsp baking powder
1 tsp vanilla extract

TO DECORATE

100 g / 3 ½ oz / ½ cup dark chocolate, chopped
40 g / 1 ½ oz / ¼ cup butter, softened
25 g / ¾ oz / ¼ cup milk chocolate, coarsely grated

- Preheat the oven to 180°C (160°C fan) / 355F / gas 4 and grease and line a deep 20 cm round loose-bottomed cake tin.
- Put all of the cake ingredients in a large mixing bowl and whisk them together with an electric whisk for 4 minutes or until pale and well whipped.
- Scrape the mixture into the tin and level the top with a spatula.
- Bake for 45–50 minutes. The cake is ready when a toothpick inserted in the centre comes out clean.
- Transfer the cake to a wire rack to cool completely.
- To make the chocolate glaze, melt the dark chocolate in a microwave or bain-marie then stir in the butter.
- Spoon the glaze over the cake and leave to set for 30 minutes.
- Sprinkle over the grated chocolate.

214
MAKES 24

Chocolate and Orange Mini Muffins

PREPARATION TIME 25 MINUTES

COOKING TIME 15–20 MINUTES

....

INGREDIENTS

1 large egg
120 ml / 4 fl. oz / ½ cup sunflower oil
120 ml / 4 fl. oz / ½ cup milk
1 orange, juice and zest
375 g / 12 ½ oz / 2 ½ cups self-raising flour, sifted
1 tsp baking powder
2 tbsp cocoa powder
75 g / 2 ½ oz / ½ cup chocolate chips
75 g / 2 ½ oz / ½ cup candied orange peel, chopped
200 g / 7 oz / ¾ cup caster (superfine) sugar

- Preheat the oven to 180°C (160°C fan) 350F / gas 4 and line a 24-hole mini muffin tin with paper cases.
- Beat the egg in a jug with the oil, milk and orange juice and zest until well mixed.
- Mix the flour, baking powder, cocoa, chocolate chips, candied peel and sugar in a bowl.
- Pour in the egg mixture and stir just enough to combine.
- Divide the mixture between the paper cases and bake for 15–20 minutes.
- Test with a wooden toothpick, if it comes out clean, the cakes are done.
- Transfer the muffins to a wire rack and leave to cool completely.

Spiced Chocolate Orange Mini Muffins
215

- Add 1 tsp of ground cinnamon and pinch of ground nutmeg to the mixture for a spiced alternative.

216
SERVES 8-10

Mirabelle Plum Cake

PREPARATION TIME 20 MINUTES

COOKING TIME 45–55 MINUTES

....

INGREDIENTS

225 g / 8 oz / 1 cup butter, softened
225 g / 8 oz / 1 cup caster (superfine) sugar
5 large eggs, beaten
225 g / 4 ½ oz / 1 ½ cups self-raising flour
350 g / 12 ½ oz / 2 ⅓ cups mirabelles, stoned

- Preheat the oven to 180°C (160°C fan) / 355F / gas 4 and grease and line a 23 cm round cake tin with greaseproof paper.
- Cream the butter and sugar together until well whipped then gradually whisk in the eggs, beating well after each addition.
- Fold in the flour then scrape the mixture into the tin and scatter over the mirabelles.
- Bake the cake for 45–55 minutes or until a skewer inserted in the centre comes out clean.
- Transfer the cake to a wire rack and leave to cool.

Damson Cake
217

- Swap the Mirabelle plums for damsons for a darker, more intense fruity cake.

Chocolate, Orange and Almond Torte

218
SERVES 6

- Preheat the oven to 180°C (160°C fan) / 355F / gas 4 and line a 20 cm round spring-form cake tin.
- Whisk the egg yolks and sugar together for 4 minutes.
- Melt the butter, cocoa and chocolate then fold into the egg yolk mixture with the almonds and orange zest.
- Whip the egg whites to stiff peaks in a very clean bowl and fold them into the cake mixture.
- Scrape the mixture into the tin, being careful to retain as many air bubbles as possible, and bake for 25–30 minutes or until the centre is just set.
- Transfer to a wire rack to cool. Heat the sugar in a small saucepan until it has all dissolved and turned a light caramel colour.
- Use a fork to dip the almonds and orange zest in the caramel and leave them to set on a non-stick baking mat.
- Cut the torte into wedges and decorate with the caramel almonds and orange zest.

Chocolate, Orange and Hazelnut Torte

219

- Change the ground almonds for ground hazelnuts (cob nuts) for a more nutty flavour.

PREPARATION TIME 30 MINUTES

COOKING TIME 25–30 MINUTES

INGREDIENTS

2 large eggs, separated
150 g / 5 ½ oz / ⅔ cup caster (superfine) sugar
75 g / 2 ½ oz / ⅓ cup butter
2 tbsp unsweetened cocoa powder
100 g / 3 ½ oz / ½ cup dark chocolate (minimum 60% cocoa solids), chopped
150 g / 5 ½ oz / 1 ½ cups ground almonds
1 orange, zest finely grated

TO DECORATE

100 g / 3 ½ oz / ½ cup caster (superfine) sugar
6 almonds
1 orange, zest finely pared

Gluten-free Sponge Cake

220
SERVES 8

- Preheat the oven to 180°C (160°C fan) / 355F / gas 4 and grease and line a 20 cm round loose-bottomed cake tin.
- Put all of the cake ingredients in a large mixing bowl and whisk them together with an electric whisk for 4 minutes or until pale and well whipped.
- Scrape the mixture into the tin and level the top with a spatula.
- Bake for 45–50 minutes. The cake is ready when a toothpick inserted in the centre comes out clean.
- Transfer the cake to a wire rack to cool completely.

Gluten-free Citrus Sponge Cake

221

- Swap the vanilla extract with a ½ teaspoon of orange essence and add 1 tbsp finely grated orange zest for a citrus flavour.

PREPARATION TIME 15 MINUTES

COOKING TIME 45–50 MINUTES

INGREDIENTS

50 g / 1 ¾ oz / ⅓ cup rice flour
50 g / 1 ¾ oz / ⅓ cup potato flour
50 g / 1 ¾ oz / ⅓ cup tapioca flour
150 g / 5 ½ oz / ⅔ cup caster (superfine) sugar
150 g / 5 ½ oz / ⅔ cup butter, softened
3 eggs
2 tsp baking powder
1 tsp vanilla extract

222

MAKES 12

Peach Cupcakes

PREPARATION TIME 35 MINUTES

COOKING TIME 15–20 MINUTES

....

INGREDIENTS

1 can peach slices, drained, syrup reserved
110 g / 4 oz / ⅔ cup self-raising flour, sifted
110 g / 4 oz / ½ cup caster (superfine) sugar
110 g / 4 oz / ½ cup butter, softened
2 large eggs
300 ml / 10 ½ fl. oz / 1 ¼ cups double (heavy) cream

- Preheat the oven to 190°C (170°C fan) / 375F / gas 5 and line a 12-hole cupcake tin with paper cases.
- Reserve 12 of the peach slices and finely chop the rest. Combine the flour, sugar, butter and eggs. Fold in the chopped peaches.
- Divide the mixture between the paper cases, then transfer the tin to the oven and bake for 15–20 minutes.
- Test with a wooden toothpick, if it comes out clean, the cakes are done.
- Transfer the cakes to a wire rack and leave to cool completely.
- Whip the cream until thick then fill a piping bag fitted with a large star nozzle and pipe a rosette on top of each cake.
- Lay a slice of peach next to the cream and drizzle a little of the reserved peach syrup on top.

223

MAKES 18

Peanut Butter Whoopie Pies

PREPARATION TIME 40 MINUTES

COOKING TIME 10–15 MINUTES

....

INGREDIENTS

110 g / 4 oz / ⅔ cup self-raising flour, sifted
2 tsp baking powder
110 g / 4 oz / ½ cup caster (superfine) sugar
110 g / 4 oz / ½ cup butter, softened
2 large eggs
75 g / 2 ½ oz / ⅔ cup peanuts, chopped

TO DECORATE
½ jar smooth peanut butter

- Preheat the oven to 190°C (170°C fan) / 375F / gas 5 and line 2 large baking trays with non-stick baking mats.
- Combine the flour, baking powder, sugar, butter, eggs and chopped peanuts in a bowl and whisk together for 2 minutes or until smooth.
- Spoon the mixture into a piping bag fitted with a large plain nozzle and pipe 18 walnut-sized domes onto each tray.
- Transfer the trays to the oven and bake for 10–15 minutes. The mixture should spread a little whilst cooking and the cakes will be ready when springy to the touch.
- Leave the cakes to cool on the tray then lift them off with a palette knife.
- Sandwich the cakes together in pairs with the peanut butter.

Chocolate and Peanut Butter Whoopie Pies

224

- Add a layer of chocolate spread on top of the peanut butter for a sweeter taste.

Peanut Muffins

225 · MAKES 12

- Preheat the oven to 180°C (160°C fan) / 355F / gas 4 and line a 12-hole muffin tin with paper cases.
- Beat the egg in a jug with the oil and milk until well mixed.
- Mix the flour, baking powder, sugar and peanuts in a bowl.
- Pour in the egg mixture and stir just enough to combine.
- Divide the mixture between the paper cases and bake for 20–25 minutes.
- Test with a wooden toothpick, if it comes out clean, the cakes are done.
- Transfer the muffins to a wire rack and leave to cool completely.

PREPARATION TIME 25 MINUTES

COOKING TIME 20–25 MINUTES

INGREDIENTS

1 large egg
120 ml / 4 fl. oz / ½ cup sunflower oil
120 ml / 4 fl. oz / ½ cup milk
375 g / 12 ½ oz / 2 ½ cups self-raising flour, sifted
1 tsp baking powder
200 g / 7 oz / ¾ cup caster (superfine) sugar
150 g / 5 ½ oz / 1 cup peanuts

Pear, Cardamom and Honey Tarts

226 · MAKES 6

PREPARATION TIME 55 MINUTES

COOKING TIME 30 MINUTES

INGREDIENTS

200 ml / 7 fl. oz / ⅔ cup runny honey
6 cardamom pods, bruised
4 ripe pears, 2 chopped and 2 sliced

FOR THE PASTRY

200 g / 7 oz / 1 ⅓ cups plain (all purpose) flour
100 g / 3 ½ oz / ½ cup butter, cubed
50 g / 1 ¾ oz / ¼ cup caster (superfine) sugar

- To make the pastry, rub the butter into the flour until the mixture resembles fine breadcrumbs. Stir in the sugar and add enough cold water to bring the pastry together into a pliable dough.
- Chill the dough for 30 minutes.
- Put the honey and cardamom in a small saucepan and bring to a simmer, then turn off the heat and leave to infuse for 30 minutes.
- Preheat the oven to 200°C (180°C fan) / 390F / gas 6.
- Roll out the pastry and use it to line 6 tartlet cases.
- Prick the pastry with a fork, line with cling film and fill with baking beans or rice.
- Bake for 10 minutes then remove the cling film and baking beans.
- Return to the oven for 8 minutes to crisp.
- Arrange the pears in the pastry cases and spoon over the cardamom honey.
- Bake for 10 minutes.

Gateau Breton with Pears

227 · SERVES 8

PREPARATION TIME 40 MINUTES

COOKING TIME 40–45 MINUTES

INGREDIENTS

250 g / 9 oz / 1 ¼ cup butter, cubed
250 g / 9 oz / ⅔ cup plain (all purpose) flour

250 g / 9 oz / 1 ¼ cup caster (superfine) sugar
6 large egg yolks
2 pears, peeled, cored and sliced

- Preheat the oven to 180°C (160°C fan) / 355F / gas 4 and butter a 23 cm round tart tin.
- Rub the butter into the flour then stir in the sugar.
- Beat 5 of the egg yolks and stir them into the dry ingredients.
- Bring the mixture together into a soft dough and divide it in two.
- Press one half into the bottom of the tart tin to form an even layer.
- Arrange the pears on top, leaving a clear border round the outside.
- Roll out the other half of the dough between 2 sheets of greaseproof paper then peel away the paper and lay it on top of the pears.
- Brush the top of the gateau with the final egg yolk then score a pattern on top.
- Bake the gateau for 40–45 minutes or until golden brown.
- Cool completely before unmoulding and cutting into slices.

228

SERVES 8

Wholemeal Raspberry Custard Tart

Wholemeal Cherry Custard Tart

229

- Swap the raspberries for the same weight in drained tinned cherries for a varied fruity taste.

Wholemeal Strawberry Custard Tart

230

- Swap the raspberries for the same weight of chopped strawberries for a sweeter flavour.

PREPARATION TIME 55 MINUTES

COOKING TIME 45–55 MINUTES

INGREDIENTS

200 g / 7 oz / 1 ⅓ cups raspberries

FOR THE PASTRY
100 g / 3 ½ oz / ½ cup butter, cubed
200 g / 7 oz / 1 ⅓ cups stoneground wholemeal flour

FOR THE CUSTARD
4 large egg yolks
75 g / 2 ½ oz / ⅓ cup caster (superfine) sugar
1 tsp vanilla extract
2 tsp cornflour (cornstarch)
450 ml / 16 fl. oz / 1 ¾ cups whole milk

- Preheat the oven to 200°C (180°C fan) / 390F / gas 6.
- Rub the butter into the flour and add just enough cold water to bind.
- Chill for 30 minutes then roll out on a floured surface. Use the pastry to line a 23 cm round tart tin.
- Prick the pastry with a fork, line with cling film and fill with baking beans or rice.
- Bake for 10 minutes then remove the cling film and baking beans and cook for another 8 minutes to crisp.
- Reduce the oven temperature to 170°C (150°C fan) / 340F / gas 3.
- Whisk together the custard ingredients and pour into the pastry case. Arrange the raspberries on top.
- Bake the tart for 25–35 minutes or until the custard is just set in the centre.

231
SERVES 8

Cranberry and Orange Loaf Cake

- Preheat the oven to 180°C (160°C fan) / 355F / gas 4 and line a loaf tin with non-stick baking paper.
- Sieve the flour into a mixing bowl and rub in the butter until it resembles fine breadcrumbs then stir in the sugar, cranberries and orange zest.
- Lightly beat the egg with the orange juice and stir it into the dry ingredients until just combined.
- Scrape the mixture into the loaf tin and bake for 55 minutes or until a skewer inserted in the centre comes out clean.
- Transfer the cake to a wire rack and leave to cool completely before dusting with icing sugar.

PREPARATION TIME 15 MINUTES

COOKING TIME 55 MINUTES

INGREDIENTS

225 g / 8oz / 1 ½ cups self raising flour
100 g / 3 ½ oz / ½ cup butter, cubed
85 g / 3oz / ⅓ cup caster (superfine) sugar
150 g / 5 ½ oz / ¾ cup dried cranberries
2 oranges, juice and zest finely grated
1 large egg
icing (confectioners') sugar to dust

Blueberry and Orange Loaf Cake   232

- Substitute the cranberries with dried blueberries for a delicious fruity change.

233
MAKES 4

Raspberry Charlottes

- Preheat the oven to 190°C (170°C fan) / 375F / gas 5 and grease and line 2 large baking trays.
- Put the egg yolks in a bowl with half of the caster sugar and the vanilla extract. Whisk with an electric whisk for 4 minutes or until very thick and pale.
- Whisk the egg whites with the cream of tartar until they reach soft peak stage, then gradually whisk in the remaining sugar.
- Sieve the flour over the egg yolk mixture and scrape in the egg whites, then carefully fold it all together.
- Spoon the mixture into a piping bag fitted with a large plain nozzle. Pipe 2 rows of 14 adjoining biscuits on each tray and sprinkle with granulated sugar.
- Bake the biscuits for 10–15 minutes.
- While the biscuits are still hot, lift them off the baking tray and curve each line round inside a ramekin dish. Leave to cool and harden.
- Unmould the charlottes and fill the centres with raspberries.
- Melt the raspberry jam in the microwave then spoon it over the top.

PREPARATION TIME 40 MINUTES

COOKING TIME 10–15 MINUTES

INGREDIENTS

4 large eggs, separated
125 g / 4 ½ oz / ½ cup caster (superfine) sugar
1 tsp vanilla extract
a pinch cream of tartar
115 g / 4 oz / ⅔ cup plain (all purpose) flour
2 tbsp granulated sugar
200 g / 7 oz / 1 ⅓ cup raspberries
4 tbsp seedless raspberry jam (jelly)

234

SERVES 8-10 Carrot Layer Cake

PREPARATION TIME 25 MINUTES

COOKING TIME 30–35 MINUTES

INGREDIENTS

175 g / 6 oz / 1 cup light brown sugar
2 large eggs
150 ml / 5 fl. oz / ⅔ cup sunflower oil
175 g / 6 oz / 1 ¼ cup stoneground
wholemeal flour
3 tsp baking powder
2 tsp ground cinnamon
½ tsp nutmeg, freshly grated
1 orange, zest finely grated
200 g / 7 oz / 1 ⅔ cup carrots, washed
and coarsely grated

FOR THE ICING

225g / 8 oz / 1 cup cream cheese
110 g / 4 oz / ½ cup butter, softened
275 g / 10 oz / 2 ½ cups icing
(confectioners') sugar
1 tsp vanilla extract

- Preheat the oven to 190°C (170°C fan) / 375F / gas 5 and line 2 x 20 cm round cake tins with greaseproof paper.
- Whisk the sugar, eggs and oil together for 3 minutes until thick.
- Fold in the flour, baking powder and spices, followed by the orange zest and carrots.
- Divide the mixture between the tins and bake for 30–35 minutes.
- Test with a wooden toothpick, if it comes out clean, the cakes are done. Transfer the cakes to a wire rack and leave to cool completely.
- To make the icing, beat the cream cheese and butter together with a wooden spoon until light and fluffy then beat in the icing sugar a quarter at a time.
- Add the vanilla extract then use a whisk to whip the mixture for 2 minutes or until smooth and light.
- Use half of the icing to sandwich the cakes together and spread the rest over the top of the cake with a palette knife. Grate over a little nutmeg to finish.

235

SERVES 12 Toffee Sponge Cake

PREPARATION TIME 20 MINUTES

COOKING TIME 45–50 MINUTES

INGREDIENTS

150 g / 5 ½ oz / 1 cup self-raising
flour
150 g / 5 ½ oz / ¾ cup light
muscovado sugar
150 g / 5 ½ oz / ⅔ cup butter,
softened
3 large eggs
1 tsp baking powder
1 tsp vanilla extract

FOR THE TOFFEE SAUCE

100 g / 3 ½ oz / ½ cup butter
100 g / 3 ½ oz / ½ cup light
muscovado sugar
100 g / 3 ½ oz / ⅓ cup golden syrup

- Preheat the oven to 180°C (160°C fan) / 355F / gas 4 and grease and line a deep 20 cm round loose-bottomed cake tin.
- Put all of the cake ingredients in a large mixing bowl and whisk them together with an electric whisk for 4 minutes or until pale and well whipped.
- Scrape the mixture into the tin and level the top with a spatula.
- Bake for 45–50 minutes. The cake is ready when a toothpick inserted in the centre comes out clean.
- Meanwhile, put the toffee sauce ingredients in a small saucepan and stir over a low heat until the butter melts and the sugar dissolves.
- Bring the toffee sauce to the boil then take it off the heat.
- When the cake comes out of the oven, prick the top with a skewer and spoon over half of the toffee sauce.
- Allow the cake to cool for at least 15 minutes then cut into wedges and serve the rest of the sauce alongside.

#

236

SERVES 8

Raspberry Upside-down Cake

- Preheat the oven to 170⁰C (150⁰C fan) / 375F / gas 3 and butter a 23 cm round cake tin.
- Sieve the flour and baking powder into a mixing bowl and add sugar, butter and eggs.
- Beat the mixture with an electric whisk for 4 minutes or until smooth and well whipped.
- Spread the jam over the base of the cake tin and arrange the raspberries on top.
- Spoon in the cake mixture and bake for 35 minutes or until a skewer inserted in the centre comes out clean.
- Leave the cake to cool for 20 minutes before turning out onto a serving plate.

PREPARATION TIME 15 MINUTES

COOKING TIME 35 MINUTES

....

INGREDIENTS

300 g / 10 ½ oz / 2 cups self-raising flour
2 tsp baking powder
250 g / 9 oz / 1 ¼ cups caster (superfine) sugar
250 g / 9 oz / 1 ¼ cups butter, softened
5 large eggs
4 tbsp raspberry jam (jelly)
200 g / 7 oz / 1 ⅓ cups raspberries

Vanilla and Honey Loaf Cake

237

SERVES 8

PREPARATION TIME 20 MINUTES

COOKING TIME 35–40 MINUTES

....

INGREDIENTS

150 g / 5 ½ oz / 1 cup self-raising flour
150 g / 5 ½ oz / ⅔ cup caster (superfine) sugar

150 g / 5 ½ oz / ⅔ cup butter, softened
3 eggs
1 tsp baking powder
2 tsp vanilla extract
200 g / 7 oz / ⅔ cup runny honey

- Preheat the oven to 180⁰C (160⁰C fan) / 355F / gas 4 and grease and line a small loaf tin.
- Put all of the cake ingredients except the honey in a large mixing bowl and whisk them together with an electric whisk for 4 minutes or until pale and well whipped.
- Scrape the mixture into the tin and level the top with a spatula.
- Bake for 35–40 minutes. The cake is ready when a toothpick inserted in the centre comes out clean.
- While the cake is cooking, put the honey in a small saucepan and heat until very liquid.
- When the cake is ready, prick all over the surface with a skewer and spoon over the hot honey.
- Leave the cake to cool completely in the tin.

Cinnamon and Lime Whoopies

238

MAKES 18

PREPARATION TIME 30 MINUTES

COOKING TIME 10–15 MINUTES

....

INGREDIENTS

110 g / 4 oz / ⅔ cup self-raising flour, sifted
2 tsp baking powder
110 g / 4 oz / ½ cup caster (superfine)

sugar
110 g / 4 oz / ½ cup butter, softened
2 large eggs
1 tsp ground cinnamon

TO DECORATE
½ jar lime curd
a few drops of green food dye

- Preheat the oven to 190⁰C (170⁰C fan) / 375F / gas 5 and line 2 large baking trays with non-stick baking mats.
- Combine the flour, baking powder, sugar, butter, eggs and cinnamon in a bowl and whisk together for 2 minutes or until smooth.
- Spoon the mixture into a piping bag fitted with a large plain nozzle and pipe 18 walnut-sized domes onto each tray.
- Transfer the trays to the oven and bake for 10–15 minutes. The mixture should spread a little whilst cooking and the cakes will be ready when springy to the touch.
- Leave the cakes to cool on the tray then lift them off with a palette knife.
- Mix the lime curd with the food colouring until evenly coloured then sandwich the cakes together in pairs.

Orange and Cardamom Rolls

Raisin, Orange and Cardamom Rolls

240

- Before rolling the pastry up, sprinkle over a handful of juicy raisins for a richer fruity taste.

Lemon and Cardamom Rolls

241

- Swap the orange zest for lemon zest for a sharper citrus flavour.

PREPARATION TIME
2 HOURS 30 MINUTES

COOKING TIME 15–20 MINUTES

....

INGREDIENTS

400 g / 14 oz / 2 ⅔ cups strong white bread flour
½ tsp easy blend dried yeast
4 tbsp caster (superfine) sugar
1 tsp fine sea salt
1 tbsp olive oil
75 g / 2 ½ oz / ½ cup dark brown sugar
25 g / ¾ oz butter, softened
1 orange, zest finely grated
1 tsp ground cardamom
1 egg, beaten
3 tbsp sugar nibs

- Mix together the flour, yeast, caster sugar and salt. Stir the oil into 280 ml of warm water then stir the liquid into the dry ingredients.
- Knead the mixture on a lightly oiled surface for 10 minutes or until the dough is smooth and elastic.
- Leave the dough to rest, covered with oiled cling film, for 1–2 hours or until doubled in size.
- Roll out the dough into a large rectangle.
- Cream the brown sugar and butter together and stir in the orange zest and cardamom.
- Spread the mixture over the surface of the dough and roll it up tightly.
- Cut the roll into 12 slices and spread them out on a greased baking tray.
- Cover the rolls with oiled cling film and leave to prove for 1 hour or until doubled in size.
- Preheat the oven to 220°C (200°C fan) / 430F / gas 7.
- Brush the rolls with beaten egg and sprinkle with sugar nibs.
- Bake the rolls for 15–20 minutes or until they are cooked through and golden brown.

242
SERVES 8

Gluten-free Orange Sponge Cake

- Preheat the oven to 180°C (160°C fan) / 355F / gas 4 and grease and line a 20 cm round loose-bottomed cake tin.
- Put all of the cake ingredients in a large mixing bowl and whisk them together with an electric whisk for 4 minutes or until pale and well whipped.
- Scrape the mixture into the tin and level the top with a spatula.
- Bake for 45–50 minutes. The cake is ready when a toothpick inserted in the centre comes out clean.
- Transfer the cake to a wire rack to cool completely.

PREPARATION TIME 10 MINUTES

COOKING TIME 45–50 MINUTES

INGREDIENTS

50 g / 1 ¾ oz / ⅓ cup rice flour
50 g / 1 ¾ oz / ⅓ cup potato flour
50 g / 1 ¾ oz / ⅓ cup tapioca flour
150 g / 5 ½ oz / ⅔ cup caster (superfine) sugar
150 g / 5 ½ oz / ⅔ cup butter, softened
3 large eggs
2 tsp baking powder
1 orange, juice and zest finely grated

Gluten-free Sultana and Orange Cake

243

- Add a handful of sultanas to the mixture to get a more fruity texture.

244
MAKES 12

Ginger Muffins

- Preheat the oven to 180°C (160°C fan) / 355F / gas 4 and oil a 12-hole silicone oval muffin mould.
- Beat the egg in a jug with the oil, milk and stem ginger until well mixed.
- Mix the flour, baking powder, ground ginger and sugar in a bowl.
- Pour in the egg mixture and stir just enough to combine.
- Divide the mixture between the moulds and bake for 20–25 minutes.
- Test with a wooden toothpick, if it comes out clean, the cakes are done.
- Transfer the muffins to a wire rack and leave to cool completely.

PREPARATION TIME 15 MINUTES

COOKING TIME 20–25 MINUTES

INGREDIENTS

1 large egg
120 ml / 4 fl. oz / ½ cup sunflower oil
120 ml / 4 fl. oz / ½ cup milk
4 pieces stem ginger in syrup, chopped
375 g / 12 ½ oz / 2 cups self-raising flour, sifted
1 tsp baking powder
1 tsp ground ginger
200 g / 7 oz / ¾ cup caster (superfine) sugar

Ginger Blueberry Muffins

245

- Mix in a handful of blueberries before cooking to give the muffins a more fruity taste.

BREADS AND BISCUITS

246

SERVES 8

Secret-centre Apple Loaf Cake

PREPARATION TIME 20 MINUTES

COOKING TIME 55 MINUTES

INGREDIENTS

300 g / 10 ½ oz / 2 cups self-raising flour
2 tsp baking powder
250 g / 9 oz / 1 ¼ cup caster (superfine) sugar
250 g / 9 oz / 1 ¼ cup butter, softened
5 large eggs
1 eating apple, cored and finely chopped
1 tsp mixed spice
4 tbsp sultanas
1 lemon, zest finely grated
2 tbsp granulated sugar

- Preheat the oven to 170°C (150°C fan) / 325F / gas 3 and line a large loaf tin with non-stick baking paper.
- Sieve the flour and baking powder into a mixing bowl and add the sugar, butter and eggs.
- Beat the mixture with an electric whisk for 4 minutes or until smooth and well whipped.
- Mix the chopped apple with the mixed spice, sultanas and lemon zest.
- Spoon half of the cake mixture into the lined tin then spoon the apple mixture on top, leaving a border round the outside.
- Spoon the rest of the cake mixture on top and level the surface then sprinkle with granulated sugar.
- Bake the cake for 55 minutes or until a skewer inserted in the centre comes out clean. Transfer the cake to a wire rack and leave to cool completely before slicing.

Secret-centre Berry Loaf Cake   247

- Replace the eating apple with 200 g / 7 oz / 1 ⅓ cups frozen mixed berries that have been thawed.

248

MAKES 12

Crusty Farmhouse Rolls

PREPARATION TIME
3 HOURS 30 MINUTES

COOKING TIME 15–20 MINUTES

INGREDIENTS

350 g / 12 ½ oz/ 2 ⅓ cups strong white bread flour, plus extra for dusting
50 g / 1 ¾ oz / ⅓ cup stoneground wholemeal flour
½ tsp easy blend dried yeast
1 tbsp caster (superfine) sugar
1 tsp fine sea salt
1 tbsp olive oil

- Mix together the flours, yeast, sugar and salt. Stir in the oil and 280 ml of warm water.
- Knead the mixture on a lightly oiled surface with your hands for 10 minutes or until smooth and elastic.
- Leave the dough to rest in an oiled bowl, covered with oiled cling film, for 2 hours. Knead it for 2 minutes then split into 12 pieces and shape into rolls.
- Transfer the rolls to a greased baking tray and cover with oiled cling film. Leave to prove for 1 hour.
- Meanwhile, preheat the oven to 220°C (200°C fan) / 425F / gas 7.
- Dust the rolls with flour and slash the tops with a knife.
- Transfer the tray to the top shelf of the oven.
- Bake for 15–20 minutes or until the rolls sound hollow when you tap them underneath.
- Transfer to a wire rack and leave to cool.

Olive Farmhouse Rolls   249

- Add 55 g / 2 oz / ⅓ cup finely chopped black olives when the dough is kneaded the second time for a more savoury taste.

250

MAKES 12

Viennese Whirls

- Preheat the oven to 170°C (150°C fan) / 325F / gas 3 and line 2 baking trays with non-stick baking paper.
- Cream the butter, sugar and vanilla extract together with an electric whisk then stir in the flour.
- Spoon the mixture into a piping bag fitted with a large star nozzle and pipe 12 rosettes onto each tray. Bake the biscuits for 15–20 minutes.
- Transfer the biscuits to a wire rack and leave to cool before dusting with icing sugar.
- To make the buttercream, beat the butter with a wooden spoon until light and fluffy then beat in the icing sugar.
- Use a whisk to incorporate the milk, then whisk for 2 minutes or until smooth and well whipped.
- Spoon the buttercream into a piping bag and pipe a swirl onto the flat side of 12 biscuits.
- Top each one with a spoonful of jam and sandwich together with the remaining biscuits.

Chocolate Viennese Whirls 251

- Replace 30 g / 1 oz of the self-raising flour with 55 g / 2 oz / ⅓ cup good-quality cocoa powder for a more decadent flavour. Add the cocoa powder at the same time as the rest of the self-raising flour.

PREPARATION TIME 30 MINUTES

COOKING TIME 15–20 MINUTES

INGREDIENTS

175 g / 6 oz / ¾ cup butter, softened
50 g / 1 ¾ oz / ¼ cup caster (superfine) sugar
½ tsp vanilla extract
175 g / 6 oz / 1 ¼ cup self-raising flour
2 tbsp icing (confectioners') sugar

FOR THE FILLING
100 g / 3 ½ oz / ½ cup butter, softened
200 g / 7oz / 2 cups icing (confectioners') sugar
1 tbsp milk
½ jar strawberry jam (jelly)

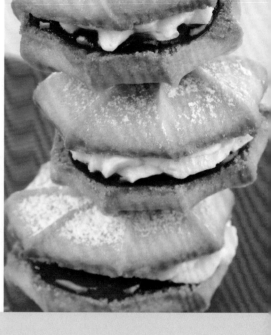

252

MAKES 36

Chocolate Chip and Hazelnut Cookies

- Preheat the oven to 170°C (150°C fan) / 325F / gas 3 and line 2 baking sheets with greaseproof paper.
- Cream together the two sugars, butter and vanilla extract until pale and well whipped then beat in the egg and yolk, followed by the flour, chocolate and hazelnuts.
- Drop tablespoons of the mixture onto the prepared trays, leaving plenty of room to spread.
- Bake the cookies in batches for 12–15 minutes or until the edges are starting to brown, but the centres are still chewy.
- Transfer to a wire rack and leave to cool.

White and Dark Chocolate Chip Cookies 253

- Replace the hazelnuts with the same weight of finely chopped white chocolate and add to the dough at the same time as the chocolate chips.

PREPARATION TIME 20 MINUTES

COOKING TIME 12–15 MINUTES

INGREDIENTS

175 g / 6 oz / ¾ cup butter, softened
225 g / 8 oz / 1 ⅓ cups dark brown sugar
100 g / 3 ½ oz / ½ cup caster (superfine) sugar
2 tsp vanilla extract
1 egg, plus 1 egg yolk
250 g / 9 oz / 1 ⅔ cups self-raising flour
175 g / 6 oz / 1 ¼ cups chocolate chips
175 g / 6 oz / 1 ½ cups hazelnuts (cob nuts), chopped

254

MAKES 36

Double Chocolate and Pistachio Cookies

Chocolate and Pistachio Cookies

255

- Replace the cocoa powder with the same weight of self-raising flour for a less chocolatey flavour.

Chocolate and Raspberry Cookies

256

- Replace the pistachios with 110 g / 4 oz / 1 ¼ cups chopped, dried raspberries for a fruitier flavour.

PREPARATION TIME 20 MINUTES

COOKING TIME 12–15 MINUTES

INGREDIENTS

175 g / 6 oz / ¾ cup butter, softened
225 g / 8 oz / 1 ⅓ cup dark brown sugar
100 g / 3 ½ oz / ½ cup caster (superfine) sugar
2 tsp vanilla extract
1 egg, plus 1 egg yolk
250 g / 9 oz / 1 ⅔ cup self-raising flour
2 tbsp unsweetened cocoa powder
175 g / 6 oz / 1 ¼ cups chocolate chips
175 g / 6 oz / 1 ½ cups pistachio nuts, chopped

- Preheat the oven to 170°C (150°C fan) / 325F / gas 3 and line 2 baking sheets with greaseproof paper.
- Cream together the two sugars, butter and vanilla extract until pale and well whipped then beat in the egg and yolk, followed by the flour, cocoa, chocolate and pistachio nuts.
- Drop tablespoons of the mixture onto the prepared trays, leaving plenty of room to spread.
- Bake the cookies in batches for 12–15 minutes or until the edges are starting to brown, but the centres are still chewy.
- Transfer to a wire rack and leave to cool.

257
MAKES 16 Cocoa Shortbread Biscuits

- Preheat the oven to 180°C (160°C fan) / 355F / gas 4 and line a baking tray with greaseproof paper.
- Mix together the flour, cocoa and caster sugar in a bowl, then rub in the butter.
- Knead gently until the mixture forms a smooth dough then form into a cylinder 6 cm in diameter and roll in granulated sugar.
- Slice the roll into 1 cm thick slices and spread them out on the baking tray.
- Bake the biscuits for 15–20 minutes, turning the tray round halfway through.
- Transfer the biscuits to a wire rack and leave to cool.

PREPARATION TIME 20 MINUTES

COOKING TIME 15–20 MINUTES

INGREDIENTS

230 g / 8 oz / 1 ½ cups plain (all purpose) flour
2 tbsp cocoa powder
75 g / 2 ½ oz / ⅓ cup caster (superfine) sugar
150 g / 5 oz / ⅔ cup butter, cubed
50 g / 1 ¾ oz / ¼ cup granulated sugar

Cocoa and Orange Shortbread Biscuits
258

- Add 1 tbsp orange flower water whilst rubbing the butter into the flour mixture.

259
MAKES 12 Chocolate Madeleines

- Heat the butter until it foams and starts to smell nutty, then leave to cool.
- Combine the flour, cocoa, ground almonds and icing sugar in a bowl and whisk in the egg whites.
- Pour the cooled butter through a sieve into the bowl and whisk into the mixture until evenly mixed.
- Leave the cake mixture to rest in the fridge for 1 hour.
- Preheat the oven to 170°C (150°C fan) / 325F / gas 3 and oil and flour a 12-hole Madeleine mould.
- Spoon the mixture into the moulds, then transfer the tin to the oven and bake for 10–15 minutes.
- Test with a wooden toothpick, if it comes out clean, the cakes are done.
- Transfer the cakes to a wire rack to cool for 5 minutes before serving.

PREPARATION TIME
1 HOUR 30 MINUTES

COOKING TIME 10–15 MINUTES

INGREDIENTS

110 g / 4 oz / ½ cup butter
55 g / 2 oz / ⅓ cup plain (all purpose) flour
28 g / 1 oz / ¼ cup unsweetened cocoa powder
55 g / 2 oz / ½ cup ground almonds
110 g / 4 oz / 1 cup icing (confectioners') sugar
3 large egg whites

Almond Madeleines
260

- Replace the cocoa powder with and additional 30 g / 1 oz / ¼ cup of ground almonds for a more traditional flavour.

261

MAKES 45-50 # Sponge Finger Biscuits

PREPARATION TIME 35 MINUTES

COOKING TIME 10–15 MINUTES

....

INGREDIENTS

4 large eggs
125 g / 4 ½ oz / ½ cup caster
(superfine) sugar
1 tsp vanilla extract
a pinch cream of tartar
115 g / 4 oz / ¾ cup plain (all
purpose) flour

- Preheat the oven to 190°C (170°C fan) / 375F / gas 5 and grease and line 2 large trays with greaseproof paper.
- Separate the eggs and put the yolks in a bowl with half of the sugar and the vanilla extract. Whisk with an electric whisk for 4 minutes or until thick and pale.
- Whisk the egg whites with the cream of tartar, making sure the whisk and bowl are completely clean.
- When the egg white reaches the soft peak stage, gradually whisk in the remaining sugar.
- Sieve the flour over the yolk mixture and scrape in the egg whites, then fold it all together with a metal spoon.
- Spoon the mixture into a piping bag fitted with a large plain nozzle. Pipe 10 cm lines onto the baking trays, leaving room for the biscuits to spread.
- Bake the biscuits for 10–15 minutes.
- Transfer to a wire rack and leave to cool completely.

Amaretto Sponge Finger Biscuits   262

- Replace the vanilla extract with 2 tbsp Amaretto, whisking it into the egg yolks at the same time as you would add the vanilla extract.

263

MAKES 36 # Iced Heart Biscuits

PREPARATION TIME
1 HOUR 15 MINUTES

COOKING TIME 25–30 MINUTES

....

INGREDIENTS

100 g / 3 ½ oz / ½ cup caster
(superfine) sugar
100 g / 3 ½ oz / ½ cup butter,
softened
1 tsp vanilla extract
1 large egg, beaten
300 g / 10 ½ oz / 2 cups plain (all
purpose) flour

TO DECORATE

150 g / 5 ½ oz / 1 ½ cups royal icing
(confectioners') sugar
pink food dye

- Cream together the sugar, butter and vanilla extract until pale and well whipped then beat in the egg, followed by the flour.
- Bring the mixture together into a ball with your hands then wrap in cling film and refrigerate for 45 minutes.
- Preheat the oven to 190°C (170°C fan) / 375F / gas 5 and line 2 baking sheets with greaseproof paper.
- Roll out the dough on a lightly floured surface to 5mm thick. Use a heart-shaped cutter to cut out the biscuits.
- Transfer the biscuits to the prepared trays in batches and bake for 8–10 minutes until pale golden.
- Transfer the biscuits to a wire rack and leave to cool.
- Whisk the royal icing sugar with a few drops of pink food dye and 25 ml water for 5 minutes.
- Spoon it into a piping bag and pipe your designs onto the biscuits.

Sugar Heart Biscuits   264

- Instead of icing the biscuits, sprinkle over 50 g / 2 oz / ¼ cup caster sugar as soon as they leave the oven. Let them cool on wire racks before serving.

Ginger Snap Biscuits

Lemon Snap Biscuits

266

- Replace the ground ginger with 2 tsp lemon extract for a tart, citrus taste to these biscuits.

Nutmeg Snap Biscuits

267

- Replace the ground ginger with 1 ½ tsp ground nutmeg.

PREPARATION TIME 10 MINUTES

COOKING TIME 12–15 MINUTES

INGREDIENTS

75 g / 2 ½ oz / ⅓ cup butter
100 g / 3 ½ oz / ⅓ cup golden syrup
225 g / 8 oz / 1 ½ cups self-raising flour
100 g / 3 ½ oz / ½ cup caster (superfine) sugar
1 tsp ground ginger
1 large egg, beaten

- Preheat the oven to 180°C (160° C fan) / 355F / gas 4 and line 2 baking sheets with greaseproof paper.
- Melt the butter and golden syrup together in a saucepan.
- Mix the flour, sugar and ground ginger together then stir in the melted butter mixture and the beaten egg.
- Use a teaspoon to portion the mixture onto the baking trays, leaving plenty of room for the biscuits to spread.
- Bake in batches for 12–15 minutes or until golden brown.
- Transfer the biscuits to a wire rack and leave to cool and harden.

268
MAKES 1 LOAF Hot Cross Bun Loaf

PREPARATION TIME
2 HOURS 30 MINUTES

COOKING TIME 35–40 MINUTES

INGREDIENTS

55 g / 2 oz / ¼ cup butter, cubed
400 g / 14 oz / 2 ⅔ cups strong white bread flour, plus extra for dusting
½ tsp easy blend dried yeast
4 tbsp caster (superfine) sugar
1 tsp fine sea salt
2 tsp mixed spice
100 g / 3 ½ oz / ½ cup mixed dried fruit
4 tbsp plain (all purpose) flour
1 egg, beaten

• Rub the butter into the bread flour and stir in the yeast, sugar, salt and spice. Stir the dried fruit into 280 ml of warm water and stir into the dry ingredients.
• Knead the mixture on a lightly oiled surface for 10 minutes or until the dough is smooth and elastic.
• Leave the dough to rest, covered with a lightly oiled bowl, for 1–2 hours or until doubled in size.
• Roll the dough into a fat sausage. Turn it 90⁰ and roll it tightly the other way then tuck the ends under and transfer to a large loaf tin. Leave to prove for 45 minutes.
• Preheat the oven to 220⁰C (200⁰C fan) / 430F / gas 7.
• Mix the plain flour with just enough water to make a thick paste and spoon it into a piping bag. Brush the loaf with egg and pipe the flour mixture on top into crosses.
• Bake for 35–40 minutes or until the underneath sounds hollow when tapped.

Raisin and Apple Loaf
269

• Replace the mixed dried fruit with 75 g / 3 oz / ⅓ cup raisins and 2 small diced eating apples that have been peeled and cored.

270
MAKES 36 Nutmeg Star Biscuits

PREPARATION TIME
1 HOUR 15 MINUTES

COOKING TIME 8–10 MINUTES

INGREDIENTS

100 g / 3 ½ oz / ½ cup caster (superfine) sugar
100 g / 3 ½ oz / ½ cup butter, softened
½ tsp nutmeg, freshly grated
1 large egg, beaten
300 g / 10 ½ oz / 2 cups plain (all purpose) flour
icing (confectioners') sugar to dust

• Cream together the sugar, butter and grated nutmeg until pale and well whipped then beat in the egg, followed by the flour.
• Bring the mixture together into a ball with your hands then wrap in cling film and refrigerate for 45 minutes.
• Preheat the oven to 190⁰C (170⁰C fan) / 375F / gas 5 and line 2 baking sheets with greaseproof paper.
• Roll out the dough on a lightly floured surface to 5mm thick. Use a star-shaped cutter to cut out the biscuits, rerolling the trimmings as necessary.
• Transfer the biscuits to the prepared trays in batches and bake for 8–10 minutes or until cooked through and golden brown.
• Transfer the biscuits to a wire rack and leave to cool completely before dusting with icing sugar.

Cinnamon Sugar Star Biscuits
271

• Instead of using icing sugar to decorate combine ½ tsp ground cinnamon with 50 g / 2 oz / ¼ cup of sugar in a food processor. Pulse and sprinkle over the biscuits.

272

MAKES 36

Cheese Wafer Biscuits

- Preheat the oven to 180°C (160°C fan) / 355F / gas 4 and line 2 baking sheets with greaseproof paper.
- Melt the butter with the cayenne pepper in a saucepan.
- Stir in the cheese and flour, beating rapidly to form a paste.
- Use a teaspoon to portion the mixture onto the baking trays and spread the biscuits out thinly with the back of the spoon.
- Bake in batches for 8–10 minutes.
- Leave the biscuits to harden on the tray for a few minutes then transfer them to a wire rack to cool.

PREPARATION TIME 20 MINUTES

COOKING TIME 8–10 MINUTES

INGREDIENTS

225 g / 8 oz / 1 cup butter
½ tsp cayenne pepper
175 g / 6 oz / 1 ¾ cups Red Leicester cheese, grated
300 g / 10 ½ oz / 2 cups plain (all purpose) flour

Cheese and Black Pepper Wafer Biscuits

273

- Combine 2 tsp of freshly ground black pepper with the grated cheese before stirring into the butter for a more piquant flavour.

274

SERVES 8

Black Cherry Crumble Cake

- Preheat the oven to 180°C (160°C fan) / 355F / gas 4 and line a loaf tin with non-stick baking paper.
- Sieve the flour into a mixing bowl and rub in the butter until it resembles fine breadcrumbs then stir in the sugar and cherries.
- Lightly beat the egg with the milk and stir it into the dry ingredients until just combined.
- Scrape the mixture into the loaf tin and level the surface.
- To make the crumble layer, rub the butter into the flour and stir in the ground almonds and brown sugar
- Take a handful of the topping and squeeze it into a clump, then crumble it over the cake mixture. Repeat with the rest of the mixture then bake the cake for 55 minutes or until a skewer inserted in the centre comes out clean.
- Transfer the cake to a wire rack and leave to cool.

PREPARATION TIME 20 MINUTES

COOKING TIME 55 MINUTES

INGREDIENTS

225 g / 8 oz / 1 ½ cups self-raising flour
100 g / 3 ½ oz / ½ cup butter, cubed
100 g / 3 ½ oz / ½ cup caster (superfine) sugar
150 g / 5 ½ oz / 1 cup black cherries, pitted
1 large egg
75 ml / 2 ½ fl. oz / ⅓ cup whole milk

FOR THE CRUMBLE
75 g / 2 ½ oz / ⅓ cup butter
50 g / 1 ¾ oz / ⅓ cup plain (all purpose) flour
25 g / 1 oz / ¼ cup ground almonds
40 g / 1 ½ oz / ¼ cup light brown sugar

Black Cherry and Almond Crumble Cake

275

- Add an additional 75 g / 3 oz / ¾ cup ground almonds to the mixture for a nuttier flavour.

276
MAKES 2

White Cob Loaf

Sun-dried Tomato Cob Loaf
277

- Add 2 tbsp drained and finely chopped sun-dried tomatoes to the dough when you knead it the first time for a Mediterranean look and flavour.

Raisin Cob Loaf
278

- Add 50 g / 2 oz / ¼ cup raisins to the dough when you knead it the first time for a fruity tasting loaf.

PREPARATION TIME
2 HOURS 30 MINUTES

COOKING TIME 35–40 MINUTES

....

INGREDIENTS

400 g / 14 oz / 2 ⅔ cups strong white bread flour, plus extra for dusting
½ tsp easy blend dried yeast
1 tbsp caster (superfine) sugar
1 tsp fine sea salt
1 tbsp olive oil

- Mix together the flour, yeast, sugar and salt. Stir the oil into 280 ml of warm water then stir it into the dry ingredients.
- Knead the mixture on a lightly oiled surface with your hands for 10 minutes or until smooth and elastic.
- Leave the dough to rest in a lightly oiled bowl, covered with oiled cling film, for 1–2 hours or until doubled in size.
- Knead it for 2 more minutes then split it into 2 even pieces and shape into 2 round loaves
- Transfer the cobs to a greased baking tray and cover with oiled cling film. Leave to prove for 1 hour or until doubled in size.
- Meanwhile, preheat the oven to 220°C (200°C fan) / 425F / gas 7.
- Dust the cobs with flour and slash a cross in the tops with a knife.
- Transfer the tray to the top shelf of the oven then close the door.
- Bake for 35–40 minutes or until the loaves sound hollow when you tap them underneath.
- Transfer to a wire rack and leave to cool.

279
MAKES 6

Olive and Pepper Millefeuille

- Preheat the oven to 220°C (200°C fan) / 430F / gas 7.
- Roll out the pastry on a floured surface and press the olive slices into the surface.
- Cut the pastry into 18 squares and transfer them to 2 baking trays
- Bake in the oven for 15–20 minutes or until golden brown and cooked through.
- Layer the pastries with the roasted peppers and serve warm.

PREPARATION TIME 20 MINUTES

COOKING TIME 15–20 MINUTES

INGREDIENTS

225 g / 8 oz / ¾ cup all-butter puff pastry
200 g / 7 oz / 1 ⅓ cups black olives, pitted and sliced
1 jar sliced roasted peppers in oil, drained

Two Olive Millefeuille

280

- Replace the pepper with 150 g / 5 oz / 1 cup pitted and sliced green olives for a savoury bite.

281
MAKES 36

Buckwheat Crackers

- Preheat the oven to 190°C (170°C fan) / 375F / gas 5 and line 2 baking sheets with greaseproof paper.
- Rub the butter into the wholemeal flour then stir in the rest of the ingredients.
- Add enough water to bind it together into a pastry-like dough and roll out on a floured surface.
- Cut the dough into square biscuits with a sharp knife, rerolling the trimmings as necessary.
- Transfer the biscuits to the prepared trays in batches and bake for 8–10 minutes or until cooked through and golden brown.
- Transfer the biscuits to a wire rack and leave to cool completely.

PREPARATION TIME 15 MINUTES

COOKING TIME 8–10 MINUTES

INGREDIENTS

110 g / 4 oz / ½ cup butter
225 g / 8 oz / 1 ½ cups stoneground wholemeal flour
225 g / 8 oz / 1 ¾ cups s buckwheat flour
1 tsp salt
1 tsp baking powder
110 g / 4 oz / ⅔ cup whole raw buckwheat

Buckwheat Crackers with Cream Cheese

282

- Once the crackers have cooled, garnish them with a teaspoon of cream cheese for a rich, creamy snack.

283
MAKES 2

Wholemeal Cob Loaf

PREPARATION TIME

2 HOURS 30 MINUTES

COOKING TIME 35–40 MINUTES

INGREDIENTS

300 g / 10 ½ oz / 2 cups stoneground wholemeal flour
100 g / 3 ½ oz / ⅔ cup strong white bread flour, plus extra for dusting
½ tsp easy blend dried yeast
2 tbsp caster (superfine) sugar
1 tsp fine sea salt
1 tbsp olive oil

- Mix together the flours, yeast, sugar and salt. Stir the oil and 280 ml of warm water into the dry ingredients.
- Knead the mixture on an oiled surface for 10 minutes.
- Leave the dough to rest in a lightly oiled bowl, covered with oiled cling film, for 1–2 hours.
- Knead it for 2 more minutes then split it into 2 even pieces and shape into 2 round loaves.
- Transfer the cobs to a greased baking tray and cover with oiled cling film. Leave to prove for 1 hour.
- Meanwhile, preheat the oven to 220⁰C (200⁰C fan) / 425F / gas 7.
- Dust with flour and slash across the tops with a knife.
- Transfer the tray to the top shelf of the oven and close the door.
- Bake for 35–40 minutes or until the loaves sound hollow when you tap them underneath.

Herbed Cob Loaf
284

- Add 1 tsp of dried rosemary, oregano and basil to the flour before mixing into a dough for an aromatic, savoury loaf.

285
MAKES 4

Wholemeal Sesame Baguettes

PREPARATION TIME

2 HOURS 30 MINUTES

COOKING TIME 25–30 MINUTES

INGREDIENTS

300 g / 10 ½ oz / 2 cups stoneground wholemeal flour
100 g / 3 ½ oz / ½ cup strong white bread flour, plus extra for dusting
½ tsp easy blend dried yeast
2 tbsp caster (superfine) sugar
1 tsp fine sea salt
1 tbsp sesame oil
1 egg, beaten
3 tbsp sesame seeds

- Mix together the flours, yeast, sugar and salt. Stir the oil and 280 ml of warm water into the dry ingredients.
- Knead the mixture on a lightly oiled surface with your hands for 10 minutes or until smooth and elastic.
- Leave the dough to rest in an oiled bowl, covered with oiled film, for 2 hours. Knead it for 2 more minutes then split it into 4 even pieces and shape into baguettes.
- Transfer the baguettes to a greased baking tray and cover with oiled cling film. Leave to prove for 1 hour.
- Preheat the oven to 220⁰C (200⁰C fan) / 430F / gas 7.
- Brush the baguettes with beaten egg and sprinkle with sesame seeds then slash across the tops with a knife.
- Transfer the tray to the top shelf of the oven then close the door.
- Bake for 25–30 minutes or until the loaves sound hollow when you tap them underneath.

Poppy Seed Baguettes
286

- Use 4 tbsp of black poppy seeds to garnish the loaves instead of the sesame seeds for a stark colour contrast.

287

MAKES 36

Chocolate Sprinkle Star Biscuits

Honey Star Biscuits

288

- Add 2 tbsp runny honey to the dough mixture before mixing. These biscuits can be garnished with grated chocolate if desired.

Multicoloured Sprinkle Star Biscuits

289

- Replace the grated chocolate garnish with multicoloured sugar sprinkles, sprinkling them over the cookies as soon as they leave the oven.

PREPARATION TIME
1 HOUR 10 MINUTES

COOKING TIME 8–10 MINUTES

....

INGREDIENTS

100 g / 3 ½ oz / ½ cup caster (superfine) sugar
100 g / 3 ½ oz / ½ cup butter, softened
1 large egg, beaten
300 g / 10 ½ oz / 2 cups plain (all purpose) flour

TO FINISH
1 egg, beaten
4 tbsp caster (superfine) sugar
30 g / 1 oz grated dark chocolate

- Cream together the sugar and butter until pale and well whipped then beat in the egg, followed by the flour.
- Bring the mixture together into a ball with your hands then wrap in cling film and refrigerate for 45 minutes.
- Preheat the oven to 190°C (170°C fan) / 375F / gas 5 and line 2 baking sheets with greaseproof paper.
- Roll out the dough on a lightly floured surface to 5mm thick. Use a star-shaped cutter to cut out the biscuits, rerolling the trimmings as necessary.
- Transfer the biscuits to the prepared trays, brush with beaten egg and sprinkle with caster sugar.
- Bake for 8–10 minutes or until cooked through and golden brown.
- Transfer the biscuits to a wire rack and leave to cool completely before sprinkling with grated chocolate.

Fondant Flower Biscuits

290

MAKES 36

Fondant Animal Biscuits 291

- Use animal-shaped cutters for the fondant to create fun animal biscuits for kids.

Ginger Flower Biscuits 292

- Add 1 heaped teaspoon of ground ginger to the butter and golden syrup when you melt them together for a spicy, warming flavour.

PREPARATION TIME 30 MINUTES

COOKING TIME 12–15 MINUTES

INGREDIENTS

75 g / 2 ½ oz / ⅓ cup butter
100 g / 3 ½ oz / ⅓ cup golden syrup
225 g / 8 oz / 1 ½ cups self-raising flour
100 g / 3 ½ oz / ½ cup caster (superfine) sugar
1 large egg, beaten

FOR THE FLOWERS

200 g / 7 oz / ½ cup ready to roll fondant icing
a few drops of food dye
sweets to decorate

- Preheat the oven to 180ºC (160ºC fan) / 355F / gas 4 and line 2 baking sheets with greaseproof paper.
- Melt the butter and golden syrup together in a saucepan.
- Mix the flour and sugar together then stir in the melted butter mixture and the beaten egg.
- Use a teaspoon to portion the mixture onto the baking trays, leaving plenty of room for the biscuits to spread.
- Bake in batches for 12–15 minutes or until golden brown.
- Transfer the biscuits to a wire rack and leave to cool and harden.
- Take a small ball of icing and knead it with your chosen food dye.
- Roll it out between 2 sheets of greaseproof paper and use a flower-shaped cutter to cut out the flowers. Repeat with the rest of the icing, using a variety of different colours.
- Wet the back of the flowers with a little water and stick them onto the biscuits. Use contrasting coloured sweets for the centres.

293
MAKES 24 Almond Biscotti

- Preheat the oven to 180°C (160°C fan) / 355F / gas 4 and line 2 baking sheets with greaseproof paper.
- Beat the eggs and butter together then add the flour, caster sugar and almonds.
- Bring the mixture together into a soft dough and shape into 2 long rolls.
- Transfer the rolls to one of the prepared trays and flatten slightly.
- Bake for 20 minutes or until golden then leave to cool for 15 minutes.
- Cut the rolls across into 1 cm thick pieces and spread them out cut side down on the baking trays.
- Bake the biscuits for 15 minutes or until golden and crisp.
- Transfer the biscuits to a wire rack and leave to cool completely.

PREPARATION TIME 35 MINUTES

COOKING TIME 35 MINUTES

INGREDIENTS

2 large eggs
55 g / 2 oz / ¼ cup butter, melted
225 g / 8 oz / 1 ½ cups self-raising flour
100 g / 3 ½ oz / ½ cup caster (superfine) sugar
100 g / 3 ½ oz / ⅔ cup blanched almonds

Lemon and Thyme Biscotti
294

- Replace the almonds in the recipe with the finely grated zest of 2 lemons and 1 tbsp finely chopped thyme leaves for a citrus and herb twist to these biscotti.

295
MAKES 24 Almond and Cranberry Biscotti

- Preheat the oven to 180°C (160°C fan) / 355F / gas 4 and line 2 baking sheets with greaseproof paper.
- Beat the eggs and butter together then add the flour, caster sugar, almonds and cranberries.
- Bring the mixture together into a soft dough and shape into 2 long rolls.
- Transfer the rolls to the prepared trays and flatten slightly.
- Bake for 20 minutes or until golden then leave to cool for 15 minutes.
- Cut the rolls across into 1 cm thick sliced and spread them out cut side down on the baking trays.
- Bake the biscuits for 15 minutes or until golden and crisp.
- Transfer the biscuits to a wire rack and leave to cool completely.

PREPARATION TIME 35 MINUTES

COOKING TIME 35 MINUTES

INGREDIENTS

2 large eggs
55 g / 2 oz / ¼ cup butter, melted
225 g / 8 oz / 1 ½ cups self-raising flour
100 g / 3 ½ oz / ½ cup caster (superfine) sugar
100 g / 3 ½ oz / ⅔ cup blanched almonds
100 g / 3 ½ oz / ⅔ cup dried cranberries

Almond and Sultana Biscotti
296

- Replace the cranberries with the same weight of sultanas; golden sultanas can be used for a brighter colour.

297

MAKES 1 LOAF

Beer and Mustard Seed Bread

PREPARATION TIME
2 HOURS 30 MINUTES

COOKING TIME 35–40 MINUTES

INGREDIENTS

200 g / 7 oz / 1 ⅓ cup strong white
bread flour, plus extra for dusting
200 g / 7 oz / 1 ⅓ cup stoneground
wholemeal flour
½ tsp easy blend dried yeast
1 tbsp caster (superfine) sugar
1 tsp fine sea salt
1 tbsp mustard seeds
280 ml / 10 fl. oz / 1 ¼ cups real ale
1 tbsp mustard oil

- Mix together the flours, yeast, sugar, salt and seeds. Stir in the oil and beer. Knead the mixture on an oiled surface. Leave to rest in an oiled bowl for 2 hours.
- Roll the dough with your hands into a fat sausage, then turn it 90° and roll it tightly the other way. Tuck the ends under and transfer the dough to a large loaf tin, keeping the seam underneath.
- Cover the tin loosely with oiled cling film and leave to prove somewhere warm for 45 minutes.
- Preheat the oven to 220°C (200°C fan) / 430F / gas 7.
- Transfer the tin to the top shelf of the oven then close the door.
- Bake for 35–40 minutes or until the loaf sounds hollow when you tap it underneath. Transfer the bread to a wire rack and leave to cool completely before slicing.

Stout and Mustard Seed Bread   298

- Replace the real ale with the same volume of stout for a richer, maltier flavour.

299

MAKES 36

Nutmeg Biscuits

PREPARATION TIME 15 MINUTES

COOKING TIME 12–15 MINUTES

INGREDIENTS

75 g / 2 ½ oz / ⅓ cup butter
100 g / 3 ½ oz / ⅓ cup golden syrup
225 g / 8 oz / 1 ½ cups self-raising
flour
100 g / 3 ½ oz / ½ cup caster
(superfine) sugar
1 tsp nutmeg, freshly grated
1 large egg, beaten

- Preheat the oven to 180°C (160°C fan) / 355F / gas 4 and line 2 baking sheets with greaseproof paper.
- Melt the butter and golden syrup together in a saucepan.
- Mix the flour, sugar and nutmeg together then stir in the melted butter mixture and the beaten egg.
- Use a teaspoon to portion the mixture onto the baking trays, leaving plenty of room for the biscuits to spread.
- Bake in batches for 12–15 minutes or until golden brown.
- Transfer the biscuits to a wire rack and leave to cool and crisp.

Cinnamon and Cocoa Biscuits   300

- Add 30 g / 1 oz / ¼ cup of cocoa powder to the flour and 1 tsp of ground cinnamon instead of the nutmeg for a chocolatey twist to these biscuits.

301
MAKES 36

Muesli Cookies

Chocolate Chip
Muesli Cookies

302

- Add 110 g / 4 oz / ⅔ cup chocolate chips to the mixture at the same time as the flour and muesli for a more luxurious cookie.

Bran and Muesli
Cookies

303

- Replace 110 g / 4 oz / 1 cup of the muesli with 110 g / 4 oz / 1 cup lightly crushed bran flakes for a different texture to these cookies.

PREPARATION TIME 20 MINUTES

COOKING TIME 12–15 MINUTES

....

INGREDIENTS

175 g / 6 oz / ¾ cup butter, softened
225 g / 8 oz / 1 ⅓ cups dark brown sugar
100 g / 3 ½ oz / ½ cup caster (superfine) sugar
2 tsp vanilla extract
1 egg, plus 1 egg yolk
250 g / 9 oz / 1 ⅔ cups self-raising flour
225 g / 8 oz / 2 ¼ cups nutty muesli

- Preheat the oven to 170°C (150°C fan) / 325F / gas 3 and line 2 baking sheets with greaseproof paper.
- Cream together the two sugars, butter and vanilla extract until pale and well whipped then beat in the egg and yolk, followed by the flour and muesli.
- Drop tablespoons of the mixture onto the prepared trays, leaving plenty of room to spread.
- Bake the cookies in batches for 12–15 minutes or until the edges are starting to brown, but the centres are still chewy.
- Transfer to a wire rack and leave to cool.

304
MAKES 1 LOAF Wholemeal Olive Bread

PREPARATION TIME

2 HOURS 30 MINUTES

COOKING TIME 35–40 MINUTES

INGREDIENTS

200 g / 7 oz / ⅓ cup strong white
bread flour, plus extra for dusting
200 g / 7 oz / 1 ⅓ cup stoneground
wholemeal flour
½ tsp easy blend dried yeast
1 tbsp caster (superfine) sugar
1 tsp fine sea salt
100 g / 3 ½ oz / ⅔ cup mixed olives,
pitted and sliced
1 tbsp olive oil

- Mix together the flours, yeast, sugar, salt and olives.
- Stir in the oil and 280 ml warm water into the dry ingredients.
- Knead the mixture on an oiled surface for 10 minutes.
- Leave the dough to rest in an oiled bowl for 1–2 hours.
- Roll the dough with your hands into a fat sausage, then turn it 90° and roll it tightly the other way. Tuck the ends under and transfer the dough to a large loaf tin, keeping the seam underneath.
- Cover the tin loosely with oiled cling film and leave to prove somewhere warm for 45 minutes.
- Preheat the oven to 220°C (200°C fan) / 430F / gas 7.
- Transfer the tin to the top shelf of the oven.
- Bake for 35–40 minutes or until the loaf sounds hollow when you tap it underneath. Transfer the bread to a wire rack and leave to cool completely before slicing.

Wholemeal Olive and Nut Bread

305

- Add 110 g / 4 oz / ¾ cup of chopped nuts of your choice to the dough when you knead it for a different texture to this bread.

306
MAKES 1 LOAF Black Olive and Feta Bread

PREPARATION TIME

2 HOURS 30 MINUTES

COOKING TIME 35–40 MINUTES

INGREDIENTS

300 g / 10 ½ oz / 2 cups strong white
bread flour, plus extra for dusting
100 g / 3 ½ oz / ⅔ cup stoneground
wholemeal flour
½ tsp easy blend dried yeast
1 tbsp caster (superfine) sugar
1 tsp fine sea salt
100 g / 3 ½ oz / ½ cup feta, cubed
100 g / 3 ½ oz / ⅔ cup black olives,
pitted and sliced

- Mix together the flours, yeast, sugar and salt. Stir in the feta, olives and 280 ml of warm water.
- Knead the mixture on a lightly oiled surface for 10 minutes or until the dough is smooth and elastic.
- Leave the dough to rest in a lightly oiled bowl, covered with oiled cling film, for 1–2 hours.
- Knead the dough for 2 more minutes then roll it into a fat sausage. Turn it 90° and roll it tightly the other way then tuck the ends under and transfer the dough to a large loaf tin, keeping the seam underneath.
- Cover the tin with oiled cling film and leave to prove for 45 minutes.
- Preheat the oven to 220°C (200°C fan) / 430F / gas 7.
- Transfer the tin to the top shelf of the oven.
- Bake for 35–40 minutes. Leave to cool completely on a wire rack before slicing.

Black Olive, Oregano and Feta Bread

307

- Add 2 tsp dried oregano to the flour before mixing the dough for an added Mediterranean flavour.

Granary Bread

308

MAKES 2

- Mix together the flours, yeast, sugar and salt. Stir in the oil and 280 ml of warm water.
- Knead the mixture on a lightly oiled surface with your hands for 10 minutes or until smooth and elastic.
- Leave the dough to rest in a lightly oiled bowl, covered with oiled cling film, for 1–2 hours.
- Knead it for 2 more minutes then split it into 2 even pieces and shape into 2 loaves
- Transfer the loaves to a greased baking tray and cover with oiled cling film. Leave to prove for 1 hour.
- Meanwhile, preheat the oven to 220°C (200°C fan) / 425F / gas 7.
- Dust with flour and slash across the tops with a knife.
- Transfer the tray to the top shelf of the oven.
- Bake for 35–40 minutes. Transfer to a wire rack and leave to cool.

PREPARATION TIME

2 HOURS 30 MINUTES

COOKING TIME 35–40 MINUTES

....

INGREDIENTS

300 g / 10 ½ oz / 2 cups malted granary flour
100 g / 3 ½ oz / ⅔ cup strong white bread flour, plus extra for dusting
½ tsp easy blend dried yeast
2 tbsp caster (superfine) sugar
1 tsp fine sea salt
1 tbsp olive oil

Seeded Granary Bread

309

- Add 55 g / 2 oz / ⅓ cup sesame seeds and 55 g / 2 oz sunflower seeds to the dough when you knead it for a crunchier texture.

Salt Crust Rolls

310

MAKES 12

- Mix together the flours, yeast, sugar and salt. Stir in the oil and 280 ml of warm water.
- Knead the mixture on a lightly oiled surface with your hands for 10 minutes or until smooth and elastic.
- Leave the dough to rest in a lightly oiled bowl, covered with oiled cling film, for 1–2 hours.
- Knead it for 2 more minutes then split it into 12 even pieces and shape into rolls.
- Transfer the rolls to a greased baking tray and cover with oiled cling film. Leave to prove for 1 hour.
- Preheat the oven to 220°C (200°C fan) / 425F / gas 7.
- Stir 2 tablespoons of warm water into the salt to dissolve.
- Brush the salt water over the rolls then transfer the tray to the top shelf of the oven. Bake for 15–20 minutes.
- Transfer to a wire rack and leave to cool.

PREPARATION TIME

2 HOURS 30 MINUTES

COOKING TIME 15–20 MINUTES

....

INGREDIENTS

350 g / 12 ½ oz / 2 ⅓ cups strong white bread flour, plus extra for dusting
50 g / 1 ¾ oz / ⅓ cup stoneground wholemeal flour
½ tsp easy blend dried yeast
1 tbsp caster (superfine) sugar
1 tsp fine sea salt
1 tbsp olive oil

TO GLAZE
2 tsp fine sea salt

Salt and Pepper Rolls

311

- Add 1 tsp ground black pepper to the glaze before brushing it on the rolls for a peppery bite to these rolls.

312
MAKES 1 LOAF Wholemeal Chocolate Bread

PREPARATION TIME
2 HOURS 30 MINUTES

COOKING TIME 35–40 MINUTES

INGREDIENTS

200 g / 7 oz / 1 ⅓ cup stoneground wholemeal flour
200 g / 7 oz / 1 ⅓ cup strong white bread flour, plus extra for dusting
½ tsp easy blend dried yeast
4 tbsp brown sugar
2 tbsp cocoa powder
1 tsp fine sea salt
1 tbsp sunflower oil
100 g / 3 ½ oz / ½ cup dark chocolate (minimum 60 % cocoa solids), grated

- In a large bowl, mix together the flours, yeast, sugar, cocoa and salt. Stir the oil and grated chocolate into 280 ml warm water.
- Stir the liquid into the dry ingredients then knead the mixture on a lightly oiled surface with your hands for 10 minutes or until the dough is smooth and elastic.
- Leave the dough to rest in a lightly oiled bowl, covered with oiled cling film, for 1–2 hours or until doubled in size.
- Punch the dough with your fist to knock out the air then knead it for 2 more minutes. Flatten the dough with your hands then roll it up tightly and tuck under the ends.
- Transfer the loaf to a greased loaf tin and cover again with oiled cling film. Leave to prove for 1 hour or until doubled in size.
- Meanwhile, preheat the oven to 220°C (200°C fan) / 430F / gas 7.
- When the dough has risen, transfer the tin to the top shelf of the oven.
- Bake for 35–40 minutes or until the loaf sounds hollow when you tap it underneath. Transfer the bread to a wire rack and leave to cool completely before slicing.

313
MAKES 36 Double Chocolate Cookies

PREPARATION TIME 20 MINUTES

COOKING TIME 12–15 MINUTES

INGREDIENTS

175 g / 6 oz / ¾ cup butter, softened
225 g / 8 oz / 1 ⅓ cup dark brown sugar
100 g / 3 ½ oz / ½ cup caster (superfine) sugar
2 tsp vanilla extract
1 egg, plus 1 egg yolk
250 g / 9 oz / 1 ⅔ cup self-raising flour
2 tbsp unsweetened cocoa powder
175 g / 6 oz / 1 ¼ cup chocolate chips

- Preheat the oven to 170°C (150°C fan) / 340F / gas 3 and line 2 baking sheets with greaseproof paper.
- Cream together the two sugars, butter and vanilla extract until pale and well whipped then beat in the egg and yolk, followed by the flour, cocoa and chocolate chips.
- Drop tablespoons of the mixture onto the prepared trays, leaving plenty of room to spread.
- Bake the cookies in batches for 12–15 minutes or until the edges are starting to brown, but the centres are still chewy.
- Transfer to a wire rack and leave to cool.

314
MAKES 36
Double Chocolate and Currant Cookies

- Preheat the oven to 170°C (150°C fan) / 340F / gas 3 and line 2 baking sheets with greaseproof paper.
- Cream together the two sugars, butter and vanilla extract until pale and well whipped then beat in the egg and yolk, followed by the flour, cocoa, chocolate and currants.
- Drop tablespoons of the mixture onto the prepared trays, leaving plenty of room to spread.
- Bake the cookies in batches for 12–15 minutes or until the edges are starting to brown, but the centres are still chewy.
- Transfer to a wire rack and leave to cool.

PREPARATION TIME 20 MINUTES

COOKING TIME 12–15 MINUTES

INGREDIENTS

175 g / 6 oz / ¾ cup butter, softened
225 g / 8 oz / 1 ⅓ cup dark brown sugar
100 g / 3 ½ oz / ½ cup caster (superfine) sugar
2 tsp vanilla extract
1 egg, plus 1 egg yolk
250 g / 9 oz / 1 ⅔ cup self-raising flour
2 tbsp unsweetened cocoa powder
175 g / 6 oz / 1 ¼ cup chocolate chips
175 g / 6 oz / 1 ¼ cup currants

Chocolate and Cinnamon Cookies
315
MAKES 36

PREPARATION TIME 20 MINUTES

COOKING TIME 12–15 MINUTES

INGREDIENTS

175 g / 6 oz / ¾ cup butter, softened
225 g / 8 oz / 1 ⅓ cup dark brown sugar
100 g / 3 ½ oz / ½ cup caster (superfine) sugar
2 tsp vanilla extract
1 egg, plus 1 egg yolk
250 g / 9 oz / 1 ⅔ cups self-raising flour
2 tbsp unsweetened cocoa powder
1 tsp ground cinnamon
175 g / 6 oz / 1 ¼ cups chocolate chips

- Preheat the oven to 170°C (150°C fan) / 340F / gas 3 and line 2 baking sheets with greaseproof paper.
- Cream together the two sugars, butter and vanilla extract until pale and well whipped then beat in the egg and yolk, followed by the flour, cocoa, cinnamon and chocolate chips.
- Drop tablespoons of the mixture onto the prepared trays, leaving plenty of room to spread.
- Bake the cookies in batches for 12–15 minutes or until the edges are starting to brown, but the centres are still chewy.
- Transfer to a wire rack and leave to cool.

Bullseye Biscuits
316
MAKES 24

PREPARATION TIME 30 MINUTES

COOKING TIME 12–15 MINUTES

INGREDIENTS

75 g / 2 ½ oz / ⅓ cup butter
100 g / 3 ½ oz / ⅓ cup golden syrup
225 g / 8 oz / 1 ½ cups self-raising flour
100 g / 3 ½ oz / ½ cup caster (superfine) sugar
1 large egg, beaten
2 tbsp unsweetened cocoa powder
24 glacé cherries

- Preheat the oven to 180°C (160°C fan) / 355F / gas 4 and line 2 baking sheets with greaseproof paper.
- Melt the butter and golden syrup together in a saucepan.
- Mix the flour and sugar together then stir in the melted butter mixture and the beaten egg.
- Spoon two thirds of the mixture into a separate bowl and stir in the cocoa powder.
- Use a teaspoon to portion the cocoa mixture onto the baking trays, leaving plenty of room for the biscuits to spread. Top with a teaspoon of the plain mixture, then half a teaspoon of the cocoa mixture. Press a cherry into the centre of each one.
- Bake the biscuits in batches for 12–15 minutes or until they have spread and set.
- Transfer the biscuits to a wire rack and leave to cool and harden.

Chocolate Caramel Cookies

Salted Caramel Cookies 318

- Replace the chocolate caramel bars with 75 ml / 3 fl. oz / ⅓ cup dulce de leche and 1 tbsp sea salt flakes when you prepare the cookie dough, for a sweet/savoury contrast.

Chocolate, Caramel and Nut Cookies 319

- Replace the chocolate caramel bars with the same weight of chopped caramel and nut chocolate bars for a nutty crunch.

PREPARATION TIME 20 MINUTES

COOKING TIME 12–15 MINUTES

....

INGREDIENTS

175 g / 6 oz / ¾ cup butter, softened
225 g / 8 oz / 1 ⅓ cup light brown sugar
100 g / 3 ½ oz / ½ cup caster (superfine) sugar
2 tsp vanilla extract
1 egg, plus 1 egg yolk
250 g / 9 oz / 1 ⅔ cups self-raising flour
150 g / 5 ½ oz / ¾ cup chocolate caramel bars, chopped

- Preheat the oven to 170°C (150°C fan) / 340F / gas 3 and line 2 baking sheets with greaseproof paper.
- Cream together the two sugars, butter and vanilla extract until pale and well whipped then beat in the egg and yolk, followed by the flour and chopped chocolate caramel bars.
- Drop tablespoons of the mixture onto the prepared trays, leaving plenty of room to spread.
- Bake the cookies in batches for 12–15 minutes or until the edges are starting to brown, but the centres are still chewy.
- Transfer to a wire rack and leave to cool.

320
MAKES 36

Marmalade Heart Biscuits

- Cream together the sugar, butter and vanilla extract until pale then stir in the flour and ground almonds.
- Bring the mixture together into a ball with your hands then wrap in cling film and refrigerate for 45 minutes.
- Preheat the oven to 140^{0}C (120^{0}C fan) / 280F / gas 1 and line 2 baking sheets with greaseproof paper.
- Roll out the dough on a lightly floured surface to 5 mm thick. Use a heart-shaped cutter to cut out 72 biscuits.
- Use a small cutter to cut a hole out of 36 of the biscuits.
- Transfer the biscuits to the prepared trays in batches and bake for 25–30 minutes or until cooked through and only just golden.
- Transfer the biscuits to a wire rack and leave to cool.
- Put a teaspoon of marmalade on the underside of the plain biscuits and top with the biscuits with the hole cut out. Dust liberally with icing sugar.

PREPARATION TIME
1 HOUR 15 MINUTES

COOKING TIME 25–30 MINUTES

INGREDIENTS

150 g / 5 ½ oz / ⅔ cup caster (superfine) sugar
350 g / 12 oz / 1 ½ cups butter, softened
1 tsp vanilla extract
300 g / 10 ½ oz / 2 cups plain (all purpose) flour
150 g / 5 ½ oz / 1 ½ cups ground almonds
200 g / 7 oz / ⅔ cup marmalade
icing (confectioners') sugar to dust

Apricot Jam Heart Biscuits
321

- Replace the marmalade with the same weight of apricot jam for an alternative fruit flavour.

322
MAKES 25

Parmesan and Herb Shortbread Biscuits

- Preheat the oven to 180^{0}C (160^{0}C fan) / 355F / gas 4 and line a baking tray with greaseproof paper.
- Rub the butter into the flour and stir in the Parmesan and herbs.
- Knead gently until the mixture forms a smooth dough then roll out on a lightly floured surface to 1 cm thick.
- Use a knife to cut the sheet into small squares and transfer them to the baking tray.
- Bake the biscuits for 12–15 minutes, turning the tray round halfway through.
- Transfer the biscuits to a wire rack and leave to cool.

PREPARATION TIME 20 MINUTES

COOKING TIME 15–20 MINUTES

INGREDIENTS

150 g / 5 oz / ⅔ cup butter, cubed
230 g / 8 oz / 1 ½ cups plain (all purpose) flour
50 g / 1 ¾ oz / ½ cup Parmesan, grated
2 tbsp dried herbes de Provence

Gruyere Shortbread Biscuits
323

- Replace the Parmesan with the same weight of Gruyere and omit the herbs for a more distinct cheese flavour to these biscuits.

324
MAKES 1

Stuffed Ring Loaf

PREPARATION TIME
2 HOURS 30 MINUTES

COOKING TIME 25–30 MINUTES

INGREDIENTS

400 g / 14 oz / 2 ⅔ cups strong white bread flour, plus extra for dusting
½ tsp easy blend dried yeast
1 tbsp caster (superfine) sugar
1 tsp fine sea salt
1 tbsp olive oil

FOR THE STUFFING

100 g / 3 ½ oz / ½ cup chorizo, chopped
75 g / 2 ½ oz / ⅓ cup sun-dried tomatoes in oil, drained and chopped
100 g / 3 ½ oz / ½ cup mozzarella, cubed
1 tbsp basil leaves, chopped

- Mix together the flour, yeast, sugar and salt. Stir in the oil and 280 ml of warm water.
- Knead the mixture on a lightly oiled surface for 10 minutes or until smooth and elastic.
- Leave the dough to rest, covered with oiled cling film, for 1–2 hours or until doubled in size.
- Combine the stuffing ingredients.
- Roll the dough out into a rectangle. Put the stuffing ingredients in a line down the middle then fold in the sides and pinch to seal.
- Curl the dough round into a ring with the seam on top and transfer to a greased baking tray. Cover with oiled cling film and leave to prove for 1 hour.
- Preheat the oven to 220°C (200°C fan) / 430F / gas 7.
- Bake for 25–30 minutes or until the loaf sounds hollow when you tap it underneath.

Spinach Stuffed Ring Loaf   325

- Replace the chorizo in the recipe with 200 g / 7 oz / 1 ⅓ cups wilted spinach for a vegetarian take on this loaf.

326
MAKES 18

Black Sesame Tuiles

PREPARATION TIME I HOUR

COOKING TIME 8–10 MINUTES

INGREDIENTS

110 g / 4 oz / ⅔ cup plain (all purpose) flour
110 g / 4 oz / ½ cup caster (superfine) sugar
2 large egg whites
110 g / 4 oz / ½ cup butter, softened
2 tbsp black sesame seeds

- Beat together the flour, sugar and egg whites until smooth, then beat in the melted butter and sesame seeds.
- Refrigerate for 30 minutes.
- Preheat the oven to 180°C (160°C fan) / 350F / gas 4 and oil 2 large baking trays.
- Spoon teaspoonfuls of the mixture onto the baking trays and spread out with the back of the spoon to make 10 cm circles.
- Bake the tuiles for 8–10 minutes then lift them off the trays with a palette knife and drape over a rolling pin while still soft. Leave to cool and harden.

Black Sesame and Orange Tuiles   327

- Add 1 tsp of orange flower water and the grated zest of ½ orange to the tuile mixture for an added citrus tang.

328
MAKES 20 Chocolate Spring Rolls

- Preheat the oven to 180°C (160°C fan) / 355F / gas 4 and grease a large baking tray.
- Cut the pile of filo sheets in half then take one halved sheet and brush it with melted butter.
- Arrange a tablespoon of chopped chocolate along one side and roll it up, tucking in the sides as you go.
- Transfer the roll to the baking tray and repeat with the rest of the filo and chocolate.
- Brush the spring rolls with beaten egg and bake for 12–15 minutes or until the filo is crisp and golden brown.
- Serve warm.

PREPARATION TIME 25 MINUTES

COOKING TIME 12–15 MINUTES

INGREDIENTS

225 g / 8 oz / 1 cup filo pastry
100 g / 3 ½ oz / ½ cup butter, melted
200 g / 7 oz / 1 ¼ cups dark chocolate (minimum 60 % cocoa solids), finely chopped
1 egg, beaten

White Chocolate and Cranberry Spring Rolls
329

- Replace the chocolate filling with 150 g / 5 oz / ¾ cup chopped white chocolate and 55 g / 2 oz / ⅓ cup dried cranberries. Combine before filling the rolls.

330
MAKES 36 Cinnamon Snap Biscuits

- Preheat the oven to 180°C (160°C fan) / 355F / gas 4 and line 2 baking sheets with greaseproof paper.
- Melt the butter and golden syrup together in a saucepan.
- Mix the flour, sugar and cinnamon together then stir in the melted butter mixture and the beaten egg.
- Use a teaspoon to portion the mixture onto the baking trays, leaving plenty of room for the biscuits to spread.
- Bake in batches for 12–15 minutes or until golden brown.
- Transfer the biscuits to a wire rack and leave to cool and harden.

PREPARATION TIME 20 MINUTES

COOKING TIME 12–15 MINUTES

INGREDIENTS

75 g / 2 ½ oz / ⅓ cup butter
100 g / 3 ½ oz / ⅓ cup golden syrup
225 g / 8 oz / 1 ½ cups self-raising flour
100 g / 3 ½ oz / ½ cup caster (superfine) sugar
1 tsp ground cinnamon
1 large egg, beaten

Spiced Snap Biscuits
331

- Instead of using just cinnamon, use 1 tsp ground mixed spice for a more varied flavour.

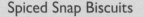

Date-filled Shortbread

Cranberry-filled Shortbread

333

- Soak 250 g / 9 oz / 1 ¼ cups of dried cranberries in enough hot water to cover them for an hour. Drain, puree and use to stuff the shortbread.

Caramel-filled Shortbread

334

- Use 200 g / 7 oz / ¾ cup dulce de leche as the filled instead of the dates for an even sweeter shortbread.

PREPARATION TIME 30 MINUTES

COOKING TIME 12–15 MINUTES

INGREDIENTS

200 g / 7 oz / 1 cup dates, pitted and chopped
150 g / 5 ½ oz / 1 cup plain (all purpose) flour
75 g / 2 ½ oz / ⅓ cup caster (superfine) sugar
150 g / 5 oz / ⅔ cup butter, cubed

- Cover the dates with boiling water and leave to soak for 1 hour. Drain well then puree in a food processor.
- Preheat the oven to 180°C (160°C fan) / 355F / gas 4 and line a baking tray with greaseproof paper.
- Mix the flour and caster sugar in a bowl, then rub in the butter.
- Knead gently until the mixture forms a smooth dough then roll out on a lightly floured surface to 5 mm thick and cut the sheet in half.
- Spread the date puree over one half of the shortbread and lay the other sheet on top.
- Cut the shortbread into 24 squares and transfer to the baking tray.
- Bake the biscuits for 12–15 minutes, turning them over half way through.
- Transfer the biscuits to a wire rack and leave to cool.

335

MAKES 1 LOAF

Curry and Pistachio Bread

- Mix together the flours, yeast, sugar, salt, curry powder and pistachios. Stir in oil and 280 ml of warm water.
- Knead the mixture on a lightly oiled surface for 10 minutes or until the dough is smooth and elastic.
- Leave the dough to rest in a lightly oiled bowl, covered with oiled cling film, for 1–2 hours.
- Knead the dough for 2 more minutes then roll it into a fat sausage. Turn it 90° and roll it tightly the other way then tuck the ends under and transfer the dough to a large loaf tin, keeping the seam underneath.
- Cover the tin with oiled cling film and leave to prove for 45 minutes.
- Preheat the oven to 220°C (200°C fan) / 430F / gas 7.
- Bake for 35–40 minutes or until the underneath sounds hollow when tapped.
- Leave to cool completely on a wire rack.

Indian Mixed Seed Bread   336

- Use 75 g / 3 oz / ⅔ cup of any combination of seeds instead of the pistachios for a nut-free bread.

PREPARATION TIME
2 HOURS 30 MINUTES

COOKING TIME 35–40 MINUTES

INGREDIENTS

300 g / 10 ½ oz / 2 cups strong white bread flour, plus extra for dusting
100 g / 3 ½ oz / ⅔ cup stoneground wholemeal flour
½ tsp easy blend dried yeast
1 tbsp caster (superfine) sugar
1 tsp fine sea salt
2 tbsp mild curry powder
75 g / 2 ½ oz / ½ cup pistachio nuts
2 tbsp olive oil

337

MAKES 24

Fruit and Nut Cookies

- Preheat the oven to 180°C (160°C fan) / 355F / gas 4 and line a baking tray with greaseproof paper.
- Rub the butter into the flour with a pinch of salt then stir in the sugar.
- Beat the egg yolks and stir them into the dry ingredients with the dried fruit and nuts.
- Bring the mixture together into a soft dough and space tablespoons of the mixture out on the baking tray.
- Bake the biscuits for 20–25 minutes or until golden brown.
- Transfer the biscuits to a wire rack and leave to cool.

Chewy Fruit Cookies   338

- Instead of using nuts, replace the flaked almonds and pistachios with the same weight of raisins and chopped glacé cherries for chewy, colourful cookies.

PREPARATION TIME 15 MINUTES

COOKING TIME 20–25 MINUTES

INGREDIENTS

125 g / 4 ½ oz / ½ cup butter, cubed
125 g / 4 ½ oz / ¾ cup plain (all purpose) flour
125 g / 4 ½ oz / ½ cup caster (superfine) sugar
3 large egg yolks
75 g / 2 ½ oz / 1 cup flaked (slivered) almonds
75 g / 2 ½ oz / ½ cup pistachios, chopped
75 g / 2 ½ oz / ⅓ cup dried apricots, chopped
75 g / 2 ½ oz / ⅓ cup sultanas

Fig and Walnut Bread

339

MAKES 1 LOAF

PREPARATION TIME
2 HOURS 30 MINUTES

COOKING TIME 35–40 MINUTES

INGREDIENTS

400 g / 14 oz / 2 ⅔ cups strong white bread flour, plus extra for dusting
½ tsp easy blend dried yeast
1 tbsp caster (superfine) sugar
1 tsp fine sea salt
100 g / 3 ½ oz / ½ cup dried figs, chopped
100 g / 3 ½ oz / ⅔ cup walnut halves

- Mix together the flour, yeast, sugar and salt. Stir in the figs, walnuts and 280 ml of warm water.
- Knead the mixture on a lightly oiled surface with your hands for 10 minutes or until the dough is elastic.
- Leave the dough to rest in a lightly oiled bowl, covered with oiled cling film, for 1–2 hours.
- Punch the dough with your fist to knock out the air then knead it for 2 more minutes. Cup your hands around the dough and move it in a circular motion whilst pressing down to form a tight round loaf.
- Transfer the dough to a greased round cake tin and cover with oiled cling film. Leave to prove for 1 hour or until doubled in size then slash a cross in the top.
- Preheat the oven to 220°C (200°C fan) / 430F / gas 7.
- Bake for 35–40 minutes or until the loaf sounds hollow when tapped. Transfer the bread to a wire rack and leave to cool completely before slicing.

Apricot and Walnut Bread

340

- Replace the figs in the recipe with 100 g / 3 ½ oz / ½ cup chopped dried apricots instead for a different flavour and texture.

Coffee Sponge Finger Biscuits

341

MAKES 40

PREPARATION TIME 30 MINUTES

COOKING TIME 10–15 MINUTES

INGREDIENTS

4 large eggs
125 g / 4 ½ oz / ½ cup caster (superfine) sugar
1 tsp instant espresso powder
a pinch cream of tartar
115 g / 4 oz / ⅔ cup plain (all purpose) flour

- Preheat the oven to 190°C (170°C fan) / 375F / gas 5 and grease and line 2 large trays with greaseproof paper.
- Separate the eggs and put the yolks in a bowl with half of the sugar and the espresso powder. Whisk with an electric whisk for 4 minutes or until very thick and pale.
- Whisk the egg whites with the cream of tartar, making sure the whisk and bowl are completely clean.
- When the egg white reaches the soft peak stage, gradually whisk in the remaining sugar.
- Sieve the flour over the egg yolk mixture and scrape in the egg whites, then carefully fold it all together with a large metal spoon, retaining as much air as possible.
- Spoon the mixture into a piping bag.
- Pipe 10 cm lines onto the baking trays, leaving room for the biscuits to spread.
- Bake the biscuits for 10–15 minutes.
- Transfer to a wire rack and leave to cool completely.

Chocolate Sponge Finger Biscuits

342

- Replace the instant espresso powder in the recipe with 1 tbsp good-quality cocoa powder for a chocolatey take on these biscuits.

343
MAKES 40 # Langues Du Chat Biscuits

- Preheat the oven to 190°C (170°C fan) / 375F / gas 5 and grease and line 2 large trays with greaseproof paper.
- Separate the eggs and put the yolks in a bowl with half of the sugar and the vanilla extract. Whisk with an electric whisk for 4 minutes or until very thick and pale.
- Whisk the egg whites with the cream of tartar, making sure the whisk and bowl are completely clean.
- When the egg white reaches the soft peak stage, gradually whisk in the remaining sugar.
- Sieve the flour over the egg yolk mixture and scrape in the egg whites, then carefully fold it all together with a large metal spoon, retaining as much air as possible.
- Spoon tablespoons of the mixture onto the tray and spread out with the spoon into tongue shapes.
- Bake the biscuits for 10–15 minutes.
- Transfer to a wire rack and leave to cool completely.

PREPARATION TIME 20 MINUTES

COOKING TIME 10–15 MINUTES

INGREDIENTS

4 large eggs
125 g / 4 ½ oz / ½ cup caster (superfine) sugar
1 tsp vanilla extract
a pinch cream of tartar
115 g / 4 oz / ⅔ cup plain (all purpose) flour

Amaretto Cat's Tongue Biscuits   344

- Replace the vanilla extract with 1 tbsp of Amaretto for a more complex flavour.

345
SERVES 12 # Galette Du Roi

- Preheat the oven to 200°C (180°C fan) / 390F / gas 6 and grease and line a baking tray with greaseproof paper.
- Roll out half the pastry on a floured surface into a large circle and transfer it to the baking tray.
- Whisk together the almonds, butter, sugar, eggs and flour until smooth then spoon the mixture on top of the pastry, leaving a clear border round the edge.
- Brush the border with a little water. Roll out the other half of the pastry and lay it over the almond paste, pressing around the outside to seal.
- Trim away the excess pastry and score a pattern in the top with a knife.
- Brush the pastry with egg yolk and bake for 35 minutes.
- Traditionally a dried bean or porcelain figurine is hidden inside the galette before baking. The person that finds it in their slice becomes king for the day.

PREPARATION TIME 30 MINUTES

COOKING TIME 35 MINUTES

INGREDIENTS

450 g / 1 lb / 1 ½ cups puff pastry
150 g / 5 ½ oz / 1 ½ cup ground almonds
150 g / 5 ½ oz / ⅔ cup butter, softened
150 g / 5 ½ oz / ⅔ cup caster (superfine) sugar
2 large eggs
2 tbsp plain (all purpose) flour
1 egg yolk

Marzipan King Cake   346

- Divide 200 g / 7 oz / ½ cup of softened natural marzipan into small balls and use them to garnish the top of the cake for an additional almond flavour.

MAKES 24 Almond Snaps

PREPARATION TIME 15 MINUTES

COOKING TIME 15–20 MINUTES

INGREDIENTS

2 large egg whites
175 g / 6 oz / 1 ¾ cup ground almonds
100 g / 3 ½ oz / 1 cup icing (confectioners') sugar
75 g / 2 ½ oz / ⅓ cup caster (superfine) sugar
1 tbsp Amaretto liqueur

• Preheat the oven to 170°C (150°C fan) / 325F / gas 3 and oil a large baking tray.
• Whisk the egg whites to stiff peaks in a very clean bowl then carefully fold in the rest of the ingredients.
• Spoon the mixture into a piping bag fitted with a large plain nozzle and pipe 8 cm circles onto the baking tray.
• Bake for 15–20 minutes or until golden brown and crisp.
• Transfer to a wire rack to cool.

Almond Kirsch Snaps   348

• Replace the Amaretto in the recipe with the same amount of kirsch for a fruity kick to these snaps.

SERVES 6 Sesame and Poppy Seed Focaccia

PREPARATION TIME
2 HOURS 30 MINUTES

COOKING TIME 25–35 MINUTES

INGREDIENTS

300 g / 10 ½ oz / 2 cups strong white bread flour
½ tsp easy blend dried yeast
1 tsp fine sea salt
2 tbsp olive oil

TO FINISH

50 ml / 1 ¾ fl. oz / ¼ cup olive oil
50 ml / 1 ¾ fl. oz / ¼ cup warm water
½ tsp fine sea salt
1 tbsp sesame seeds
1 tbsp poppy seeds

• Mix together the flour, yeast and salt. Stir in the oil and 280 ml of warm water.
• Knead the mixture on a lightly oiled surface for 10 minutes or until smooth and elastic.
• Leave the dough to rest, covered with oiled cling film, for 1–2 hours or until doubled in size.
• Oil a rectangular cake tin then stretch out the dough to cover the base.
• Cover the focaccia with oiled cling film and leave to prove for 1 hour or until doubled in size.
• Preheat the oven to 220°C (200°C fan) / 430F / gas 7.
• Put the oil, water and salt in a jar and shake well.
• Pour it all over the dough then sprinkle with the seeds.
• Bake for 25–35 minutes or until the top is golden and the base is cooked through.
• Leave to cool on a wire rack before cutting into squares.

Sesame and Onion Seed Focaccia   350

• Replace the poppy seeds in the recipe with black onion seeds (nigella seeds) for a different flavour and appearance.

Double Chocolate Ice Cream Cookies

Chocolate Chip Ice Cream Cookies

352

- Remove the cocoa powder from the cookie recipe and increase the amount of chocolate chips used by 30 g / 1 oz.

Triple Chocolate Ice Cream Cookies

353

- Replace 100 g / 3 ½ oz / ⅔ cup of the chocolate chips with 100 g / 3 ½ oz / ⅔ cup of finely chopped white chocolate.

PREPARATION TIME 25 MINUTES

COOKING TIME 12–15 MINUTES

....

INGREDIENTS

175 g / 6 oz / ¾ cup butter, softened
225 g / 8 oz / 1 ⅓ cups dark brown sugar
100 g / 3 ½ oz / ½ cups caster (superfine) sugar
2 tsp vanilla extract
1 egg, plus 1 egg yolk
250 g / 9 oz / 1 ⅔ cups self-raising flour
2 tbsp unsweetened cocoa powder
175 g / 6 oz / 1 ¼ cups chocolate chips

TO SERVE

1 l / 1 pt 15 fl. oz / 4 cups strawberry ice cream

- Leave the ice cream out of the freezer for 15 minutes to soften then scoop it onto a large sheet of cling film.
- Form it into a log shape and roll it in the cling film then freeze for 1 hour or until firm.
- Preheat the oven to 170°C (150°C fan) / 340F / gas 3 and line 2 baking sheets with greaseproof paper.
- Cream together the two sugars, butter and vanilla extract until pale and well whipped then beat in the egg and yolk, followed by the flour, cocoa and chocolate chips.
- Drop tablespoons of the mixture onto the prepared trays, leaving plenty of room to spread.
- Bake the cookies in batches for 12–15 minutes or until the edges are starting to brown, but the centres are still chewy.
- Transfer to a wire rack and leave to cool completely.
- When you're ready to serve, cut the ice cream log into 18 slices and sandwich each one between two cookies.

354
MAKES 36

Sandwich Biscuits

PREPARATION TIME
I HOUR I5 MINUTES

COOKING TIME 25–30 MINUTES

INGREDIENTS

150 g / 5 ½ oz / ⅔ cup caster (superfine) sugar
350 g / 12 oz / 1 ½ cups butter, softened
1 tsp vanilla extract
300 g / 10 ½ oz / 2 cups plain (all purpose) flour
150 g / 5 ½ oz / 1 ½ cups ground almonds
icing (confectioners') sugar, to dust

TO FILL
strawberry jam (jelly)
marmalade
coconut spread

- Cream together the sugar, butter and vanilla extract until pale then stir in the flour and ground almonds.
- Bring the mixture together into a ball with your hands then wrap in cling film and refrigerate for 45 minutes.
- Preheat the oven to 140⁰C (120⁰C fan) / 280F / gas 1 and line 2 baking sheets with greaseproof paper.
- Roll out the dough on a lightly floured surface to 5 mm thick. Use a fluted pastry cutter to cut out 72 biscuits.
- Use small cutters to cut the centre out of 36 of the biscuits.
- Transfer the biscuits to the prepared trays in batches and bake for 25–30 minutes.
- Transfer the biscuits to a wire rack and leave to cool.
- Put a teaspoon of jam, marmalade or coconut spread on the underside of the plain rounds and sandwich each one with a cut-out biscuit. Dust liberally with icing sugar.

Coconut Sandwich Biscuits
355

- Instead of using strawberry jam and marmalade to fill the biscuits, use only coconut spread and sprinkle with desiccated coconut before sandwiching them for a tropical taste.

356
MAKES 1

Spelt Bread

PREPARATION TIME
2 HOURS 30 MINUTES

COOKING TIME 35–40 MINUTES

INGREDIENTS

200 g / 7 oz / 1 ⅓ cups strong white bread flour, plus extra for dusting
200 g / 7 oz / 1 ⅓ cups spelt flour
½ tsp easy blend dried yeast
1 tbsp caster (superfine) sugar
1 tsp fine sea salt
1 tbsp olive oil

- Mix together the flours, yeast, sugar and salt. Stir in the oil and 280 ml of warm water.
- Knead on a lightly oiled surface for 10 minutes or until the dough is elastic.
- Leave the dough to rest, covered with oiled cling film, for 1–2 hours or until doubled in size.
- Knead the dough for 2 more minutes, then shape it into a round loaf.
- Transfer the loaf to a greased baking tray and cover again with oiled cling film. Leave to prove for 1 hour or until doubled in size.
- Preheat the oven to 220⁰C (200⁰C fan) / 430F / gas 7.
- When the dough has risen, score the top with a knife and dust with flour.
- Bake for 35–40 minutes. Transfer the bread to a wire rack and leave to cool.

Spelt Granary Bread
357

- Replace half of the strong white bread flour 100 g / 3 ½ oz / ⅔ cup of malted granary flour if you'd like a maltier tasting bread.

358
MAKES 12 Lemon Cakes

- Preheat the oven to 190°C (170°C fan) / 375F / gas 5 and line a 12-hole cupcake tin with shallow paper cases.
- Combine the flour, sugar, butter, eggs and lemon zest in a bowl and whisk together for 2 minutes or until smooth.
- Divide the mixture between the paper cases, then transfer the tin to the oven and bake for 15–20 minutes.
- Test with a wooden toothpick, if it comes out clean, the cakes are done.
- Transfer the cakes to a wire rack and leave to cool completely.

PREPARATION TIME 20 MINUTES

COOKING TIME 15–20 MINUTES

INGREDIENTS

110 g / 4 oz / ⅔ cup self-raising flour, sifted
110 g / 4 oz / ½ cup caster (superfine) sugar
110 g / 4 oz / ½ cup butter, softened
2 large eggs
1 lemon, zest finely grated

Lemon and Thyme Cupcakes 359
- Add 1 tsp dried thyme to the batter before mixing for a fragrant savoury twist on these cupcakes.

360
MAKES 1 Kamut Bread

- Mix together the flours, yeast, sugar and salt. Stir in the oil and 280 ml of warm water.
- Knead on a lightly oiled surface for 10 minutes.
- Leave the dough to rest, covered with oiled cling film, for 1–2 hours or until doubled in size.
- Knead the dough for 2 more minutes, then shape it into a round loaf.
- Transfer the loaf to a greased baking tray and cover again with oiled cling film. Leave to prove for 1 hour or until doubled in size.
- Preheat the oven to 220°C (200°C fan) / 430F / gas 7.
- When the dough has risen, score the top with a knife and dust with flour.
- Bake for 35–40 minutes or until the loaf sounds hollow when tapped. Transfer the bread to a wire rack and leave to cool.

PREPARATION TIME
2 HOURS 30 MINUTES

COOKING TIME 35–40 MINUTES

INGREDIENTS

200 g / 7 oz / 1 ⅓ cups strong white bread flour, plus extra for dusting
200 g / 7 oz / 1 ⅓ cups kamut flour
½ tsp easy blend dried yeast
1 tbsp caster (superfine) sugar
1 tsp fine sea salt
1 tbsp olive oil

Raisin Kamut Bread 361
- Knead 100 g / 3 ½ oz / ½ cup of raisins into the dough before proving, shaping and baking.

362
MAKES 1

Treacle Bread

PREPARATION TIME

2 HOURS 30 MINUTES

COOKING TIME 35–40 MINUTES

INGREDIENTS

400 g / 14 oz / 2 ⅔ cups strong white
bread flour, plus extra for dusting
½ tsp easy blend dried yeast
3 tbsp treacle
1 tsp fine sea salt
1 tbsp olive oil

- Mix together the flour, yeast and salt. Stir the oil and treacle into 280 ml of warm water.
- Stir the liquid into the dry ingredients then knead on a lightly oiled surface for 10 minutes.
- Leave the dough to rest, covered with oiled cling film, for 1–2 hours or until doubled in size. Knead the dough for 2 minutes, then shape it into a round loaf.
- Transfer the loaf to a greased baking tray and cover again with oiled cling film. Leave to prove for 1 hour or until doubled in size.
- Preheat the oven to 220°C (200°C fan) / 430F / gas 7.
- When the dough has risen, score the top with a knife and dust with flour.
- Bake for 35–40 minutes or until the loaf sounds hollow when tapped. Transfer the bread to a wire rack and leave to cool.

Golden Syrup Bread   363

- Replace the treacle with the same amount of golden syrup for a sweeter, milder tasting bread.

364
MAKES 1

Chocolate Chip Baton

PREPARATION TIME

2 HOURS 30 MINUTES

COOKING TIME 25–30 MINUTES

INGREDIENTS

400 g / 14 oz / 2 ⅔ cups strong white
bread flour, plus extra for dusting
½ tsp easy blend dried yeast
1 tbsp caster (superfine) sugar
1 tsp fine sea salt
1 tbsp sunflower oil
200 g / 7 oz / 1 ⅓ cups chocolate
chips

- Mix together the flour, yeast, sugar and salt. Stir in the oil and 280 ml of warm water.
- Knead the mixture on a lightly oiled surface for 10 minutes or until smooth and elastic.
- Leave the dough to rest, covered with oiled cling film, for 1–2 hours or until doubled in size.
- Sprinkle over the chocolate chips and knead for 2 more minutes then roll it up tightly into a baton.
- Transfer the loaf to a greased baking tray and cover with oiled cling film. Leave to prove for 1 hour.
- Preheat the oven to 220°C (200°C fan) / 430F / gas 7.
- Slash the top diagonally with a knife and transfer the tray to the top shelf of the oven.
- Bake for 25–30 minutes or until the loaf sounds hollow when you tap it underneath.

Fruit Baton   365

- Replace the chocolate chips with 150 g / 5 oz / ¾ cup mixed candied peel for a fruity, colourful version of this baton.

Crusty Finger Rolls

366

MAKES 12

Wholemeal Finger Rolls

367

- Replace 300 g / 10 ½ oz / 2 cups of the strong white bread flour with wholemeal flour before kneading the dough.

Crusty Parmesan Finger Rolls

368

- Incorporate 75 g / 3 oz / ¾ cup of grated Parmesan into the dough before kneading for a cheesy take on these rolls.

PREPARATION TIME
2 HOURS 30 MINUTES

COOKING TIME 15–20 MINUTES

INGREDIENTS

400 g / 14 oz / 2 ⅔ cups strong white bread flour, plus extra for dusting
½ tsp easy blend dried yeast
1 tbsp caster (superfine) sugar
1 tsp fine sea salt
1 tbsp olive oil

- Mix together the flour, yeast, sugar and salt. Stir the oil into 280 ml of warm water then stir it into the dry ingredients.
- Knead the mixture on a lightly oiled surface with your hands for 10 minutes or until smooth and elastic.
- Leave the dough to rest in a lightly oiled bowl, covered with oiled cling film, for 1–2 hours or until doubled in size.
- Knead it for 2 more minutes then split it into 12 even pieces and shape into finger rolls.
- Transfer the rolls to a greased baking tray and cover with oiled cling film. Leave to prove for 1 hour or until doubled in size.
- Meanwhile, preheat the oven to 220⁰C (200⁰C fan) / 425F / gas 7.
- Dust the rolls with flour and slash along the tops with a knife.
- Transfer the tray to the top shelf of the oven.
- Bake for 15–20 minutes or until the rolls sound hollow when you tap them underneath.
- Transfer to a wire rack and leave to cool.

369
MAKES 24

Mixed Nut Cookies

PREPARATION TIME 15 MINUTES

COOKING TIME 20–25 MINUTES

INGREDIENTS

125 g / 4 ½ oz / ½ cup butter, cubed
125 g / 4 ½ oz / ¾ cup plain (all purpose) flour
125 g / 4 ½ oz / ½ cup caster (superfine) sugar
3 large egg yolks
75 g / 2 ½ oz / 1 cup flaked (slivered) almonds
75 g / 2 ½ oz / ⅔ cup almonds, chopped
75 g / 2 ½ oz / ⅔ cup walnuts, chopped
75 g / 2 ½ oz / ⅔ cup hazelnuts (cob nuts), chopped

- Preheat the oven to 180⁰C (160⁰C fan) / 355F / gas 4 and line a baking tray with greaseproof paper.
- Rub the butter into the flour with a pinch of salt then stir in the sugar.
- Beat the egg yolks and stir them into the dry ingredients with the nuts.
- Bring the mixture together into a soft dough and space tablespoons of the mixture out on the baking tray.
- Bake the biscuits for 20–25 minutes or until golden brown.
- Transfer the biscuits to a wire rack and leave to cool.

Mixed Nut and Caramel Cookies   370

- Add 55 g / 2 oz / ¼ cup of dulce de leche and an additional 30 g / 1 oz of plain (all purpose) flour to the cookie dough before shaping and baking for a sweeter crunch.

371
MAKES 36

Treacle and Oat Cookies

PREPARATION TIME 20 MINUTES

COOKING TIME 12–15 MINUTES

INGREDIENTS

225 g / 8 oz / 1 ⅓ cup dark brown sugar
75 g / 2 ½ oz / ⅓ cup caster (superfine) sugar
175 g / 6 oz / ¾ cup butter, softened
2 tbsp treacle
1 egg, plus 1 egg yolk
250 g / 9 oz / 1 ⅔ cups self-raising flour
100 g / 3 ½ oz / 1 cup porridge oats

- Preheat the oven to 170⁰C (150⁰C fan) / 340F / gas 3 and line 2 baking sheets with greaseproof paper.
- Cream together the two sugars, butter and treacle until pale and well whipped then beat in the egg and yolk, followed by the flour and oats.
- Drop tablespoons of the mixture onto the prepared trays, leaving plenty of room to spread.
- Bake the cookies in batches for 12–15 minutes or until the edges are starting to brown, but the centres are still chewy.
- Transfer to a wire rack and leave to cool.

Golden Syrup and Oat Cookies   372

- Replace the treacle with the same amount of golden syrup for a lighter cookie in taste and appearance.

373

MAKES 24

Sesame and Tapenade Shortbread

- Preheat the oven to 180°C (160°C fan) / 355F / gas 4 and line a baking tray with greaseproof paper.
- Rub the butter into the flour and stir in the tapenade.
- Knead gently until the mixture forms a smooth dough then roll out on a lightly floured surface to 1 cm thick.
- Use a round cookie cutter to cut out the biscuits and transfer them to the baking tray.
- Sprinkle with sesame seeds then bake for 12–15 minutes, turning the tray round halfway through.
- Transfer the biscuits to a wire rack and leave to cool.

PREPARATION TIME 20 MINUTES

COOKING TIME 12–15 MINUTES

INGREDIENTS

150 g / 5 oz / ⅔ cup butter, cubed
230 g / 8 oz / 1 ½ cups plain (all purpose) flour
50 g / 1 ¾ oz / ¼ cup black olive tapenade
2 tbsp sesame seeds

Poppy and Tapenade Shortbread   374

- Replace the sesame seeds with mixed poppy seeds for a different looking shortbread.

375

MAKES 1 LOAF

Onion Bread

- Fry the onions in the oil for 15 minutes or until starting to caramelise. Leave to cool.
- Mix together the flours, yeast, sugar and salt. Stir the onions and onion seeds into 280 ml of warm water and stir into the dry ingredients.
- Knead the mixture on a lightly oiled surface for 10 minutes or until the dough is smooth and elastic.
- Leave the dough to rest in a lightly oiled bowl, covered with oiled cling film, for 1–2 hours.
- Roll the dough into a fat sausage. Turn it 90° and roll it tightly the other way then tuck the ends under and transfer the dough to a lined loaf tin, keeping the seam underneath.
- Cover the tin with oiled cling film and leave for 1 hour.
- Preheat the oven to 220°C (200°C fan) / 430F / gas 7.
- Bake the loaf for 35–40 minutes or until the underneath sounds hollow when tapped.

PREPARATION TIME
2 HOURS 30 MINUTES

COOKING TIME 35–40 MINUTES

INGREDIENTS

2 large onions, peeled, quartered and sliced
3 tbsp olive oil
300 g / 10 ½ oz / 2 cups strong white bread flour, plus extra for dusting
100 g / 3 ½ oz / ⅔ cup stoneground wholemeal flour
½ tsp easy blend dried yeast
1 tbsp caster (superfine) sugar
1 tsp fine sea salt
2 tbsp black onion seeds

Onion Cheddar Bread   376

- Incorporate 100 g / 3 ½ oz / 1 cup grated Cheddar into the dough before kneading for an additional cheese flavour.

377

MAKES 36

Date and Oat Cookies

PREPARATION TIME 20 MINUTES

COOKING TIME 12–15 MINUTES

INGREDIENTS

175 g / 6 oz / ¾ cup butter, softened
225 g / 8 oz / 1 ⅓ cup dark brown sugar
100 g / 3 ½ oz / ½ cup caster (superfine) sugar
2 tsp vanilla extract
1 egg, plus 1 egg yolk
250 g / 9 oz / 1 ⅔ cups self-raising flour
100 g / 3 ½ oz / 1 cup porridge oats
100 g / 3 ½ oz / ½ cup dates, stoned and finely chopped

- Preheat the oven to 170°C (150°C fan) / 340F / gas 3 and line 2 baking sheets with greaseproof paper.
- Cream together the two sugars, butter and vanilla extract until pale and well whipped then beat in the egg and yolk, followed by the flour, oats and dates.
- Drop tablespoons of the mixture onto the prepared trays, leaving plenty of room to spread.
- Bake the cookies in batches for 12–15 minutes or until the edges are starting to brown, but the centres are still chewy.
- Transfer to a wire rack and leave to cool.

Vanilla Oat Cookies

378

- Remove the dates from the recipe and add an additional 1 tsp of vanilla extract for an added vanilla flavour.

379

MAKES 36

Cinnamon Oat Cookies

PREPARATION TIME 20 MINUTES

COOKING TIME 12–15 MINUTES

INGREDIENTS

225 g / 8 oz / 1 ⅓ cups dark brown sugar
100 g / 3 ½ oz / ½ cup caster (superfine) sugar
175 g / 6 oz / ¾ cup butter, softened
2 tsp vanilla extract
1 egg, plus 1 egg yolk
250 g / 9 oz / 1 ⅔ cups self-raising flour
2 tsp ground cinnamon
100 g / 3 ½ oz / 1 cup porridge oats

- Preheat the oven to 170°C (150°C fan) / 340F / gas 3 and line 2 baking sheets with greaseproof paper.
- Cream together the two sugars, butter and vanilla extract until pale and well whipped then beat in the egg and yolk, followed by the flour, cinnamon and oats.
- Drop tablespoons of the mixture onto the prepared trays, leaving plenty of room to spread.
- Bake the cookies in batches for 12–15 minutes or until the edges are starting to brown, but the centres are still chewy.
- Transfer to a wire rack and leave to cool.

Cinnamon and Pumpkin Seed Cookies

380

- Stud each of the cookies with ½ tsp pumpkin seeds before baking for a crunchy, nutty addition to these cookies.

MAKES 1 LOAF

Walnut Bread

381

Walnut and Pumpkin Bread

382

- Add 55 g / 2 oz / ¼ cup canned pumpkin as well as an additional 30 g / 1 oz wholemeal flour to the dough and incorporate well before kneading.

Walnut and Raisin Bread

383

- Add 100 g / 3 ½ oz / ½ cup raisins to the dough, incorporating them well before kneading.

PREPARATION TIME
2 HOURS 30 MINUTES

COOKING TIME 35–40 MINUTES

....

INGREDIENTS

200 g / 7 oz / 1 ⅓ cups strong white bread flour, plus extra for dusting
200 g / 7 oz / 1 ⅓ cups stoneground wholemeal flour
½ tsp easy blend dried yeast
1 tbsp caster (superfine) sugar
1 tsp fine sea salt
100 g / 3 ½ oz / ¾ cup walnuts, chopped
1 tbsp walnut oil

- Mix together the flours, yeast, sugar, salt and walnuts. Stir the oil into 280 ml of warm water.
- Stir the liquid into the dry ingredients then knead on a lightly oiled surface for 10 minutes or until the dough is smooth and elastic.
- Leave the dough to rest, covered with oiled cling film, for 1–2 hours or until doubled in size.
- Knead the dough for 2 more minutes, then shape it into a long loaf.
- Transfer the loaf to a greased baking tray and cover again with oiled cling film. Leave to prove for 1 hour or until doubled in size.
- Meanwhile, preheat the oven to 220°C (200°C fan) / 430F / gas 7.
- When the dough has risen, slash the top with a knife.
- Transfer the tray to the top shelf of the oven.
- Bake for 35–40 minutes or until the loaf sounds hollow when tapped. Transfer the bread to a wire rack and leave to cool.

384

MAKES 1 LOAF

Potato Bread

PREPARATION TIME

2 HOURS 30 MINUTES

COOKING TIME 35–40 MINUTES

INGREDIENTS

400 g / 14 oz / 2 ⅔ cups strong white bread flour, plus extra for dusting
½ tsp easy blend dried yeast
1 tbsp caster (superfine) sugar
1 tsp fine sea salt
1 tbsp olive oil
150 g / 5 ½ oz / ⅔ cup mashed potato

- Mix together the flour, yeast, sugar and salt. Stir the oil and 150 ml of warm water into the mashed potato.
- Stir the liquid into the dry ingredients then knead on a lightly oiled surface for 10 minutes or until the dough is smooth and elastic.
- Leave the dough to rest, covered with oiled cling film, for 1–2 hours or until doubled in size.
- Knead the dough for 2 more minutes, then shape it into a long loaf.
- Transfer the loaf to a greased baking tray and cover again with oiled cling film. Leave to prove for 1 hour or until doubled in size.
- Meanwhile, preheat the oven to 220°C (200°C fan) / 430F / gas 7.
- When the dough has risen, slash the top with a knife.
- Transfer the tray to the top shelf of the oven.
- Bake for 35–40 minutes or until the loaf sounds hollow when tapped. Transfer the bread to a wire rack and leave to cool.

385

MAKES 24

Parmesan and Black Pepper Shortbread

PREPARATION TIME 20 MINUTES

COOKING TIME 12–15 MINUTES

INGREDIENTS

150 g / 5 oz / ⅔ cup butter, cubed
230 g / 8 oz / 1 ½ cups plain (all purpose) flour
50 g / 1 ¾ oz / ½ cup Parmesan, grated
2 tsp cracked black pepper

- Preheat the oven to 180°C (160°C fan) / 355F / gas 4 and line a baking tray with greaseproof paper.
- Rub the butter into the flour and stir in the Parmesan and black pepper.
- Knead gently until the mixture forms a smooth dough then roll out on a lightly floured surface to 5 mm thick.
- Use a cookie cutter to cut out circles and transfer them to the baking tray.
- Bake the biscuits for 12–15 minutes, turning the tray round halfway through.
- Transfer the biscuits to a wire rack and leave to cool.

386
MAKES 36 Pecan Snap Biscuits

- Preheat the oven to 180⁰C (160⁰C fan) / 355F / gas 4 and line 2 baking sheets with greaseproof paper.
- Melt the butter and golden syrup together in a saucepan.
- Mix the flour, sugar and pecans together then stir in the melted butter mixture and the beaten egg.
- Use a teaspoon to portion the mixture onto the baking trays, leaving plenty of room for the biscuits to spread.
- Bake in batches for 12–15 minutes or until golden brown.
- Transfer the biscuits to a wire rack and leave to cool and harden.

PREPARATION TIME 15 MINUTES

COOKING TIME 12–15 MINUTES

INGREDIENTS

75 g / 2 ½ oz / ⅓ cup butter
100 g / 3 ½ oz / ⅓ cup golden syrup
225 g / 8 oz / 1 ½ cups self-raising flour
100 g / 3 ½ oz / ½ cup caster (superfine) sugar
75 g / 2 ½ oz / ⅔ cup pecan nuts, finely chopped
1 large egg, beaten

387

MAKES 36

Waffle Biscuits

PREPARATION TIME 10 MINUTES

COOKING TIME 1 MINUTE

INGREDIENTS

110 g / 4 oz / ½ cup butter, softened
3 large eggs, beaten
150 g / 5 ½ oz / ⅔ cup caster (superfine) sugar

2 tsp baking powder
225 g / 8 oz / 1 ½ cups self-raising flour
1 tsp ground star anise

- Beat all the ingredients together until smooth.
- Heat a pizzelle iron on the hob until very hot, then add a heaped teaspoon of batter to each waffle indent and close the two halves together.
- Cook the waffles for 30 seconds to 1 minute or until cooked through.
- Repeat with the rest of the mixture, allowing the waffles to cool and crisp on a wire rack.

388
Pine Nut Crescent Biscuits

MAKES 20

PREPARATION TIME 20 MINUTES

COOKING TIME 15–20 MINUTES

INGREDIENTS

175 g / 6 oz / 1 ¼ cups plain (all purpose) flour
55 g / 2 oz / ½ cup ground almonds

75 g / 2 ½ oz / ½ cup light brown sugar
150 g / 5 oz / ⅔ cup butter, cubed
100 g / 3 ½ oz / ¾ cup pine nuts

- Preheat the oven to 180⁰C (160⁰C fan) / 355F / gas 4 and line a baking tray with greaseproof paper.
- Mix together the flour, ground almonds and brown sugar in a bowl, then rub in the butter.
- Knead gently with the pine nuts until the mixture forms a smooth dough.
- Divide the dough into 20 balls and then roll them into a sausage shape and curve round into crescents.
- Bake the biscuits for 15–20 minutes, turning the tray round halfway through.
- Transfer the biscuits to a wire rack and leave to cool.

389

MAKES 24

Raspberry Viennese Shortbread

PREPARATION TIME 10 MINUTES

COOKING TIME 15–20 MINUTES

INGREDIENTS

175 g / 6 oz / ¾ cup butter, softened
50 g / 1 ¾ oz / ¼ cup caster
(superfine) sugar
4 tbsp raspberry syrup
175 g / 6 oz / 1 ¼ cups self-raising
flour

- Preheat the oven to 170°C (150°C fan) / 340F / gas 3 and line 2 baking trays with non-stick baking mats.
- Cream the butter, sugar and raspberry syrup together with an electric whisk until pale and well whipped then stir in the flour.
- Spoon the mixture into a piping bag fitted with a large star nozzle and pipe 12 swirls onto each tray.
- Bake the biscuits for 15–20 minutes or until they are lightly golden.
- Transfer the biscuits to a wire rack and leave to cool completely.

Almond Viennese Shortbread

390

- Replace the raspberry syrup in the recipe with almond syrup for a nutty hint to these shortbreads.

391

MAKES 24

Pistachio Cookies

PREPARATION TIME 15 MINUTES

COOKING TIME 20–25 MINUTES

INGREDIENTS

125 g / 4 ½ oz / ½ cup butter, cubed
125 g / 4 ½ oz / ¾ cup plain (all
purpose) flour
125 g / 4 ½ oz / ½ cup caster
(superfine) sugar
3 large egg yolks
200 g / 7 oz / 1 ⅔ cups pistachio nuts,
finely chopped

- Preheat the oven to 180°C / (160°C fan) / 355F / gas 4 and line a baking tray with greaseproof paper.
- Rub the butter into the flour with a pinch of salt then stir in the sugar.
- Beat the egg yolks and stir them into the dry ingredients.
- Bring the mixture together into a soft dough and space tablespoons of the mixture out on the baking tray. Sprinkle the biscuits liberally with chopped pistachios.
- Bake the biscuits for 20–25 minutes or until golden brown.
- Transfer the biscuits to a wire rack and leave to cool.

Pistachio White
Chocolate Cookies

392

- Replace 100 g / 3 ½ oz / ¾ cup of the pistachios with the same weight of chopped white chocolate for a different flavour and texture.

393

MAKES 12

Raisin Rock Cookies

Raisin, Sultana and Currant Rock Cookies

394

- Replace 55 g / 2 oz / ¼ cup of the raisins with 30 g / 1 oz each of currants and sultanas for added flavour and texture.

Raisin Marshmallow Rock Cookies

395

- Replace 55 g / 2 oz / ¼ cup of the raisins with the same weight of mini marshmallows for a chewy texture.

PREPARATION TIME 15 MINUTES

COOKING TIME 10–12 MINUTES

INGREDIENTS

100 g / 3 ½ oz / ½ cup butter
200 g / 7 oz / 1 ⅓ cups self-raising flour
100 g / 3 ½ oz / ½ cup caster (superfine) sugar
100 g / 3 ½ oz / 1 ⅔ cups raisins
1 large egg
2 tbsp whole milk

- Preheat the oven to 200°C (180°C fan) / 390F / gas 6 and grease a large baking tray.
- Rub the butter into the flour until the mixture resembles fine breadcrumbs then stir in the sugar and raisins.
- Beat the egg with the milk and stir it into the dry ingredients to make a sticky dough.
- Use a dessert spoon to portion the mixture onto the baking tray, flattening the cookies a bit with the back of the spoon but leaving the surface quite rough.
- Bake the cookies for 15 minutes then transfer them to a wire rack and leave to cool.

MAKES 1 LOAF # Wholemeal Honey and Nut Bread

Honey and Nut Bread 397

- Replace the stoneground wholemeal flour in the recipe with an additional 200 g / 7 oz / 1 ⅓ cups of strong white bread flour for a white version of this bread.

Wholemeal Honey Oat Bread 398

- Instead of using nuts for the topping, use 30 g / 1 oz / ¼ cup rolled porridge oats for a softer texture to the topping.

PREPARATION TIME
2 HOURS 30 MINUTES

COOKING TIME 35–40 MINUTES

INGREDIENTS

200 g / 7 oz / 1 ⅓ cups strong white bread flour, plus extra for dusting
200 g / 7 oz / 1 ⅓ cups stoneground wholemeal flour
½ tsp easy blend dried yeast
4 tbsp runny honey
1 tsp fine sea salt
1 tbsp olive oil

FOR THE TOPPING

3 tbsp runny honey
2 tbsp sunflower seeds
25 g / 1 oz / ¼ cup blanched almonds
25 g / 1 oz / ¼ cup walnuts, chopped

- Mix together the flours, yeast and salt.
- Stir the oil and honey into 280 ml warm water, then mix with the dry ingredients.
- Knead the mixture on a lightly oiled surface for 10 minutes or until smooth and elastic.
- Leave the dough to rest in an oiled bowl for 1–2 hours or until doubled in size.
- Roll the dough with your hands into a fat sausage, then turn it 90⁰ and roll it tightly the other way. Tuck the ends under and transfer the dough to a large loaf tin, keeping the seam underneath.
- Cover the tin loosely with oiled cling film and leave to prove for 45 minutes.
- Preheat the oven to 220⁰C (200⁰C fan) / 430F / gas 7.
- Bake for 35–40 minutes or until the loaf sounds hollow when you tap it underneath.
- Mix the honey with the seeds and nuts and spoon it over the loaf.
- Transfer the bread to a wire rack and leave to cool completely before slicing.

399

MAKES 36

Raisin Cookies

- Preheat the oven to 170°C (150°C fan) / 340F / gas 3 and line 2 baking sheets with greaseproof paper.
- Cream together the two sugars, butter and vanilla extract until pale and well whipped then beat in the egg and yolk, followed by the flour and raisins.
- Drop tablespoons of the mixture onto the prepared trays, leaving plenty of room to spread.
- Bake the cookies in batches for 12–15 minutes or until the edges are starting to brown, but the centres are still chewy.
- Transfer to a wire rack and leave to cool.

PREPARATION TIME 20 MINUTES

COOKING TIME 12–15 MINUTES

INGREDIENTS

175 g / 6 oz / ¾ cup butter, softened
225 g / 8 oz / 1 ⅓ cups light brown sugar
100 g / 3 ½ oz / ½ cup caster (superfine) sugar
1 tsp vanilla extract
1 egg, plus 1 egg yolk
250 g / 9 oz / 1 ⅔ cups self-raising flour
100 g / 3 ½ oz / ½ cup raisins

Sultana Cherry Cookies

400

- Replace the raisins in the recipe with 75 g / 3 oz / ⅓ cup of sultanas and 30 g / 1 oz of chopped cocktail cherries.

401

MAKES 12

Raspberry Rock Cookies

- Preheat the oven to 200°C (180°C fan) / 390F / gas 6 and grease a large baking tray.
- Rub the butter into the flour until the mixture resembles fine breadcrumbs then stir in the sugar and raspberries.
- Beat the egg with the milk and stir it into the dry ingredients to make a sticky dough.
- Use a dessert spoon to portion the mixture onto the baking tray, flattening the cookies a bit with the back of the spoon but leaving the surface quite rough.
- Bake the cookies for 15 minutes then transfer them to a wire rack and leave to cool.

PREPARATION TIME 15 MINUTES

COOKING TIME 15 MINUTES

INGREDIENTS

100 g / 3 ½ oz / ½ cup butter
200 g / 7 oz / 1 ⅓ cups self-raising flour
100 g / 3 ½ oz / ½ cup caster (superfine) sugar
100 g / 3 ½ oz / ⅔ cup raspberries
1 large egg
2 tbsp whole milk

Mixed Berry Rock Cookies

402

- Use 100 g / 3 ½ oz / ⅔ cup frozen mixed berries that have been thawed instead of the raspberries for a more complex tasting rock cookies.

403
MAKES 1 LOAF

Rice Bread

PREPARATION TIME
2 HOURS 30 MINUTES

COOKING TIME 35–40 MINUTES

....

INGREDIENTS

300 g / 10 ½ oz / 2 cups strong white
bread flour, plus extra for dusting
½ tsp easy blend dried yeast
1 tbsp caster (superfine) sugar
1 tsp fine sea salt
300 g / 10 ½ oz / 1 ¾ cups cooked
white rice, cooled
1 tbsp olive oil

- Mix together the flour, yeast, sugar, and salt. Stir the rice and oil into 280 ml of warm water and mix with the dry ingredients.
- Knead the dough on a lightly oiled surface for 10 minutes or until smooth and elastic.
- Leave the dough to rest, covered with oiled cling film, for 1–2 hours or until doubled in size.
- Roll the dough into a fat sausage. Turn it 90⁰ and roll it tightly the other way then tuck the ends under and transfer the dough to a greased loaf tin, keeping the seam underneath.
- Cover the tin and leave to prove for 1 hour.
- Preheat the oven to 220⁰C (200⁰C fan) / 430F / gas 7.
- Bake for 35–40 minutes or until the loaf sounds hollow when you tap it underneath.

Rice and Soy Bread

404

- Add 2 tbsp soy sauce to the water before incorporating into the dry ingredients for an added savoury, Japanese flavour to the bread.

405
MAKES 1 LOAF

Spiced Wholemeal Bread

PREPARATION TIME
2 HOURS 30 MINUTES

COOKING TIME 35–40 MINUTES

....

INGREDIENTS

200 g / 7 oz / 1 ⅓ cups strong white
bread flour, plus extra for dusting
200 g / 7 oz / 1 ⅓ cups stone-ground
wholemeal flour
½ tsp easy blend dried yeast
1 tbsp caster (superfine) sugar
1 tsp fine sea salt
½ tsp ground cloves
½ tsp ground nutmeg
½ tsp ground star anise
½ tsp ground cardamom
½ tsp ground cinnamon
1 tbsp sunflower oil

- Mix together the flours, yeast, sugar, salt and spices.
- Stir the oil into 280 ml of warm water and add to mixture.
- Knead on a lightly oiled surface for 10 minutes until the dough is smooth and elastic.
- Leave the dough to rest, covered with oiled clingfilm, for 1–2 hours or until doubled in size.
- Knead the dough for 2 more minutes, then shape it into a loaf.
- Transfer the loaf to a greased baking tray and cover again with oiled clingfilm. Leave to prove for 1 hour or until doubled in size.
- Preheat the oven to 220°C (200°C fan) / 425F / gas 7.
- When the dough has risen, slash the top with a sharp knife. Transfer the tray to the top shelf of the oven.
- Bake for 35–40 minutes, until the loaf sounds hollow when tapped.

Spiced Wholemeal Raisin Bread

406

- Add 150 g of raisins to the dough when you add the water.

407
MAKES 1 LOAF

Dried Fig and Honey Bread

- Mix together the flour, yeast, figs and salt.
  Stir the oil and honey into 280 ml of warm water.
- Stir the liquid into the dry ingredients then knead on
  a lightly oiled surface for 10 minutes or until the dough
  is smooth and elastic.
- Leave the dough to rest, covered with oiled cling film,
  for 1–2 hours or until doubled in size.
- Knead the dough for 2 more minutes, then shape it into
  a round loaf.
- Transfer the loaf to a greased baking tray and cover
  again with oiled cling film. Leave to prove for 1 hour.
- Preheat the oven to 220°C (200°C fan) / 430F / gas 7.
- When the dough has risen, slash the top with a knife
  and dust with flour.
- Bake for 35–40 minutes. Transfer the bread to a wire
  rack and leave to cool.

PREPARATION TIME
2 HOURS 30 MINUTES

COOKING TIME 35–40 MINUTES

INGREDIENTS

400 g / 14 oz / 2 ⅔ cups strong white
bread flour, plus extra for dusting
½ tsp easy blend dried yeast
3 tbsp runny honey
100 g / 3 ½ oz / ½ cup dried figs,
quartered
1 tsp fine sea salt
1 tbsp olive oil

Raisin and Honey Bread   408

- Instead of using figs in the bread,
  use 75 g / 3 oz / ⅓ cup raisins incorporating
  them well into the dough before kneading.

409
MAKES 1

Wholemeal Sesame Bread

- Mix together the flours, yeast, sugar, half of the sesame
  seeds and the salt. Stir the oil into 280 ml of warm water
  then stir it into the dry ingredients.
- Knead the mixture on a lightly oiled surface with your
  hands for 10 minutes or until smooth and elastic.
- Leave the dough to rest in a lightly oiled bowl, covered
  with oiled cling film, for 1–2 hours.
- Knead it for 2 more minutes, then shape into a long loaf
  on a greased baking tray.
- Cover with oiled cling film and prove for 1 hour.
- Preheat the oven to 220°C (200°C fan) / 430F / gas 7.
- Sprinkle the bread with the remaining sesame seeds
  then slash the top with a knife.
- Bake for 25–30 minutes or until the loaf sounds hollow
  when you tap it underneath.
- Transfer to a wire rack and leave to cool.

PREPARATION TIME
2 HOURS 30 MINUTES

COOKING TIME 25–30 MINUTES

INGREDIENTS

300 g / 10 ½ oz / 2 cups stoneground
wholemeal flour
100 g / 3 ½ oz / ⅔ cup strong white
bread flour, plus extra for dusting
½ tsp easy blend dried yeast
2 tbsp caster (superfine) sugar
50 g / 1 ¾ oz / ½ cup sesame seeds
1 tsp fine sea salt
1 tbsp sesame oil
1 egg, beaten

Sesame and Orange Bread   410

- Incorporate 1 tbsp orange flower water
  and the finely grated zest of 1 orange into
  the dough before kneading for a citrus
  take on this bread.

411

MAKES 16

Lemon and Semolina Shortbread

PREPARATION TIME 20 MINUTES

COOKING TIME 15–20 MINUTES

INGREDIENTS

175 g / 6 oz / 1 ¼ cups plain (all purpose) flour
55 g / 2 oz / ½ cup fine semolina
75 g / 2 ½ oz / ⅓ cup caster (superfine) sugar
150 g / 5 oz / ⅔ cup butter, cubed
1 lemon, zest finely grated

- Preheat the oven to 180°C (160°C fan) / 355F / gas 4 and line a baking tray with greaseproof paper.
- Mix together the flour, semolina and caster sugar in a bowl, then rub in the butter and lemon zest.
- Knead gently until the mixture forms a smooth dough then form into a cylinder 6 cm in diameter.
- Slice the roll into 1 cm thick slices and spread them out on the baking tray.
- Bake the biscuits for 15–20 minutes, turning the tray round halfway through.
- Transfer the biscuits to a wire rack and leave to cool.

Orange Polenta Shortbread

412

- Replace the lemon in the recipe with the same amount of orange zest and use polenta instead of semolina for a crunchier texture.

413

MAKES 16

Sultana Shortbread Biscuits

PREPARATION TIME 20 MINUTES

COOKING TIME 15–20 MINUTES

INGREDIENTS

230 g / 8 oz / 1 ½ cups plain (all purpose) flour
75 g / 2 ½ oz / ⅓ cup caster (superfine) sugar
150 g / 5 oz / ⅔ cup butter, cubed
50 g / 1 ¾ oz / ¼ cup sultanas

- Preheat the oven to 180°C (160°C fan) / 355F / gas 4 and line a baking tray with greaseproof paper.
- Mix together the flour and caster sugar in a bowl, then rub in the butter.
- Knead gently with the sultanas until the mixture forms a smooth dough then form into a cylinder 6 cm in diameter.
- Slice the roll into 1 cm thick slices and spread them out on the baking tray.
- Bake the biscuits for 15–20 minutes, turning the tray round halfway through.
- Transfer the biscuits to a wire rack and leave to cool.

Sultana Cherry Shortbread Biscuits

414

- Replace half of the sultanas with the same weight of chopped cocktail cherries.

Nutmeg Cross Biscuits

415

MAKES 36

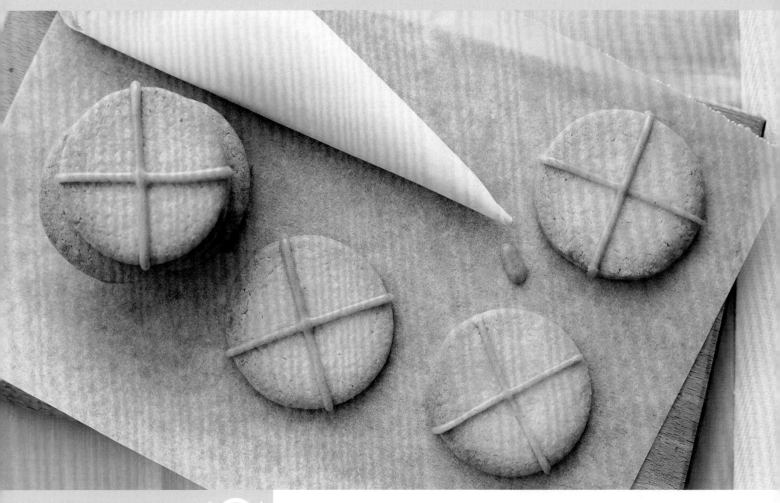

Cinnamon Cross Biscuits

416

- Use 1 tsp of ground cinnamon in the icing instead of the nutmeg for an alternative spiced flavour.

Ginger Cross Biscuits

417

- Use 1 tsp of ground ginger in the icing instead of the nutmeg for a spicy, warming flavour.

PREPARATION TIME 25 MINUTES

COOKING TIME 12–15 MINUTES

INGREDIENTS

75 g / 2 ½ oz / ⅓ cup butter
100 g / 3 ½ oz / ⅓ cup golden syrup
225 g / 8 oz / 1 ½ cups self-raising flour
100 g / 3 ½ oz / ½ cup caster (superfine) sugar
1 tsp nutmeg, freshly grated
1 large egg, beaten

TO DECORATE

4 tbsp icing (confectioners') sugar
1 tsp nutmeg, freshly grated

- Preheat the oven to 180°C (160°C fan) / 355F / gas 4 and line 2 baking sheets with greaseproof paper.
- Melt the butter and golden syrup together in a saucepan.
- Mix the flour, sugar and nutmeg together then stir in the melted butter mixture and the beaten egg.
- Use a teaspoon to portion the mixture onto the baking trays, leaving plenty of room for the biscuits to spread.
- Bake in batches for 12–15 minutes or until golden brown.
- Transfer the biscuits to a wire rack and leave to cool and harden.
- To make the icing, mix the icing sugar and nutmeg together then add enough water, drop by drop, to form a thick icing. Spoon it into a piping bag and pipe a cross onto each biscuit.

418
MAKES 1 LOAF

Hedgehog Rye Bread

PREPARATION TIME
2 HOURS 30 MINUTES

COOKING TIME 35–40 MINUTES

INGREDIENTS

200 g / 7 oz / 1 ⅓ cups strong white
bread flour, plus extra for dusting
200 g / 7 oz / 1 ⅓ cups rye flour
½ tsp easy blend dried yeast
1 tbsp caster (superfine) sugar
1 tsp fine sea salt
1 tbsp olive oil

- Mix together the flours, yeast, sugar and salt. Stir in the oil and 280 ml of warm water.
- Knead on a lightly oiled surface for 10 minutes or until the dough is smooth and elastic.
- Leave the dough to rest, covered with oiled cling film, for 1–2 hours or until doubled in size.
- Knead the dough for 2 more minutes, then shape it into a round loaf.
- Transfer the loaf to a greased baking tray and cover again with oiled cling film. Leave to prove for 1 hour.
- Preheat the oven to 220°C (200°C fan) / 430F / gas 7.
- When the dough has risen, use a pair of oiled scissors to snip the top into points.
- Bake for 35–40 minutes or until the loaf sounds hollow when tapped. Transfer the bread to a wire rack and leave to cool.

Hedgehog Granary Bread 419

- Instead of using rye flour, use the same weight of malted granary flour for an alternative flour and texture to the bread.

420
MAKES 1 LOAF

Cinnamon and Walnut Bread

PREPARATION TIME
2 HOURS 30 MINUTES

COOKING TIME 35–40 MINUTES

INGREDIENTS

200 g / 7 oz / 1 ⅓ cups strong white
bread flour, plus extra for dusting
200 g / 7 oz / 1 ⅓ cup stoneground
wholemeal flour
½ tsp easy blend dried yeast
1 tbsp caster (superfine) sugar
2 tsp ground cinnamon
1 tsp fine sea salt
100 g / 3 ½ oz / ¾ cup walnuts,
chopped
1 tbsp walnut oil

- Mix together the flours, yeast, sugar, cinnamon, salt and walnuts. Stir the oil into 280 ml of warm water and add to the dry ingredients.
- Knead on a lightly oiled surface for 10 minutes or until the dough is smooth and elastic.
- Leave the dough to rest, covered with oiled cling film, for 1–2 hours or until doubled in size.
- Knead the dough for 2 more minutes, then shape it into a round loaf.
- Transfer the loaf to a greased baking tray and cover again with oiled cling film. Leave to prove for 1 hour.
- Preheat the oven to 220°C (200°C fan) / 430F / gas 7.
- When the dough has risen, slash the top with a knife.
- Bake for 35–40 minutes or until the loaf sounds hollow when tapped. Transfer the bread to a wire rack and leave to cool.

Walnut Allspice Bread 421

- Use 1 tbsp ground allspice in place of the ground cinnamon for an alternative wintery flavour to the bread.

Chestnut and Chorizo Bread

422

MAKES 1 LOAF

- Mix together the flours, yeast, sugar and salt. Stir the chorizo into 280 ml of warm water and stir it into the dry ingredients.
- Knead the mixture on a lightly oiled surface for 10 minutes or until the dough is smooth and elastic.
- Leave the dough to rest in a lightly oiled bowl, covered with oiled cling film, for 1–2 hours.
- Punch the dough with your fist to knock out the air then knead it for 2 more minutes.
- Transfer the dough to a greased baking tray and cover with oiled cling film. Leave to prove for 1 hour or until doubled in size.
- Preheat the oven to 220°C (200°C fan) / 430F / gas 7.
- Bake for 35–40 minutes or until the loaf sounds hollow when you tap it underneath. Transfer the bread to a wire rack and leave to cool completely before slicing.

Smoked Paprika Chorizo Bread

423

- Replace the chestnut flour with the same weight of strong white bread flour and add 1 tbsp of smoked paprika to the flour mixture before mixing for a smoky, Spanish flavour.

**PREPARATION TIME
2 HOURS 30 MINUTES**

COOKING TIME 35–40 MINUTES

INGREDIENTS

200 g / 7 oz / 1 ⅓ cups strong white bread flour, plus extra for dusting
200 g / 7 oz / 1 ⅓ cups chestnut flour
½ tsp easy blend dried yeast
1 tbsp caster (superfine) sugar
1 tsp fine sea salt
200 g / 7 oz / 1 cup cooking chorizo, cubed

Rye Bread

424

MAKES 1 LOAF

- Mix together the flour, yeast and salt. Stir the oil, treacle and malt extract into 280 ml of warm water.
- Stir the liquid into the dry ingredients then knead on a lightly oiled surface for 10 minutes.
- Leave the dough to rest, covered with oiled cling film, for 1–2 hours or until doubled in size.
- Knead the dough for 2 more minutes, then shape it into a round loaf.
- Transfer the loaf to a greased baking tray and cover again with oiled cling film. Leave to prove for 1 hour or until doubled in size.
- Preheat the oven to 220°C (200°C fan) / 430F / gas 7.
- When the dough has risen, score the top with a knife and dust with flour.
- Bake for 35–40 minutes or until the loaf sounds hollow when tapped. Transfer the bread to a wire rack and leave to cool.

Rye Whisky Bread

425

- Add 2 tbsp of whisky, preferably rye, to the wet ingredients for an added complex flavour to the bread.

**PREPARATION TIME
2 HOURS 30 MINUTES**

COOKING TIME 35–40 MINUTES

INGREDIENTS

400 g / 14 oz / 2 ⅔ cups rye flour, plus extra for dusting
1 tsp easy blend dried yeast
1 tbsp treacle
1 tbsp malt extract
1 tsp fine sea salt
1 tbsp olive oil

Fig, Rosemary and Prosciutto Loaf Cake

426

SERVES 8

PREPARATION TIME 20 MINUTES

COOKING TIME 55 MINUTES

INGREDIENTS

300 g / 10 ½ oz / 2 cups self-raising flour
2 tsp baking powder
250 g / 9 oz / 1 ¼ cups butter, softened
5 large eggs
100 g 3 ½ oz / ½ cup dried figs, chopped
6 slices prosciutto, chopped
2 tbsp fresh rosemary, chopped

- Preheat the oven to 170⁰C (150⁰C fan) / 340F / gas 3 and line a large loaf tin with non-stick baking paper.
- Sieve the flour and baking powder into a mixing bowl and add the butter and eggs.
- Beat the mixture with an electric whisk for 4 minutes or until smooth and well whipped.
- Fold in the figs, prosciutto and rosemary then scrape the mixture into the loaf tin.
- Bake for 55 minutes or until a skewer inserted in the centre comes out clean.
- Transfer the cake to a wire rack and leave to cool completely before serving.

427

MAKES 8

Seeded Rolls

**PREPARATION TIME
2 HOURS 30 MINUTES**

COOKING TIME 10–12 MINUTES

INGREDIENTS

200 g / 7 oz / 1 ⅓ cups strong white bread flour, plus extra for dusting
200 g / 7 oz / 1 ⅓ cups stoneground wholemeal flour
½ tsp easy blend dried yeast
1 tbsp caster (superfine) sugar
1 tsp fine sea salt
1 tbsp olive oil

FOR THE SEED MIX
2 tbsp sunflower seeds
2 tbsp hemp seeds
3 tbsp sesame seeds
3 tbsp poppy seeds

- Mix together the flours, yeast, sugar and salt. Stir the oil into 280 ml of warm water then stir the liquid into the dry ingredients.
- Knead the mixture with half of the seed mix on a lightly oiled surface for 10 minutes or until smooth and elastic.
- Leave the dough to rest, covered with oiled cling film, for 1–2 hours or until doubled in size.
- Divide the dough into 8 evenly-sized pieces and shape into rolls on a greased baking tray.
- Cover the rolls with oiled cling film and leave to prove for 1 hour or until doubled in size.
- Preheat the oven to 220⁰C (200⁰C fan) / 430F / gas 7.
- When the rolls have risen, sprinkle with the rest of the seeds.
- Transfer the tray to the top shelf of the oven.
- Bake for 10–12 minutes or until the rolls sound hollow when you tap them underneath.

428
MAKES 12

Olive and Parmesan Rolls

- Mix together the flour, yeast, sugar, salt, olives and Parmesan. Stir in the oil and 280 ml of warm water.
- Knead the mixture on a lightly oiled surface for 10 minutes or until smooth and elastic.
- Leave the dough to rest, covered with oiled cling film, for 1–2 hours or until doubled in size.
- Shape the dough into 2 flat round loaves then cut each one into 6 wedges.
- Transfer the rolls to a greased baking tray and cover with oiled cling film. Leave to prove for 1 hour.
- Meanwhile, preheat the oven to 220⁰C (200⁰C fan) / 425 F / gas 7.
- Bake for 15–20 minutes or until the rolls sound hollow when you tap them underneath.
- Transfer to a wire rack and leave to cool.

PREPARATION TIME
2 HOURS 30 MINUTES
COOKING TIME 15–20 MINUTES

INGREDIENTS

400 g / 14 oz / 2 ⅔ cups strong white bread flour, plus extra for dusting
½ tsp easy blend dried yeast
1 tbsp caster (superfine) sugar
1 tsp fine sea salt
75 g / 2 ½ oz / ½ cup green olives, pitted and chopped
75 g / 2 ½ oz / ¾ cup Parmesan, finely grated
1 tbsp olive oil

429
MAKES 12

Muesli Rolls

PREPARATION TIME
2 HOURS 30 MINUTES
COOKING TIME 15–20 MINUTES

INGREDIENTS

350 g / 12 ½ oz / 2 ⅓ cups strong white bread flour, plus extra for dusting

50 g / 1 ¾ oz / ⅓ cup stoneground wholemeal flour
75 g / 2 ½ oz / ¾ cup muesli
½ tsp easy blend dried yeast
1 tbsp caster (superfine) sugar
1 tsp fine sea salt
1 tbsp olive oil

- Mix together the flours, muesli, yeast, sugar and salt. Stir in the oil and 280 ml of warm water. Knead the mixture on a lightly oiled surface for 10 minutes.
- Leave the dough to rest, covered with oiled cling film, for 1–2 hours.
- Knead it for 2 more minutes then split it into 12 even pieces and shape into rolls
- Transfer the rolls to a greased baking tray and cover with oiled cling film. Leave to prove for 1 hour or until doubled in size.
- Preheat the oven to 220⁰C (200⁰C fan) / 430F / gas 7.
- Dust the rolls with flour and slash the tops with a knife.
- Bake for 15–20 minutes or until the rolls sound hollow when you tap them underneath.
- Transfer to a wire rack and leave to cool.

430
MAKES 12

Treacle and Raisin Rolls

PREPARATION TIME
2 HOURS 30 MINUTES
COOKING TIME 15–20 MINUTES

INGREDIENTS

350 g / 12 ½ oz / 2 ⅓ cups strong white bread flour, plus extra for dusting

50 g / 1 ¾ oz / ⅓ cup stoneground wholemeal flour
75 g / 2 ½ oz / ⅓ cup raisins
½ tsp easy blend dried yeast
1 tbsp caster (superfine) sugar
1 tsp fine sea salt
1 tbsp olive oil
4 tbsp treacle

- Mix together the flours, raisins, yeast, sugar and salt. Stir in the oil, treacle and 280 ml of warm water.
- Knead the mixture on a lightly oiled surface for 10 minutes.
- Leave the dough to rest, covered with oiled cling film, for 1–2 hours.
- Knead it for 2 more minutes then split it into 12 even pieces and shape into rolls.
- Transfer the rolls to a greased baking tray and cover with oiled cling film. Leave to prove for 1 hour.
- Preheat the oven to 220⁰C (200⁰C fan) / 430F / gas 7.
- Bake for 15–20 minutes or until the rolls sound hollow when you tap them underneath.
- Transfer to a wire rack and leave to cool.

431

MAKES 36

Chocolate Chip and Cinnamon Cookies

PREPARATION TIME 20 MINUTES

COOKING TIME 12–15 MINUTES

INGREDIENTS

175 g / 6 oz / ¾ cup butter, softened
225 g / 8 oz / 1 ⅓ cups light brown sugar
100 g / 3 ½ oz / ½ cup caster (superfine) sugar
2 tsp vanilla extract
1 egg, plus 1 egg yolk
250 g / 9 oz / 1 ⅔ cups self-raising flour
150 g / 5 oz / 1 cup milk chocolate chips
2 tsp ground cinnamon

- Preheat the oven to 170°C (150°C fan) / 340F / gas 3 and line 2 baking sheets with greaseproof paper.
- Cream together the two sugars, butter and vanilla extract until pale and well whipped then beat in the egg and yolk, followed by the flour, chocolate chips and cinnamon.
- Drop tablespoons of the mixture onto the prepared trays, leaving plenty of room to spread.
- Bake the cookies in batches for 12–15 minutes or until the edges are starting to brown, but the centres are still chewy.
- Transfer to a wire rack and leave to cool.

Coconut and Cinnamon Cookies   432

- Instead of using chocolate chips, add 110 g / 4 oz / 1 cup desiccated coconut to the cookie dough before shaping and baking for a tropical taste.

433

MAKES 24

Coconut Kisses

PREPARATION TIME 20 MINUTES

COOKING TIME 10–15 MINUTES

INGREDIENTS

2 large egg whites
110 g / 4 oz / ½ cup caster (superfine) sugar
250 g / 9 oz / 2 ½ cups unsweetened shredded coconut

- Preheat the oven to 170°C (150°C fan), 325F, gas 3 and oil and line a large baking sheet with baking parchment.
- Whisk the egg whites to stiff peaks in a very clean bowl then carefully fold in the sugar and coconut.
- Spoon the mixture into a piping bag fitted with a large star nozzle and pipe small rosettes onto the prepared baking tray.
- Bake for 10–15 minutes or until they start to turn golden on top.
- Transfer to a wire rack to cool.

Coconut Cherry Kisses   434

- Substitute 75 g / 3 oz / ¾ cup of the shredded coconut for the same weight of chopped glacé cherries for a fruity alternative.

MAKES 16

Milk Rolls

435

Herb Milk Rolls

436

- Add 1 tbsp chopped mixed herbs to the dough before kneading for an additional colour and flavour to these rolls.

Raisin Milk Rolls

437

- Add 100 g / 3 ½ oz / ½ cup raisins to the dough before kneading for a fruity addition to the rolls.

PREPARATION TIME
2 HOURS 30 MINUTES

COOKING TIME 15–20 MINUTES

INGREDIENTS

400 g / 7 oz / 2 ⅔ cups strong white bread flour, plus extra for dusting
½ tsp easy blend dried yeast
1 tbsp caster (superfine) sugar
1 tsp fine sea salt
280 ml / 10 fl.oz / 1 ¼ cups whole milk, warmed

- Mix together the flours, yeast, sugar and salt then stir in the warm milk.
- Knead the mixture on a lightly oiled surface with your hands for 10 minutes or until smooth and elastic.
- Leave the dough to rest in a lightly oiled bowl, covered with oiled cling film, for 1–2 hours or until doubled in size.
- Knead it for 2 more minutes then split it into 16 even pieces and shape into rolls
- Transfer the rolls to a greased baking tray and cover with oiled cling film. Leave to prove for 1 hour or until doubled in size.
- Meanwhile, preheat the oven to 220°C (200°C fan) / 425F / gas 7.
- Transfer the tray to the top shelf of the oven.
- Bake for 15–20 minutes or until the rolls sound hollow when you tap them underneath.
- Transfer to a wire rack and leave to cool.

SAVOURIES

438
MAKES 12 Sun-dried Tomato and Basil Muffins

PREPARATION TIME 25 MINUTES

COOKING TIME 20–25 MINUTES

....

INGREDIENTS

2 large eggs
120 ml / 4 fl. oz / ½ cup sunflower oil
180 ml / 6 fl. oz / ⅔ cup Greek yoghurt
110 g / 4 oz / 1 cup Parmesan, grated
75 g / 2 ½ oz / ⅓ cup sundried tomatoes, chopped
2 tbsp basil leaves, shredded
225 g / 8 oz / 1 ½ cups plain (all purpose) flour
2 tsp baking powder
½ tsp bicarbonate of (baking) soda
½ tsp salt

- Preheat the oven to 180°C (160°C fan) / 350F / gas 4 and line a 12-hole muffin tin with paper cases.
- Beat the egg in a jug with the oil, yoghurt and cheese until well mixed.
- Mix the sundried tomatoes, basil, flour, raising agents and salt in a bowl, then pour in the egg mixture and stir just enough to combine.
- Divide the mixture between the paper cases, then bake in the oven for 20–25 minutes.
- Test with a wooden toothpick, if it comes out clean, the muffins are done.
- Transfer the muffins to a wire rack and leave to cool completely.

Sun-dried Tomato and Caper Muffins
439

- Add 2 tbsp of capers to the cake mixture.

440
SERVES 8 Artichoke and Pine Nut Loaf Cake

PREPARATION TIME 20 MINUTES

COOKING TIME 55 MINUTES

....

INGREDIENTS

300 g / 10 ½ oz / 2 cups self-raising flour
2 tsp baking powder
250 g / 9 oz / 1 ¼ cups butter, softened
4 large eggs
75 g / 2 ½ oz / ¾ cup Parmesan, grated
300 g / 11 oz / 1 ½ cups artichoke hearts in oil, drained & sliced
75 g / 2 ½ oz / ⅔ cup pine nuts

- Preheat the oven to 170°C (150°C fan) 340F / gas 3 and line a large loaf tin with non-stick baking paper.
- Sieve the flour and baking powder into a mixing bowl and add the butter, eggs and Parmesan.
- Beat the mixture with an electric whisk for 4 minutes or until smooth and well whipped.
- Fold in the sliced artichokes and pine nuts then scrape the mixture into the loaf tin.
- Bake for 55 minutes or until a skewer inserted in the centre comes out clean.
- Transfer the cake to a wire rack and leave to cool completely before serving.

Artichoke and Pesto Loaf Cake
441

- Add 4 tbsp of pesto to the cake mixture.

442

SERVES 8

Smoked Bacon and Feta Loaf Cake

- Preheat the oven to 170°C (150°C fan) / 340F / gas 3 and line a large loaf tin with non-stick baking paper.
- Sieve the flour and baking powder into a mixing bowl and add the butter and eggs.
- Beat the mixture with an electric whisk for 4 minutes or until smooth and well whipped.
- Fold in the feta and smoked bacon then scrape the mixture into the loaf tin.
- Bake for 55 minutes or until a skewer inserted in the centre comes out clean.
- Transfer the cake to a wire rack and leave to cool completely before serving.

PREPARATION TIME 20 MINUTES

COOKING TIME 55 MINUTES

INGREDIENTS

300 g / 10 ½ oz / 2 cups self-raising flour
2 tsp baking powder
250 g / 9 oz / 1 ¼ cups butter, softened
5 large eggs
150 g / 5 oz / ¾ cup feta, cubed
150 g / 5 oz / ¾ cup smoked streaky bacon, cubed

Bacon and Egg Loaf Cake   443

- Soft-boil and peel 4 eggs. Spoon half the cake mixture into the tin, then arrange the eggs in a line down the centre of the tin before topping with the rest of the cake mixture and baking as before.

444

SERVES 8

Chicken and Tarragon Loaf Cake

- Preheat the oven to 180°C (160°C fan) /350F / gas 4 and line a loaf tin with greaseproof paper.
- Fry the chicken breast pieces in the olive oil for 5 minutes or until cooked through. Leave to cool.
- Beat the eggs in a jug with the sunflower oil, yoghurt and cheese until well mixed.
- Mix the chicken, tarragon, flour, raising agents and salt in a bowl, then pour in the egg mixture and stir just enough to combine.
- Scrape the mixture into the tin, then bake in the oven for 20–25 minutes.
- Test with a wooden toothpick, if it comes out clean, the cake is done.
- Transfer the loaf to a wire rack and leave to cool completely.

PREPARATION TIME 25 MINUTES

COOKING TIME 20–25 MINUTES

INGREDIENTS

2 skinless chicken breasts, cubed
2 tbsp olive oil
2 large eggs
120 ml / 4 fl. oz / ½ cup sunflower oil
180 ml / 6 fl. oz / ⅔ cup Greek yoghurt
110 g / 4 oz / 1 cup Parmesan, grated
2 tbsp tarragon leaves, chopped
225 g / 8 oz / 1 ½ cups plain (all purpose) flour
2 tsp baking powder
½ tsp bicarbonate of (baking) soda
½ tsp salt

Chicken and Tarragon Muffins   445

- Bake the mixture in a 12-hole silicone muffin tray and reduce the cooking time to 15–20 minutes.

446

SERVES 8

Red Onion and Rosemary Loaf Cake

PREPARATION TIME 25 MINUTES

COOKING TIME 55 MINUTES

....

INGREDIENTS

2 red onions, sliced
2 tbsp olive oil
300 g / 10 ½ oz / 2 cups self-raising flour
2 tsp baking powder
250 g / 9 oz / 1 ¼ cups butter, softened
5 large eggs
2 tbsp rosemary leaves

- Preheat the oven to 170°C (150°C fan) / 340F / gas 3 and line a loaf tin with a paper case.
- Fry the onions in the oil for 10 minutes or until softened and starting to caramelise. Leave to cool.
- Sieve the flour and baking powder into a mixing bowl and add the butter and eggs.
- Beat the mixture with an electric whisk for 4 minutes or until smooth and well whipped.
- Fold in the onions and rosemary then scrape the mixture into the loaf tin.
- Bake for 55 minutes or until a skewer inserted comes out clean.
- Transfer the cake to a wire rack and leave to cool completely before serving.

Red Onion and Thyme Loaf Cake 447

- Replace the rosemary with fresh thyme.

448

MAKES 1 LOAF

Chorizo Bread

PREPARATION TIME
2 HOURS 30 MINUTES

COOKING TIME 35–40 MINUTES

....

INGREDIENTS

400 g / 14 oz / 2 ⅔ cups strong white bread flour, plus extra for dusting
½ tsp easy blend dried yeast
1 tbsp caster (superfine) sugar
1 tsp fine sea salt
200 g / 7 oz / 1 cup chorizo slices, chopped

- In a large bowl, mix together the flour, yeast, sugar and salt. Stir in the chorizo and 280 ml of warm water.
- Knead the mixture on a lightly oiled surface with your hands for 10 minutes or until the dough is elastic.
- Leave the dough to rest in a lightly oiled bowl, covered with oiled cling film, for 1–2 hours.
- Punch the dough with your fist to knock out the air then knead it for 2 more minutes. Cup your hands around the dough and move it in a circular motion whilst pressing down to form a tight round loaf.
- Transfer the dough to a greased round cake tin and cover with oiled cling film. Leave to prove for 1 hour.
- Meanwhile, preheat the oven to 220°C (200°C fan) / 430F / gas 7.
- Bake for 35–40 minutes or until the loaf sounds hollow when you tap it underneath. Transfer the bread to a wire rack and leave to cool completely before slicing.

Chorizo and Rosemary Bread 449

- Add 2 tbsp of fresh rosemary leaves to the flour before adding the water.

Bacon and Chicory Tarte Tatin

450

SERVES 8

Chicory and Stilton Tarte Tatin

451

- Replace the bacon with 100 g / 3 ½ oz / ½ cup of Stilton, cut into small cubes.

Leek and Bacon Tarte Tatin

452

- Replace the chicory with 6 leeks. Remove the green part of the stem and cut each leek lengthways in half.

PREPARATION TIME 25 MINUTES

COOKING TIME 25 MINUTES

INGREDIENTS

2 tbsp olive oil
4 rashers streaky bacon, chopped
4 small heads chicory, halved
250 g / 9 oz / ¾ cup all-butter puff pastry

- Preheat the oven to 220°C (200°C fan) / 425F / gas 7.
- Heat the oil in a large ovenproof frying pan and fry the bacon for 5 minutes or until browned. Remove it from the pan with a slotted spoon and reserve.
- Arrange the chicory in the pan, cut side up and cook over a medium heat for 5 minutes until it starts to soften.
- Turn the chicory over so it lays cut side down and sprinkle over the bacon pieces. Season with salt and pepper.
- Roll out the pastry on a floured surface and cut out a circle slightly larger than the frying pan.
- Lay the pastry over the chicory and tuck in the edges. Pierce with a knife then transfer the pan to the oven and bake for 25 minutes or until the pastry is golden brown and cooked through.
- Using oven gloves, put a large plate on top of the frying pan and turn them both over in one smooth movement to unmould the tart.

453

MAKES 24

Chorizo and Olive Canapés

PREPARATION TIME 20 MINUTES

COOKING TIME 10–15 MINUTES

INGREDIENTS

250 g / 9 oz / ¾ cup all-butter puff pastry
1 egg, beaten
8 slices chorizo, finely chopped
10 green olives, pitted and sliced
60 g / 2 oz / ½ cup Parmesan, finely grated

- Preheat the oven to 220°C (200°C fan) / 430F / gas 7 and line a baking tray with non-stick baking paper.
- Roll out the pastry on a floured surface until 3 mm thick.
- Use a round cookie cutter to cut out discs of the pastry and transfer them to the prepared baking tray.
- Brush the surface with egg and scatter over the chorizo and olives.
- Sprinkle over the grated Parmesan then bake for 10–15 minutes or until golden brown and cooked through.
- Transfer the pastries to a wire rack to cool a little and serve warm.

Pine Nut and Sun-dried Tomato Canapés

454

- Replace the chorizo and olives with pine nuts and chopped sun-dried tomatoes.

455

MAKES 1 LOAF

Bacon and Black Olive Bread

PREPARATION TIME
2 HOURS 30 MINUTES

COOKING TIME 35–40 MINUTES

INGREDIENTS

400 g / 14 oz / 2 ⅔ cups strong white bread flour, plus extra for dusting
½ tsp easy blend dried yeast
1 tbsp caster (superfine) sugar
1 tsp fine sea salt
100 g / 3 ½ oz / ⅔ cup streaky bacon, chopped
100 g / 3 ½ oz / ⅔ cup black olives, pitted and sliced

- Mix together the flour, yeast, sugar and salt. Stir in the bacon, olives and 280 ml of warm water.
- Knead the mixture on a lightly oiled surface for 10 minutes or until the dough is smooth and elastic.
- Leave the dough to rest in a lightly oiled bowl, covered with oiled cling film, for 1–2 hours.
- Knead the dough for 2 more minutes then roll it into a fat sausage. Turn it 90° and roll it tightly the other way then tuck the ends under and transfer the dough to a greased loaf tin, keeping the seam underneath.
- Cover the tin loosely with oiled cling film and leave to prove for 45 minutes.
- Preheat the oven to 220°C (200°C fan) / 430F / gas 7.
- Bake for 35–40 minutes or until the underneath sounds hollow when tapped.
- Leave to cool completely on a wire rack before slicing.

Bacon and Artichoke Bread

456

- Replace the olives with preserved artichokes in oil, roughly chopped.

457

MAKES 1 LOAF

Courgette and Feta Loaf Cake

- Preheat the oven to 170°C (150°C fan) / 340F / gas 3 and either line a loaf tin with non-stick baking paper or grease a 12-hole silicone muffin mould.
- Sieve the flour and baking powder into a mixing bowl and add the butter and eggs.
- Beat the mixture with an electric whisk for 4 minutes or until smooth and well whipped.
- Fold in the feta and courgette then scrape the mixture into the loaf tin or muffin mould.
- Bake for 55 minutes for the loaf or 25 minutes for the muffins, or until a skewer inserted in the centre comes out clean.
- Transfer the cake to a wire rack and leave to cool completely before serving.

PREPARATION TIME 20 MINUTES

COOKING TIME 55 MINUTES

INGREDIENTS

300 g / 10 ½ oz / 2 cups self-raising flour
2 tsp baking powder
250 g / 9 oz / 1 ¼ cups butter, softened
5 large eggs
150 g / 5 oz / 1 cup feta, cubed
1 courgette (zucchini), grated

Courgette and Caraway Loaf Cake

458

- Omit the feta and add 1 tsp of caraway seeds to the flour.

459

SERVES 8

Aubergine, Feta and Pesto Loaf Cake

- Preheat the oven to 180°C (160°C fan) / 355F / gas 4 and line a loaf tin with greaseproof paper.
- Brush the aubergines with olive oil and spread out on a baking tray. Sprinkle with salt and pepper then roast for 15 minutes or until softened. Leave to cool.
- Beat the eggs in a jug with the sunflower oil, yoghurt and pesto until well mixed.
- Mix the feta, aubergine, flour, raising agents and salt in a bowl, then pour in the egg mixture and stir just enough to combine.
- Scrape the mixture into the tin, then bake in the oven for 20–25 minutes.
- Test with a wooden toothpick, if it comes out clean, the cake is done.
- Transfer the loaf to a wire rack and leave to cool completely.

PREPARATION TIME 25 MINUTES

COOKING TIME 35–40 MINUTES

INGREDIENTS

1 aubergine (eggplant), quartered and sliced
2 tbsp olive oil
2 large eggs
120 ml / 4 fl. oz / ½ cup sunflower oil
180 ml / 6 fl. oz / ⅔ cup Greek yoghurt
110 g / 4 oz / ⅓ cup pesto
110 g / 4 oz / ½ cup feta, cubed
225 g / 8 oz / 1 ½ cups plain (all purpose) flour
2 tsp baking powder
½ tsp bicarbonate of (baking) soda
½ tsp salt

Aubergine and Tapenade Loaf Cake

460

- Replace the pesto with an equal quantity of green olive tapenade.

461

SERVES 8

Ham, French Bean and Carrot Loaf

PREPARATION TIME 25 MINUTES

COOKING TIME 55 MINUTES

....

INGREDIENTS

2 carrots, diced
100 g / 3 ½ oz / ½ cup French beans, chopped
300 g / 10 ½ oz / 2 cups self-raising flour
2 tsp baking powder
250 g / 9 oz / 1 ¼ cups butter, softened
5 large eggs
100 g / 3 ½ oz / ¾ cup ham, chopped

- Preheat the oven to 170°C (150° C fan) / 340F / gas 3 and line a large loaf tin with non-stick baking paper.
- Blanch the carrots and beans in boiling salted water for 5 minutes then plunge into cold water and drain well.
- Sieve the flour and baking powder into a mixing bowl and add the butter and eggs.
- Beat the mixture with an electric whisk for 4 minutes or until smooth and well whipped.
- Fold in the vegetables and ham then scrape the mixture into the loaf tin.
- Bake for 55 minutes or until a skewer inserted in the centre comes out clean.
- Transfer the cake to a wire rack and leave to cool completely before serving.

Carrot, Bean and Chorizo Loaf Cake

462

- Replace the ham with 100 g / 3 ½ oz / ¾ cup of chorizo in small cubes.

463

SERVES 8

Bacon and Olive Loaf

PREPARATION TIME 25 MINUTES

COOKING TIME 20–25 MINUTES

....

INGREDIENTS

2 large eggs
120 ml / 4 fl. oz / ½ cup sunflower oil
180 ml / 6 fl. oz / ¾ cup Greek yoghurt
110 g / 4 oz / ¾ cup streaky bacon, chopped
55 g / 2 oz / ⅓ cup green olives, pitted and sliced
55 g / 2 oz / ⅓ cup black olives, pitted and sliced
225 g / 8 oz / 1 ½ cups plain (all purpose) flour
2 tsp baking powder
½ tsp bicarbonate of (baking) soda
½ tsp salt

- Preheat the oven to 180°C (160°C fan) / 355F / gas 4 and line a loaf tin with greaseproof paper.
- Beat the eggs in a jug with the oil, yoghurt, bacon and olives until well mixed.
- Mix the flour, raising agents and salt in a bowl, then pour in the egg mixture and stir just enough to combine.
- Scrape the mixture into the tin, then bake in the oven for 20–25 minutes.
- Test with a wooden toothpick, if it comes out clean, the cake is done.
- Transfer the loaf to a wire rack and leave to cool completely.

Bacon and Basil Loaf Cake

464

- Omit the olives and stir 3 tbsp of shredded basil leaves into the cake mixture.

SERVES 8 # Cheese and Herb Loaf

Cheese, Herb and Pine Nut Loaf Cake

466

- Add 2 tbsp toasted pine nuts to the cake mixture.

Cheese, Herb and Chestnut Loaf Cake

467

- Add 75 g / 2 ½ oz / ⅔ cup of chopped, cooked chestnuts to the cake mixture.

PREPARATION TIME 20 MINUTES

COOKING TIME 55 MINUTES

INGREDIENTS

300 g / 10 ½ oz / 2 cups self-raising flour
2 tsp baking powder
250 g / 9 oz / 1 ¼ cups butter, softened
5 large eggs
100 g / 3 ½ oz / 1 cup Cheddar, grated
2 tbsp flat leaf parsley, chopped
2 tbsp chives, chopped

- Preheat the oven to 170°C (150°C fan) / 340F / gas 3 and line a large loaf tin with non-stick baking paper.
- Sieve the flour and baking powder into a mixing bowl and add the butter and eggs.
- Beat the mixture with an electric whisk for 4 minutes or until smooth and well whipped.
- Fold in the cheese and herbs then scrape the mixture into the loaf tin.
- Bake for 55 minutes or until a skewer inserted in the centre comes out clean.
- Transfer the cake to a wire rack and leave to cool completely before serving.

468

SERVES 8

Fig and Prosciutto Loaf

PREPARATION TIME 20 MINUTES

COOKING TIME 55 MINUTES

....

INGREDIENTS

300 g / 10 ½ oz / 2 cups self-raising flour
2 tsp baking powder
250 g / 9 oz / 1 ¼ cups butter, softened
5 large eggs
4 fresh figs, cut into eighths
6 slices prosciutto, chopped
2 tbsp fresh thyme leaves

- Preheat the oven to 170°C (150°C fan) / 340F / gas 3 and line a large loaf tin with non-stick baking paper.
- Sieve the flour and baking powder into a mixing bowl and add the butter and eggs.
- Beat the mixture with an electric whisk for 4 minutes or until smooth and well whipped.
- Fold in the figs, prosciutto and thyme then scrape the mixture into the loaf tin.
- Bake for 55 minutes or until a skewer inserted in the centre comes out clean.
- Transfer the cake to a wire rack and leave to cool completely before serving.

Fig and Roquefort Loaf Cake
469

- Replace the prosciutto with 100 g / 3 ½ oz / ½ cup of cubed Roquefort.

470

SERVES 8

Feta, Ham and Broccoli Loaf

PREPARATION TIME 20 MINUTES

COOKING TIME 55 MINUTES

....

INGREDIENTS

300 g / 10 ½ oz / 2 cups self-raising flour
2 tsp baking powder
250 g / 9 oz / 1 ¼ cups butter, softened
5 large eggs
75 g / 2 ½ oz / ½ cup feta, cubed
4 slices ham, chopped
75 g / 2 ½ oz / ½ cup broccoli, finely chopped

- Preheat the oven to 170°C (150°C fan) / 340F / gas 3 and line a large loaf tin with non-stick baking paper.
- Sieve the flour and baking powder into a mixing bowl and add the butter and eggs.
- Beat the mixture with an electric whisk for 4 minutes or until smooth and well whipped.
- Fold in the feta, ham and broccoli then scrape the mixture into the loaf tin.
- Bake for 55 minutes or until a skewer inserted in the centre comes out clean.
- Transfer the cake to a wire rack and leave to cool completely before serving.

Feta, Ham and Broccoli Muffins
471

- Bake the mixture in a 12-hole muffin tin and reduce the cooking time to 35 minutes.

472

SERVES 8

Feta, Olive and Roasted Pepper Loaf

- Preheat the oven to 170°C (150°C fan) / 340F / gas 3 and line a large loaf tin with non-stick baking paper.
- Sieve the flour and baking powder into a mixing bowl and add the butter and eggs.
- Beat the mixture with an electric whisk for 4 minutes or until smooth and well whipped.
- Fold in the olives, peppers and feta then scrape the mixture into the loaf tin.
- Bake for 55 minutes or until a skewer inserted in the centre comes out clean.
- Transfer the cake to a wire rack and leave to cool completely before serving.

PREPARATION TIME 20 MINUTES

COOKING TIME 55 MINUTES

....

INGREDIENTS

300 g / 10 ½ oz / 2 cups self-raising flour
2 tsp baking powder
250 g / 9 oz / 1 ¼ cups butter, softened
5 large eggs
75 g / 2 ½ oz / ½ cup black olives, pitted and sliced
75 g / 2 ½ oz / ½ cup chopped roasted peppers in oil, drained
75 g / 2 ½ oz / ½ cup feta, cubed

Wholemeal Mediterranean Loaf Cake

473

- Use wholemeal self-raising flour in place of the usual self-raising flour.

474

SERVES 8

Gorgonzola, Rosemary and Honey Loaf

- Preheat the oven to 170°C (150°C fan) / 340F / gas 3 and line a large loaf tin with non-stick baking paper.
- Sieve the flour and baking powder into a mixing bowl and add the rosemary, butter, eggs and honey.
- Beat the mixture with an electric whisk for 4 minutes or until smooth and well whipped.
- Spoon half of the mixture into the loaf tin and scatter over the Gorgonzola.
- Top with the remaining cake mixture and bake for 55 minutes or until a skewer inserted in the centre comes out clean.
- Transfer the cake to a wire rack and leave to cool completely before serving.

PREPARATION TIME 20 MINUTES

COOKING TIME 55 MINUTES

....

INGREDIENTS

300 g / 10 ½ oz / 2 cups self-raising flour
2 tsp baking powder
2 tbsp rosemary, finely chopped
250 g / 9 oz / 1 ¼ cups butter, softened
5 large eggs
4 tbsp runny honey
110 g / 4 oz / ½ cup Gorgonzola, cubed

Fig, Rosemary and Honey Loaf Cake

475

- Replace the Gorgonzola with 4 finely chopped dried figs.

Chicken, Olive and Sun-dried Tomato Loaf

476

SERVES 10

PREPARATION TIME 25 MINUTES

COOKING TIME 20–25 MINUTES

INGREDIENTS

2 skinless chicken breasts, cubed
2 tbsp olive oil
2 large eggs
120 ml / 4 fl. oz / ½ cup sunflower oil
180 ml / 6 fl. oz / ¾ cup Greek
yoghurt
110 g / 4 oz / 1 cup Parmesan, grated
75 g / 2 ½ oz / ⅓ cup sun-dried
tomatoes in oil, drained
75 g / 2 ½ oz / ½ cup black olives,
pitted and chopped
225 g / 8 oz / 1 ½ cups plain (all
purpose) flour
2 tsp baking powder
½ tsp bicarbonate of (baking) soda
½ tsp salt

- Preheat the oven to 180°C (160°C fan) / 350F / gas 4 and line a long, thin loaf tin with greaseproof paper.
- Fry the chicken breast pieces in the olive oil for 5 minutes or until cooked through. Leave to cool.
- Beat the eggs in a jug with the sunflower oil, yoghurt and cheese until well mixed.
- Mix the chicken, tomatoes, olives, flour, raising agents and salt in a bowl, then pour in the egg mixture and stir just enough to combine.
- Scrape the mixture into the tin, then bake in the oven for 20–25 minutes.
- Test with a wooden toothpick, if it comes out clean, the cake is done.
- Transfer the loaf to a wire rack and leave to cool completely before slicing.

Chicken and Artichoke Loaf Cake   477

- Replace the olives and sundried tomatoes with 150 g / 5 oz / ¾ cup of preserved artichokes in oil, roughly chopped.

478

SERVES 8

Ham and Mushroom Slice

PREPARATION TIME 30 MINUTES

COOKING TIME 25–30 MINUTES

INGREDIENTS

500 ml / 17 ½ fl. oz / 2 cups milk
35 g / 1 ¼ oz butter
2 tbsp plain (all purpose) flour
100 g / 3 ½ oz / ⅔ cup button
mushrooms, chopped
100 g / 3 ½ oz / ⅔ cup ham, cubed
450 g / 1 lb / 1 ¼ cup all-butter puff
pastry
1 egg, beaten

- Preheat the oven to 220°C (200°C fan) / 430F / gas 7.
- Heat the milk to simmering point and set aside.
- Heat the butter in a small saucepan and stir in the flour. Slowly add the hot milk, stirring constantly, and cook until the sauce is thick and smooth.
- Stir in the mushrooms and ham and season with salt and pepper, then leave to cool completely.
- Roll out the pastry and divide into 2 equal rectangles.
- Transfer one rectangle to a baking tray and spread over the filling, leaving a 2 cm border round the outside.
- Brush the edge of the pastry with beaten egg and lay the other pastry sheet on top. Squeeze the edges to seal and trim the pastry to neaten.
- Score a pattern on top with a sharp knife.
- Bake in the oven for 25–35 minutes or until the top is golden brown.

Chicken and Mushroom Slice   479

- Replace the ham with an equal weight of chopped cooked chicken breast.

480

SERVES 6-8

Onion and Thyme Quiche

- Rub the butter into the flour until the mixture resembles breadcrumbs, stir in enough cold water to bind; chill for 30 minutes.
- Preheat the oven to 190°C (170°C fan) / 375F / gas 5.
- Roll out the pastry and use it to line a square tart tin.
- Prick the pastry, line with cling film and fill with baking beans or rice. Bake for 10 minutes then remove the cling film and baking beans.
- Brush with beaten egg and bake for 8 minutes. Lower the oven to 150°C (130°C fan) / 300F / gas 2.
- Fry the onions in the butter for 15 minutes. Add the garlic and cook for 2 more minutes.
- Whisk the eggs with the double cream then stir in the onions, thyme and half of the Gruyere. Season with salt and pepper.
- Pour the filling into the pastry case and scatter the rest of the cheese on top. Bake for 35–40 minutes.

Chorizo and Onion Quiche   481

- Add 100 g / 3 ½ oz / ½ cup of chorizo in small cubes when you fry the garlic.

PREPARATION TIME 1 HOUR

COOKING TIME 55–60 MINUTES

INGREDIENTS

3 onions, thinly sliced
50 g / 1 ¾ oz / ¼ cup butter
2 cloves garlic, crushed
3 large eggs
225 ml / 8 fl. oz / ¾ cup double (heavy) cream
2 tbsp thyme leaves
150 g / 5 ½ oz / 1 ½ cups Gruyere, grated

FOR THE PASTRY

100 g / 3 ½ oz / ½ cup butter, cubed
200 g / 7 oz / 1 ⅓ cups plain (all purpose) flour
1 large egg, beaten

482

SERVES 8

Pear and Roquefort Loaf

- Preheat the oven to 170°C (150°C fan) / 340F / gas 3 and line a large loaf tin with non-stick baking paper.
- Sieve the flour and baking powder into a mixing bowl and add the butter and eggs.
- Beat the mixture with an electric whisk for 4 minutes or until smooth and well whipped.
- Fold in the pears and Roquefort then scrape the mixture into the loaf tin.
- Bake for 55 minutes or until a skewer inserted in the centre comes out clean.
- Transfer the cake to a wire rack and leave to cool completely before serving.

Pear, Roquefort and Walnut Loaf Cake   483

- Add 75 g / 3 oz / ⅔ cup of chopped walnuts to the cake mixture.

PREPARATION TIME 20 MINUTES

COOKING TIME 55 MINUTES

INGREDIENTS

300 g / 10 ½ oz / 2 cups self-raising flour
2 tsp baking powder
250 g / 9 oz / 1 ¼ cups butter, softened
5 large eggs
2 pears, peeled, cored and chopped
150 g / 5 ½ oz / ⅔ cup Roquefort, cubed

484

SERVES 8

Three-cheese Loaf Cake

PREPARATION TIME 20 MINUTES

COOKING TIME 20–25 MINUTES

....

INGREDIENTS

2 large eggs
120 ml / 4 fl. oz / ½ cup sunflower oil
180 ml / 6 fl. oz / ⅔ cup Greek yoghurt
110 g / 4 oz / 1 cup Cheddar, grated
110 g / 4 oz / ⅔ goats' cheese, cubed
110 g / 4 oz / ⅔ Roquefort, cubed
225 g / 8 oz / 1 ½ cups plain (all purpose) flour
2 tsp baking powder
½ tsp bicarbonate of (baking) soda
½ tsp salt

- Preheat the oven to 180°C (160°C fan) / 355F / gas 4 and line a loaf tin with greaseproof paper.
- Beat the eggs in a jug with the oil, yoghurt and cheeses until well mixed.
- Mix the flour, raising agents and salt in a bowl, then pour in the egg mixture and stir just enough to combine.
- Scrape the mixture into the tin, then bake in the oven for 20–25 minutes.
- Test with a wooden toothpick, if it comes out clean, the cake is done.
- Transfer the loaf to a wire rack and leave to cool completely.

Four-cheese Loaf Cake

485

- Spoon half the mixture into the tin then add a layer of sliced mozzarella before topping with the rest of the cake mixture.

486

SERVES 8

Cherry Tomato Loaf Cake

PREPARATION TIME 15 MINUTES

COOKING TIME 30–35 MINUTES

....

INGREDIENTS

2 large eggs
120 ml / 4 fl. oz / ½ cup sunflower oil
180 ml / 6 fl. oz / ⅔ cup Greek yoghurt
110 g / 4 oz / 1 cup Parmesan, grated
450 g / 1 lb / 2 ½ cherry tomatoes
225 g / 8 oz / 1 ½ cups plain (all purpose) flour
2 tsp baking powder
½ tsp bicarbonate of (baking) soda
½ tsp salt

- Preheat the oven to 180°C (160°C fan) / 355F / gas 4 and line a loaf tin with greaseproof paper.
- Beat the eggs in a jug with the oil, yoghurt and Parmesan until well mixed.
- Mix the flour, raising agents and salt in a bowl, then pour in the egg mixture.
- Reserve 16 of the tomatoes and cut the rest into quarters. Add them to the bowl and stir everything just enough to combine.
- Scrape the mixture into the tin, and stud with the reserved tomatoes.
- Bake in the oven for 30–35 minutes.
- Test with a wooden toothpick, if it comes out clean, the cake is done.
- Transfer the loaf to a wire rack and leave to cool completely.

Tomato and Bacon Loaf Cake

487

- Add 100 g / 3 ½ oz / ½ cup of smoked bacon lardons to the cake mixture.

Olive and Rosemary Mini Muffins

488

MAKES 24

Goats' Cheese and Rosemary Mini Muffins

489

- Replace the olives with 150 g / 5 oz / ⅔ cup of goats' cheese in small cubes.

Chorizo and Rosemary Mini Muffins

490

- Replace the olives with 100 g / 3 ½ oz / ⅔ cup of chorizo in small cubes.

PREPARATION TIME 15 MINUTES

COOKING TIME 10–15 MINUTES

....

INGREDIENTS

2 large eggs
120 ml / 4 fl. oz / ½ cup sunflower oil
180 ml / 6 fl. oz / ⅔ cup Greek yoghurt
2 tbsp Parmesan, finely grated
225 g / 8 oz / 1 ½ cups plain (all purpose) flour
2 tsp baking powder
½ tsp bicarbonate of (baking) soda
½ tsp salt
75 g / 2 ½ oz / ½ cup black olives, stoned and chopped
2 tbsp fresh rosemary, chopped

- Preheat the oven to 180°C (160°C fan) / 350F / gas 4 and line a 24-hole mini muffin tin with paper cases.
- Beat the egg in a jug with the oil, yoghurt and cheese until well mixed.
- Mix the flour, raising agents, salt, olives and rosemary in a bowl, then pour in the egg mixture and stir just enough to combine.
- Divide the mixture between the paper cases, then bake in the oven for 10–15 minutes.
- Test with a wooden toothpick, if it comes out clean, the muffins are done.
- Serve warm.

491
SERVES 8
Cream Cheese and Salmon Loaf

PREPARATION TIME 15 MINUTES

COOKING TIME 30–35 MINUTES

....

INGREDIENTS

2 large eggs
120 ml / 4 fl. oz / ½ cup sunflower oil
180 ml / 6 fl. oz / ⅔ cup Greek yoghurt
3 tbsp cream cheese
110 g / 4 oz / ⅔ cup smoked salmon, chopped
2 tbsp dill, chopped
225 g / 8 oz / 1 ½ cups plain (all purpose) flour
2 tsp baking powder
½ tsp bicarbonate of (baking) soda
½ tsp salt

- Preheat the oven to 180⁰C (160⁰C fan) / 355F / gas 4 and line a loaf tin with greaseproof paper.
- Beat the eggs in a jug with the oil, yoghurt and cream cheese until well mixed.
- Mix the salmon, dill, flour, raising agents and salt in a bowl, then pour in the egg mixture and stir just enough to combine.
- Scrape the mixture into the tin, then bake in the oven for 30–35 minutes.
- Test with a wooden toothpick, if it comes out clean, the cake is done.
- Transfer the loaf to a wire rack and leave to cool completely.

Smoked Mackerel Loaf Cake   492

- Replace the smoked salmon with 2 smoked mackerel fillets that have been skinned and flaked.

493
MAKES 12
Squash and Parmesan Mini Loaf Cakes

PREPARATION TIME 40 MINUTES

COOKING TIME 40 MINUTES

....

INGREDIENTS

200 g / 7 oz / 1 cup butternut squash, cubed
300 g / 10 ½ oz / 2 cups self-raising flour
2 tsp baking powder
250 g / 9 oz / 1 ¼ cups butter, softened
5 large eggs
75 g / 2 ½ oz / ¾ cup Parmesan, grated
2 tbsp chives, chopped

- Preheat the oven to 190⁰C (170⁰C fan) / 375F / gas 5 and oil a 12-hole silicone mini loaf cake mould.
- Put the squash in a roasting tin and cover with foil then bake for 20 minutes. Tip it into a sieve and leave to drain and cool completely.
- Sieve the flour and baking powder into a mixing bowl and add the butter, eggs and Parmesan.
- Beat the mixture with an electric whisk for 4 minutes or until smooth and well whipped.
- Fold in the squash and chives then spoon the mixture into the moulds.
- Bake for 15–20 minutes or until a skewer inserted in the centre comes out clean.
- Serve warm.

Squash and Stilton Mini Loaf Cakes   494

- Replace the Parmesan with 100 g / 3 ½ oz / ½ cup of Stilton in small cubes.
of Stilton in small cubes.

Carrot and Roquefort Loaf
SERVES 8

- Preheat the oven to 170°C (150°C fan) / 340F / gas 3 and line a large loaf tin with non-stick baking paper.
- Boil the carrots for 8 minutes or until tender then drain well and leave to cool.
- Sieve the flour and baking powder into a mixing bowl and add the butter and eggs.
- Beat the mixture with an electric whisk for 4 minutes or until smooth and well whipped.
- Fold in the carrots, Roquefort and Parmesan then scrape the mixture into the loaf tin.
- Bake for 55 minutes or until a skewer inserted in the centre comes out clean.
- Transfer the cake to a wire rack and leave to cool completely before serving.

PREPARATION TIME 35 MINUTES

COOKING TIME 55 MINUTES

INGREDIENTS

2 carrots, peeled and chopped
300 g / 10 ½ oz / 2 cups self-raising flour
2 tsp baking powder
250 g / 9 oz / 1 ¼ cups butter, softened
5 large eggs
150 g / 5 ½ oz / ⅔ cup Roquefort, cubed
75 g / 2 ½ oz / ¾ cup Parmesan, grated

Parsnip and Roquefort Loaf Cake   496

- Replace the carrots with parsnips and cook as before.

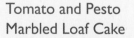
497

Tomato, Sage and Mozzarella Loaf
SERVES 8

- Preheat the oven to 170°C (150°C fan) / 340F / gas 3 and line a large loaf tin with non-stick baking paper.
- Sieve the flour and baking powder into a mixing bowl and add the butter, tomato puree and eggs.
- Beat the mixture with an electric whisk for 4 minutes or until smooth and well whipped.
- Fold in the mozzarella and sage then scrape the mixture into the loaf tin.
- Bake for 55 minutes or until a skewer inserted in the centre comes out clean.
- Transfer the cake to a wire rack and leave to cool completely before serving.

PREPARATION TIME 20 MINUTES

COOKING TIME 55 MINUTES

INGREDIENTS

300 g / 10 ½ oz / 2 cups self-raising flour
2 tsp baking powder
250 g / 9 oz / 1 ¼ cups butter, softened
2 tbsp tomato puree
4 large eggs
150 g / 5 ½ oz / ⅔ cup mozzarella, cubed
2 tbsp sage leaves, chopped

Tomato and Pesto Marbled Loaf Cake   498

- Divide the cake mixture in two and stir the tomato puree into one half. Stir 3 tbsp pesto into the other half then marble together in the tin.

Parmesan and Red Pepper Loaf Cake

499

SERVES 8

Parmesan and Sun-dried Tomato Loaf Cake

500

- Replace the red pepper layer with sun-dried tomatoes.

Parmesan and Aubergine Loaf Cake

501

- Replace the red pepper layer with char grilled aubergines in oil.

PREPARATION TIME 20 MINUTES

COOKING TIME 55 MINUTES

INGREDIENTS

300 g / 10 ½ oz / 2 cups self-raising flour
2 tsp baking powder
250 g / 9 oz / 1 ¼ cups butter, softened
150 g / 5 ½ oz / 1 ½ cups Parmesan, grated
4 large eggs
1 jar roasted red peppers in oil, drained

- Preheat the oven to 170⁰C (150⁰C fan) / 340F / gas 3 and line a large loaf tin with non-stick baking paper.
- Sieve the flour and baking powder into a mixing bowl and add the butter, Parmesan and eggs.
- Beat the mixture with an electric whisk for 4 minutes or until smooth and well whipped.
- Spoon half of the mixture into the loaf tin and top with the red peppers.
- Top with the rest of the cake mixture and bake for 55 minutes or until a skewer inserted in the centre comes out clean.
- Transfer the cake to a wire rack and leave to cool completely before serving.

502

SERVES 8 # Halloumi, Tomato and Basil Loaf Cake

- Preheat the oven to 180°C (160°C fan) / 355F / gas 4 and line a loaf tin with greaseproof paper.
- Beat the eggs in a jug with the oil, yoghurt and tomato puree until well mixed.
- Mix the Halloumi, tomatoes, basil, flour, raising agents and salt in a bowl, then pour in the egg mixture and stir everything just enough to combine.
- Scrape the mixture into the tin and bake for 30–35 minutes.
- Test with a wooden toothpick, if it comes out clean, the cake is done.
- Transfer the loaf to a wire rack and leave to cool completely.

PREPARATION TIME 15 MINUTES

COOKING TIME 30–35 MINUTES

INGREDIENTS

2 large eggs
120 ml / 4 fl. oz / ½ cup sunflower oil
180 ml / 6 fl. oz / ⅔ cup Greek yoghurt
2 tbsp tomato puree
225 g / 8 oz / 1 cup Halloumi, cubed
110 g / 8 oz / ⅔ cup cherry tomatoes, quartered
2 tbsp basil, finely chopped
225 g / 8 oz / 1 ½ cups plain (all purpose) flour
2 tsp baking powder
½ tsp bicarbonate of (baking) soda
½ tsp salt

Halloumi, Olive and Basil Loaf Cake

503

- Replace the cherry tomatoes with 75 g / 3 oz / ½ cup of chopped black olives.

504

SERVES 8 # Asparagus and Bacon Loaf Cake

- Preheat the oven to 180°C (160°C fan) / 355F / gas 4 and line a loaf tin with greaseproof paper.
- Blanch the asparagus in boiling, salted water for 2 minutes then refresh in cold water and drain.
- Beat the eggs in a jug with the oil and yoghurt.
- Mix the bacon, flour, raising agents and salt in a bowl, then pour in the egg mixture and stir to combine.
- Scrape half of the mixture into the tin and lay all but 2 of the asparagus spears on top. Spoon over the rest of the cake mixture and level the top, then lay 2 pieces of asparagus diagonally on top.
- Bake the cake for 30–35 minutes.
- Test with a wooden toothpick, if it comes out clean, the cake is done.
- Transfer the loaf to a wire rack and leave to cool completely before slicing.

PREPARATION TIME 20 MINUTES

COOKING TIME 30–35 MINUTES

INGREDIENTS

8 asparagus spears, halved lengthways
2 large eggs
120 ml / 4 fl. oz / ½ cup sunflower oil
180 ml / 6 fl. oz / ⅔ cup Greek yoghurt
110 g / 4 oz / ⅔ cup streaky bacon, chopped
225 g / 8 oz / 1 ½ cups plain (all purpose) flour
2 tsp baking powder
½ tsp bicarbonate of (baking) soda
½ tsp salt

Asparagus and Pesto Loaf Cake

505

- Omit the bacon and stir 3 tbsp of pesto into the cake mixture.

506

SERVES 8

Stilton and Walnut Loaf

PREPARATION TIME 15 MINUTES

COOKING TIME 30–35 MINUTES

....

INGREDIENTS

2 large eggs
120 ml / 4 fl. oz / ½ cup sunflower oil
180 ml / 6 fl. oz / ⅔ cup Greek
yoghurt
225 g / 8 oz / 1 cup Stilton, cubed
110 g / 3 ½ oz / ¾ cup walnuts,
chopped
225 g / 8 oz / 1 ½ cups plain (all
purpose) flour
2 tsp baking powder
½ tsp bicarbonate of (baking) soda
½ tsp salt

- Preheat the oven to 180°C (160°C fan) / 355F / gas 4 and line a loaf tin with greaseproof paper.
- Beat the eggs in a jug with the oil and yoghurt until well mixed.
- Mix the Stilton, walnuts, flour, raising agents and salt in a bowl, then pour in the egg mixture and stir everything just enough to combine.
- Scrape the mixture into the tin and bake for 30–35 minutes.
- Test with a wooden toothpick, if it comes out clean, the cake is done.
- Transfer the loaf to a wire rack and leave to cool completely.

Stilton and Fig Loaf Cake   507

- Replace the walnuts with 4 finely chopped dried figs.

508

SERVES 8

Carrot, Gruyere and Poppy Seed Loaf

PREPARATION TIME 20 MINUTES

COOKING TIME 55 MINUTES

....

INGREDIENTS

300 g / 10 ½ oz / 2 cups self-raising
flour
2 tsp baking powder
250 g / 9 oz / 1 ¼ cups butter,
softened
5 large eggs
2 carrots, grated
150 g / 5 ½ oz / 1 ½ cups Gruyere,
grated
2 tbsp poppy seeds

- Preheat the oven to 170°C (150°C fan) / 340F / gas 3 and line a large loaf tin with non-stick baking paper.
- Sieve the flour and baking powder into a mixing bowl and add the butter and eggs.
- Beat the mixture with an electric whisk for 4 minutes or until smooth and well whipped.
- Fold in the carrots, cheese and poppy seeds then scrape the mixture into the loaf tin.
- Bake for 55 minutes or until a skewer inserted in the centre comes out clean.
- Transfer the cake to a wire rack and leave to cool completely before serving.

Parsnip and Gruyere Loaf Cake   509

- Replace the carrot with grated parsnip.

Roquefort, Pine Nut and Tomato Loaf

510

SERVES 10

Wholemeal Roquefort Loaf Cake

511

- Replace the flour with wholemeal self-raising flour.

Roquefort and Dried Apple Loaf Cake

512

- Replace the sun-dried tomatoes with 75 g / 3 oz / ½ cup of chopped dried apple slices.

PREPARATION TIME 25 MINUTES

COOKING TIME 20–25 MINUTES

INGREDIENTS

2 large eggs
120 ml / 4 fl. oz / ½ cup sunflower oil
180 ml / 6 fl. oz / ⅔ cup Greek yoghurt
110 g / 4 oz / ½ cup Roquefort, cubed
75 g / 2 ½ oz / ⅓ cup sun-dried tomatoes in oil, drained
75 g / 2 ½ oz / ⅔ cup pine nuts
225 g / 8 oz / 1 ½ cups plain (all purpose) flour
2 tsp baking powder
½ tsp bicarbonate of (baking) soda
½ tsp salt

- Preheat the oven to 180⁰C (160⁰C fan) / 350F / gas 4 and line a long, thin loaf tin with greaseproof paper.
- Beat the eggs in a jug with the oil, yoghurt and cheese until well mixed.
- Mix the tomatoes, pine nuts, flour, raising agents and salt in a bowl, then pour in the egg mixture and stir just enough to combine.
- Scrape the mixture into the tin, then bake in the oven for 20–25 minutes.
- Test with a wooden toothpick, if it comes out clean, the cake is done.
- Transfer the loaf to a wire rack and leave to cool completely before slicing.

Parmesan, Thyme and Peppercorn Cookies

513

MAKES 36

PREPARATION TIME 15 MINUTES

COOKING TIME 10–15 MINUTES

INGREDIENTS

2 large eggs
110 ml / 4 fl. oz / ½ cup sunflower oil
110 ml / 4 fl. oz / ⅔ cup Greek yoghurt
110 g / 4 oz / 1 cup Parmesan, grated
225 g / 8 oz / 1 ½ cups plain (all purpose) flour
2 tsp baking powder
½ tsp bicarbonate of (baking) soda
½ tsp salt
2 tbsp fresh thyme leaves
1 tbsp pink peppercorns, crushed

- Preheat the oven to 180°C (160°C fan) / 355F / gas 4 and line 2 baking trays with greaseproof paper.
- Beat the eggs in a jug with the oil, yoghurt and Parmesan until well mixed.
- Mix the flour, raising agents, salt, thyme and peppercorns in a bowl, then pour in the egg mixture.
- Stir everything just enough to combine.
- Drop heaped teaspoons of the mixture spaced out on the baking trays and bake in batches for 10–15 minutes or until golden brown.
- Transfer to a wire rack and leave to cool.

Parmesan and Rosemary Cookies

514

- Replace the thyme with 2 tbsp of chopped fresh rosemary.

515

MAKES 6

Chicken and Almond Pastilla

PREPARATION TIME 25 MINUTES

COOKING TIME 25-30 MINUTES

INGREDIENTS

1 onion, finely chopped
2 tbsp olive oil
2 chicken breasts, finely chopped
2 cloves garlic, crushed
1 lemon, zest finely grated
100 g / 3 ½ oz / ¾ cup blanched almonds, chopped
3 tbsp coriander (cilantro) leaves, chopped
225 g / 8 oz / 1 cup filo pastry
100 g / 3 ½ oz / ½ cup butter, melted
icing (confectioners') sugar to dust

- Preheat the oven to 180°C (160°C fan) / 355F / gas 4 and grease a large baking tray.
- Fry the onion in the oil for 5 minutes then add the chicken and garlic and stir-fry for 3 minutes. Turn off the heat and stir in the lemon zest, almonds and coriander. Season with salt and pepper and leave to cool a little.
- Brush the pastry sheets with butter and layer them to create 6 separate stacks.
- Divide the chicken mixture between the filo stacks and fold in the edges.
- Turn the parcels over and transfer to the baking tray. Brush with a little extra butter then bake for 25–30 minutes or until the pastry is crisp and golden.
- Dust the pastillas with icing sugar before serving.
- To create the char marks, heat up a skewer with a blow torch or gas hob and burn lines in the icing sugar.

Pigeon and Almond Pastilla

516

- Replace the chicken breasts with 6 cubed pigeon breasts and add 1 tsp ground cinnamon when you add the lemon zest.

517

SERVES 8

Black Olive and Parsnip Loaf Cake

- Preheat the oven to 180°C (160°C fan) / 355F / gas 4 and butter a baking dish.
- Beat the eggs in a jug with the oil, yoghurt, parsnip and olives until well mixed.
- Mix the flour, raising agents and salt in a bowl, then pour in the egg mixture and stir just enough to combine.
- Scrape the mixture into the dish, then bake in the oven for 20–25 minutes.
- Test with a wooden toothpick, if it comes out clean, the cake is done.
- Serve warm.

PREPARATION TIME 25 MINUTES

COOKING TIME 20–25 MINUTES

....

INGREDIENTS

2 large eggs
120 ml / 4 fl. oz / ½ cup sunflower oil
180 ml / 6 fl. oz / ⅔ cup Greek yoghurt
110 g / 4 oz / ¾ cup parsnip, grated
110 g / 4 oz / ⅔ cup black olives, pitted and sliced
225 g / 8 oz / 1 ½ cups plain (all purpose) flour
2 tsp baking powder
½ tsp bicarbonate of (baking) soda
½ tsp salt

Black Olive and Sweetcorn Loaf Cake

518

- Replace the parsnip with 200 g / 7 oz / 1 ⅓ cup of sweetcorn.

519

MAKES 1

Granary Corn Bread

- Mix together the flours, yeast, sugar and salt. Stir in the oil and 280 ml of warm water.
- Knead the mixture on a lightly oiled surface for 10 minutes or until smooth and elastic.
- Leave the dough to rest, covered with oiled cling film, for 1–2 hours or until doubled in size.
- Knead for 2 more minutes then roll the dough into a fat sausage. Roll it up the other way and drop it into a loaf tin with the seam underneath.
- Cover the tin with oiled cling film and leave for 1 hour.
- Preheat the oven to 220°C (200°C fan) / 430F / gas 7.
- Bake for 35–40 minutes or until the loaf sounds hollow when you tap it underneath.
- Transfer to a wire rack and leave to cool.

PREPARATION TIME
2 HOURS 30 MINUTES

COOKING TIME 35–40 MINUTES

....

INGREDIENTS

200 g / 7 oz / 1 ⅓ cups malted granary flour
200 g / 7 oz / 1 ⅓ cups fine corn meal
1 tsp easy blend dried yeast
2 tbsp caster (superfine) sugar
1 tsp fine sea salt
1 tbsp olive oil

Corn Bread Loaf

520

- Replace the malted granary flour with strong white bread flour.

521
SERVES 8

Bacon and Caraway Loaf Cake

PREPARATION TIME 20 MINUTES

COOKING TIME 55 MINUTES

....

INGREDIENTS

300 g / 10 ½ oz / 2 cups self-raising
flour
2 tsp baking powder
250 g / 9 oz / 1 ¼ cups butter,
softened
5 large eggs
150 g / 5 oz / ¾ cup streaky bacon,
cubed
2 tbsp caraway seeds

- Preheat the oven to 170°C (150°C fan) / 340F / gas 3 and line a large loaf tin with non-stick baking paper.
- Sieve the flour and baking powder into a mixing bowl and add the butter and eggs.
- Beat the mixture with an electric whisk for 4 minutes or until smooth and well whipped.
- Fold in the bacon and half of the caraway seeds then scrape the mixture into the loaf tin.
- Sprinkle the top with the rest of the caraway and freshly ground black pepper.
- Bake for 55 minutes or until a skewer inserted in the centre comes out clean.
- Transfer the cake to a wire rack and leave to cool completely before serving.

Bacon and Fennel Loaf Cake   522

- Replace the caraway seeds with 1 tbsp of fennel seeds.

523
MAKES 1 LOAF

Chorizo and Thyme Bread

PREPARATION TIME
2 HOURS 30 MINUTES

COOKING TIME 35–40 MINUTES

....

INGREDIENTS

300 g / 10 ½ oz / 2 cups strong white
bread flour, plus extra for dusting
100 g / 3 ½ oz / ⅔ cup stoneground
wholemeal flour
½ tsp easy blend dried yeast
1 tbsp caster (superfine) sugar
1 tsp fine sea salt
100 g / 3 ½ oz / ½ cup chorizo, cubed
4 tbsp fresh thyme leaves

- Mix together the flours, yeast, sugar and salt. Stir in the chorizo, half of the thyme and 280 ml of warm water.
- Knead the mixture on a lightly oiled surface for 10 minutes or until the dough is smooth and elastic.
- Leave the dough to rest in a lightly oiled bowl, covered with oiled cling film, for 1–2 hours.
- Knead the dough for 2 more minutes then roll it into a fat sausage. Turn it 90° and roll it tightly the other way then tuck the ends under and transfer the dough to a greased loaf tin, keeping the seam underneath.
- Cover the tin with oiled cling film and leave for 45 minutes.
- Preheat the oven to 220°C (200°C fan) / 430F / gas 7 and sprinkle the rest of the thyme over the loaf.
- Bake for 35–40 minutes or until the underneath sounds hollow when tapped.
- Leave to cool completely on a wire rack before slicing.

Fig and Chorizo Mini Loaf Cakes

Fig and Walnut
Mini Loaf Cakes

525

- Replace the chorizo with 75 g / 3 oz / ⅔ cup of chopped walnuts.

Double Fig Mini
Loaf Cakes

526

- Replace the chorizo with 75 g / 3 oz / ½ cup of dried figs, cut into small pieces.

Fig and Stilton
Mini Loaf Cakes

527

- Replace the chorizo with 100 g / 3 ½ oz / ½ cup of Stilton in small cubes.

PREPARATION TIME 15 MINUTES

COOKING TIME 10–15 MINUTES

INGREDIENTS

2 large eggs
120 ml / 4 fl. oz / ½ cup sunflower oil
180 ml / 6 fl. oz / ¾ cup Greek yoghurt
2 tbsp Parmesan, finely grated
150 g / 5 ½ oz / ¾ cup chorizo, cubed
4 fresh figs, chopped
225 g / 8 oz / 1 ½ cups plain (all purpose) flour
2 tsp baking powder
½ tsp bicarbonate of (baking) soda
½ tsp salt

- Preheat the oven to 180°C (160°C fan) / 350F / gas 4 and line a 24 hole mini loaf tin with greaseproof paper.
- Beat the eggs in a jug with the oil, yoghurt, Parmesan, chorizo and figs until well mixed.
- Mix the flour, raising agents and salt in a bowl, then pour in the egg mixture and stir just enough to combine.
- Divide the mixture between the cases, then bake in the oven for 10–15 minutes.
- Test with a wooden toothpick, if it comes out clean, the cakes are done.

528
MAKES 24 Parmesan and Pistachio Mini Muffins

PREPARATION TIME 15 MINUTES

COOKING TIME 10–15 MINUTES

INGREDIENTS

2 large eggs
120 ml / 4 fl. oz / ½ cup sunflower oil
180 ml / 6 fl. oz / ¾ cup Greek yoghurt
100 g / 3 ½ oz / 1 cup Parmesan, grated
225 g / 8 oz / 1 ½ cups plain (all purpose) flour
2 tsp baking powder
½ tsp bicarbonate of (baking) soda
½ tsp salt
75 g / 2 ½ oz / ½ cup pistachio nuts

- Preheat the oven to 180°C (160°C fan) / 350F / gas 4 and line a 24-hole mini muffin tin with paper cases.
- Beat the eggs in a jug with the oil, yoghurt and cheese until well mixed.
- Mix the flour, raising agents, salt and pistachios in a bowl, then pour in the egg mixture and stir just enough to combine.
- Divide the mixture between the paper cases, then bake in the oven for 10–15 minutes.
- Test with a wooden toothpick, if it comes out clean, the muffins are done.
- Serve warm.

Parmesan and Hazelnut Mini Muffins
529
- Replace the pistachios with hazelnuts (cob nuts).

530
SERVES 10 King Prawn and Sun-dried Tomato Loaf

PREPARATION TIME 25 MINUTES

COOKING TIME 20–25 MINUTES

INGREDIENTS

2 large eggs
120 ml / 4 fl. oz / ½ cup sunflower oil
180 ml / 6 fl. oz / ¾ cup Greek yoghurt
110 g / 4 oz / ½ cup king prawns (shrimp), cooked and peeled
75 g / 2 ½ oz / ⅓ cup sun-dried tomatoes in oil, drained
2 tbsp fresh thyme leaves
225 g / 8 oz / 1 ½ cups plain (all purpose) flour
2 tsp baking powder
½ tsp bicarbonate of (baking) soda
½ tsp salt

- Preheat the oven to 180°C (160°C fan) / 350F / gas 4 and line a long, thin loaf tin with greaseproof paper.
- Beat the eggs in a jug with the oil and yoghurt until well mixed.
- Mix the prawns, tomatoes, thyme, flour, raising agents and salt in a bowl, then pour in the egg mixture and stir just enough to combine.
- Scrape the mixture into the tin, then bake in the oven for 20–25 minutes.
- Test with a wooden toothpick, if it comes out clean, the cake is done.
- Transfer the loaf to a wire rack and leave to cool completely before slicing.

King Prawn and Pepper Loaf Cake
531
- Replace the sun-dried tomatoes with a jar of roasted red peppers in oil, drained.

532

SERVES 8

Vegetable and Goats' Cheese Loaf Cake

- Preheat the oven to 170°C (150°C fan) / 340F / gas 3 and line a large loaf tin with non-stick baking paper.
- Sieve the flour and baking powder into a mixing bowl and add the butter and eggs.
- Beat the mixture with an electric whisk for 4 minutes or until smooth and well whipped.
- Fold in the grated vegetables, goats' cheese and Parmesan then scrape the mixture into the loaf tin.
- Bake for 55 minutes or until a skewer inserted in the centre comes out clean.
- Transfer the cake to a wire rack and leave to cool completely before serving.

Vegetable and Feta Loaf Cake 533

- Substitute feta for the goats' cheese.

PREPARATION TIME 20 MINUTES

COOKING TIME 55 MINUTES

INGREDIENTS

300 g / 10 ½ oz / 2 cups self-raising flour
2 tsp baking powder
250 g / 9 oz / 1 ¼ cups butter, softened
5 large eggs
1 carrot, grated
1 parsnip, grated
1 courgette, grated
150 g / 5 ½ oz / ⅔ cup goats' cheese, cubed
75 g / 2 ½ oz / ¾ cup Parmesan, grated

534

MAKES 1 LOAF

Goats' Cheese and Sage Bread

- Mix together the flour, yeast, sugar and salt. Stir in the goats' cheese, sage and 280 ml of warm water.
- Knead the mixture on a lightly oiled surface for 10 minutes or until the dough is smooth and elastic.
- Leave the dough to rest in a lightly oiled bowl, covered with oiled cling film, for 1–2 hours.
- Knead the dough for 2 more minutes then roll it into a fat sausage. Turn it 90° and roll it tightly the other way then tuck the ends under and transfer the dough to a greased loaf tin, keeping the seam underneath.
- Cover the tin with oiled cling film and leave for 45 minutes.
- Preheat the oven to 220°C (200°C fan) / 430F / gas 7.
- Bake for 35–40 minutes or until the underneath sounds hollow when tapped.
- Leave to cool completely on a wire rack before slicing.

**PREPARATION TIME
2 HOURS 30 MINUTES**

COOKING TIME 35–40 MINUTES

INGREDIENTS

400 g / 14 oz / 2 ⅔ cups strong white bread flour
½ tsp easy blend dried yeast
1 tbsp caster (superfine) sugar
1 tsp fine sea salt
100 g / 3 ½ oz / ½ cup goats' cheese, cubed
2 tbsp sage leaves, chopped

Cheddar and Watercress Loaf Cake

535

SERVES 8

Cheddar and Spinach Loaf Cake

536

- Replace the watercress with chopped baby leaf spinach.

Goats' Cheese and Watercress Loaf Cake

537

- Replace the cheddar with 100g / 3 ½ oz / ½ cup of goats' cheese in small cubes.

Bacon and Watercress Loaf Cake

538

- Add 4 chopped rashers of smoked streaky bacon to the cake mixture.

PREPARATION TIME 25 MINUTES

COOKING TIME 20–25 MINUTES

INGREDIENTS

2 large eggs
120 ml / 4 fl. oz / ½ cup sunflower oil
180 ml / 6 fl. oz / ¾ cup Greek yoghurt
75 g / 2 ½ oz / 1 cup watercress, chopped
110 g / 4 oz / 1 cup Cheddar, grated
225 g / 8 oz / 1 ½ cups plain (all purpose) flour
2 tsp baking powder
½ tsp bicarbonate of (baking) soda
½ tsp salt

- Preheat the oven to 180°C (160°C fan) / 355F / gas 4 and line a loaf tin with greaseproof paper.
- Beat the eggs in a jug with the oil, yoghurt, watercress and half of the Cheddar until well mixed.
- Mix the flour, raising agents and salt in a bowl, then pour in the egg mixture and stir just enough to combine.
- Scrape the mixture into the tin and sprinkle over the rest of the cheese, then bake in the oven for 20–25 minutes.
- Test with a wooden toothpick, if it comes out clean, the cake is done.
- Transfer the loaf to a wire rack and leave to cool completely.

539
SERVES 8
Olive, Mushroom and Ham Loaf Cake

- Preheat the oven to 180°C (160°C fan) / 350F / gas 4 and line a large loaf tin with non-stick baking paper.
- Sieve the flour and baking powder into a mixing bowl and add the butter and eggs.
- Beat the mixture with an electric whisk for 4 minutes or until smooth and well whipped.
- Fold in the olives, mushrooms and ham then scrape the mixture into the loaf tin.
- Bake for 55 minutes or until a skewer inserted in the centre comes out clean.
- Transfer the cake to a wire rack and leave to cool completely before serving.

PREPARATION TIME 10 MINUTES

COOKING TIME 55 MINUTES

INGREDIENTS

300 g / 10 ½ oz / 2 cups self-raising flour
2 tsp baking powder
250 g / 9 oz / 1 ¼ cups butter, softened
5 large eggs
75 g / 2 ½ oz / ½ cup green olives, pitted and halved
50 g / 1 ¾ oz / ⅔ cup mushrooms, diced
75 g / 2 ½ oz ham, cubed

Olive Mushroom and Ham Cupcakes
540

- Line a 12-hole cupcake tin with paper cases and spoon in the cake mixture. Reduce the cooking time to 25 minutes.

541
MAKES 12
Ham and Olive Sponge Squares

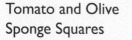

- Preheat the oven to 170°C (150°C fan) / 340F / gas 3 and line a square cake tin with greaseproof paper.
- Sieve the flour and baking powder into a mixing bowl and add the butter and eggs.
- Beat the mixture with an electric whisk for 4 minutes or until smooth and well whipped.
- Fold in the olives and ham then scrape the mixture into the loaf tin.
- Bake for 35 minutes or until a skewer inserted in the centre comes out clean.
- Transfer the cake to a wire rack and leave to cool completely before cutting into squares.

PREPARATION TIME 20 MINUTES

COOKING TIME 35 MINUTES

INGREDIENTS

300 g / 10 ½ oz / 2 cups self-raising flour
2 tsp baking powder
250 g / 9 oz / 1 ¼ cups butter, softened
5 large eggs
75 g / 2 ½ oz / ½ cup green olives, pitted and halved
75 g / 2 ½ oz / ½ cup ham, cubed

Tomato and Olive Sponge Squares
542

- Replace the ham with 4 finely chopped sundried tomatoes.

543
SERVES 8
Rocket and Parmesan Loaf Cake

PREPARATION TIME 20 MINUTES

COOKING TIME 55 MINUTES

....

INGREDIENTS

300 g / 10 ½ oz / 2 cups self-raising
flour
2 tsp baking powder
250 g / 9 oz / 1 ¼ cups butter,
softened
150 g / 5 ½ oz / 1 ½ cups Parmesan,
grated
4 large eggs
50 g / 1 ¾ oz / ⅔ cup rocket (arugula)
leaves, chopped

- Preheat the oven to 170°C (150°C fan) / 340F / gas 3 and line a large loaf tin with greaseproof paper.
- Sieve the flour and baking powder into a mixing bowl and add the butter, Parmesan and eggs.
- Beat the mixture with an electric whisk for 4 minutes or until smooth and well whipped.
- Fold in the rocket and spoon into the tin.
- Bake for 55 minutes or until a skewer inserted in the centre comes out clean.
- Transfer the cake to a wire rack and leave to cool completely before serving.

544
MAKES 4
Pretzels

PREPARATION TIME
2 HOURS 30 MINUTES

COOKING TIME 10 MINUTES

....

INGREDIENTS

300 g / 10 ½ oz / 2 cups strong white
bread flour
½ tsp easy blend dried yeast
1 tbsp butter, melted
1 tsp salt
1 egg, beaten
1 tbsp sugar nibs

- Mix the flour, yeast, butter and salt together in a bowl and stir in 210ml of warm water.
- Bring the mixture into a dough with your hands and knead for 10 minutes.
- Leave to rest in a warm place for 1 hour or until doubled in size.
- Divide the dough into 4 even pieces and roll each one into a long sausage.
- Twist into a classic pretzel shape and transfer to an oiled baking tray.
- Prove for 45 minutes in a warm place.
- Preheat the oven to 220°C (200°C fan) / 425F / gas 7.
- When the pretzels are well risen, brush them with egg and sprinkle with sugar nibs then bake for 10 minutes or until golden brown and cooked through.

545 SERVES 8
Olive and Guacamole Loaf Cake

- Preheat the oven to 180°C (160°C fan) / 355F / gas 4 and line a loaf tin with greaseproof paper.
- Beat the eggs in a jug with the oil, yoghurt, avocado, chilli, spring onion and olives until well mixed.
- Mix the flour, raising agents and salt in a bowl, then pour in the egg mixture and stir just enough to combine.
- Scrape the mixture into the tin, then bake in the oven for 30–35 minutes.
- Test with a wooden toothpick, if it comes out clean, the cake is done.
- Transfer the loaf to a wire rack and leave to cool completely.

PREPARATION TIME 25 MINUTES

COOKING TIME 30–35 MINUTES

INGREDIENTS

2 large eggs
120 ml / 4 fl. oz / ½ cup sunflower oil
180 ml / 6 fl. oz / ¾ cup Greek yoghurt
2 avocados, peeled, stoned and diced
2 red chillies, finely chopped
2 spring onions, finely chopped
110 g / 4 oz / ⅔ cup mixed olives, pitted and sliced
225 g / 8 oz / 1 ½ cups plain (all purpose) flour
2 tsp baking powder
½ tsp bicarbonate of (baking) soda
½ tsp salt

Olive and Thyme Mini Loaf Cakes
546 MAKES 12

PREPARATION TIME 15 MINUTES

COOKING TIME 10–15 MINUTES

INGREDIENTS

2 large eggs
120 ml / 4 fl. oz / ½ cup sunflower oil
180 ml / 6 fl. oz / ¾ cup Greek yoghurt
2 tbsp Parmesan, finely grated
150 g / 5 ½ oz / 1 cup green olives, pitted
2 tbsp fresh thyme leaves
225 g / 8 oz / 1 ½ cups plain (all purpose) flour
2 tsp baking powder
½ tsp bicarbonate of (baking) soda
½ tsp salt

- Preheat the oven to 180°C (160°C fan) / 350F / gas 4 and oil a 24-hole silicone mini loaf mould.
- Beat the egg in a jug with the oil, yoghurt, Parmesan, olives and thyme until well mixed.
- Mix the flour, raising agents and salt in a bowl, then pour in the egg mixture and stir just enough to combine.
- Divide the mixture between the moulds, then bake in the oven for 10–15 minutes.
- Test with a wooden toothpick, if it comes out clean, the cakes are done.

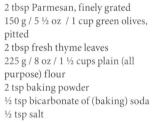

Ham, Sage and Onion Loaf Cake
547 SERVES 8

PREPARATION TIME 20 MINUTES

COOKING TIME 55 MINUTES

INGREDIENTS

2 onions, quartered and sliced
2 tbsp olive oil
300 g / 10 ½ oz / 2 cups self-raising flour
2 tsp baking powder
250 g / 9 oz / 1 ¼ cups butter, softened
5 large eggs
100 g / 3 ½ oz / ⅔ cup ham, cubed
2 tbsp fresh sage leaves, chopped

- Preheat the oven to 170°C (150°C fan) / 325F / gas 3 and line a loaf tin with greaseproof paper.
- Fry the onions in the oil for 10 minutes or until softened. Leave to cool.
- Sieve the flour and baking powder into a mixing bowl and add the butter and eggs.
- Beat the mixture with an electric whisk for 4 minutes or until smooth and well whipped.
- Fold in the onions, ham and sage then scrape the mixture into the loaf tin.
- Bake for 55 minutes or until a skewer inserted in the centre comes out clean.
- Transfer the cake to a wire rack and leave to cool completely before serving.

548

MAKES 2

Tuna and Black Olive Loaf Cake

Smoked Mackerel and Black Olive Loaf Cake

549

- Replace the tuna with 2 fillets of smoked mackerel that have been skinned and flaked.

Tuna and Sweetcorn Loaf Cake

550

- Replace the olives with 100 g / 3 ½ oz / ⅔ cup of canned sweetcorn kernels.

PREPARATION TIME 20 MINUTES

COOKING TIME 30–35 MINUTES

....

INGREDIENTS

2 large eggs
120 ml / 4 fl. oz / ½ cup sunflower oil
180 ml / 6 fl. oz / ¾ cup Greek yoghurt
300 g / 10 ½ oz / 1 ½ cups canned tuna, drained
100 g / 2 ½ oz / ⅔ cup black olives, pitted and sliced
225 g / 8 oz / 1 ½ cups plain (all purpose) flour
2 tsp baking powder
½ tsp bicarbonate of (baking) soda
½ tsp salt

- Preheat the oven to 180°C (160°C fan) / 355F / gas 4 and line 2 small loaf tins with greaseproof paper.
- Beat the eggs in a jug with the oil and yoghurt until well mixed.
- Mix the tuna, olives, flour, raising agents and salt in a bowl, then pour in the egg mixture and stir just enough to combine.
- Divide the mixture between the tins, then bake in the oven for 30–35 minutes.
- Test with a wooden toothpick, if it comes out clean, the cakes are done.
- Transfer the loaves to a wire rack and leave to cool completely.

551

SERVES 8 Spinach and Pine Nut Loaf Cake

- Preheat the oven to 180°C (160°C fan) / 350F / gas 4 and line a loaf tin with greaseproof paper.
- Put the spinach in a saucepan with 2 tbsp water and cook with the lid on for 3 minutes. When cool enough to handle, squeeze out all the moisture and chop.
- Beat the eggs in a jug with the oil, yoghurt and chopped spinach until well mixed.
- Mix the pine nuts, flour, raising agents and salt in a bowl, then pour in the egg mixture and stir just enough to combine.
- Scrape the mixture into the tin, then bake in the oven for 20–25 minutes.
- Test with a wooden toothpick, if it comes out clean, the cake is done.
- Transfer the loaf to a wire rack and leave to cool completely before slicing.

PREPARATION TIME 25 MINUTES

COOKING TIME 20–25 MINUTES

INGREDIENTS

110 g / 4 oz / 1 ⅓ cups spinach
2 large eggs
120 ml / 4 fl. oz / ½ cup sunflower oil
180 ml / 6 fl. oz / ¾ cup Greek yoghurt
75 g / 2 ½ oz / ⅔ cup pine nuts
225 g / 8 oz / 1 ½ cups plain (all purpose) flour
2 tsp baking powder
½ tsp bicarbonate of (baking) soda
½ tsp salt

Watercress and Pine Nut Loaf Cake   552

- Replace the spinach with an equal weight of watercress and wilt as before.

553

SERVES 8 Bacon and Black Olive Loaf Cake

- Preheat the oven to 180°C (160°C fan) / 355F / gas 4 and line a loaf tin with greaseproof paper.
- Beat the eggs in a jug with the oil, yoghurt, bacon and olives until well mixed.
- Mix the flour, raising agents and salt in a bowl, then pour in the egg mixture and stir just enough to combine.
- Scrape the mixture into the tin, then bake in the oven for 20–25 minutes.
- Test with a wooden toothpick, if it comes out clean, the cake is done.
- Transfer the loaf to a wire rack and leave to cool completely.

PREPARATION TIME 25 MINUTES

COOKING TIME 20–25 MINUTES

INGREDIENTS

2 large eggs
120 ml / 4 fl. oz / ½ cup sunflower oil
180 ml / 6 fl. oz / ¾ cup Greek yoghurt
110 g / 4 oz / ⅔ cup streaky bacon, chopped
110 g / 4 oz / ⅔ cup black olives, pitted and sliced
225 g / 8 oz / 1 ½ cups plain (all purpose) flour
2 tsp baking powder
½ tsp bicarbonate of (baking) soda
½ tsp salt

Bacon and Sage Loaf Cake   554

- Omit the olives and add 2 tbsp of chopped fresh sage leaves to the cake mixture.

555
SERVES 8

Gluten-free Bacon and Black Olive Loaf

PREPARATION TIME 25 MINUTES

COOKING TIME 20–25 MINUTES

INGREDIENTS

2 large eggs
120 ml / 4 fl. oz / ½ cup sunflower oil
180 ml / 6 fl. oz / ¾ cup Greek
yoghurt
110 g / 4 oz / ⅔ cup streaky bacon,
chopped
110 g / 4 oz / ⅔ cup black olives,
pitted and sliced
225 g / 8 oz / 1 ½ cups rice flour
2 tsp baking powder
½ tsp bicarbonate of (baking) soda
½ tsp salt

- Preheat the oven to 180⁰C (160⁰C fan) / 355F / gas 4 and line a loaf tin with greaseproof paper.
- Beat the eggs in a jug with the oil, yoghurt, bacon and olives until well mixed.
- Mix the flour, raising agents and salt in a bowl, then pour in the egg mixture and stir just enough to combine.
- Scrape the mixture into the tin, then bake in the oven for 20–25 minutes.
- Test with a wooden toothpick, if it comes out clean, the cake is done.
- Transfer the loaf to a wire rack and leave to cool completely.

Gluten-free Olive and Caper Loaf Cake

556

- Omit the bacon and add 2 tbsp of capers to the cake mixture.

557
SERVES 10

Caper and Sun-dried Tomato Loaf Cake

PREPARATION TIME 25 MINUTES

COOKING TIME 20–25 MINUTES

INGREDIENTS

2 large eggs
120 ml / 4 fl. oz / ½ cup sunflower oil
180 ml / 6 fl. oz / ¾ cup Greek
yoghurt
3 tbsp capers, drained
75 g / 2 ½ oz / ⅓ cup sun-dried
tomatoes in oil, drained
225 g / 8 oz / 1 ½ cups plain (all
purpose) flour
2 tsp baking powder
½ tsp bicarbonate of (baking) soda
½ tsp salt

- Preheat the oven to 180⁰C (160⁰C fan) / 350F / gas 4 and butter a baking dish or loaf tin.
- Beat the eggs in a jug with the oil and yoghurt until well mixed.
- Mix the capers, tomatoes, flour, raising agents and salt in a bowl, then pour in the egg mixture and stir just enough to combine.
- Scrape the mixture into the dish, then bake in the oven for 20–25 minutes.
- Test with a wooden toothpick, if it comes out clean, the cake is done.
- Transfer the loaf to a wire rack and leave to cool completely before slicing.

Caper and Tomato Loaf Cake

558

- Replace the sun-dried tomatoes with 100 g / 3 ½ oz / ½ cup of cherry tomatoes, cut into quarters.

559

MAKES 12 # Roasted Pepper Rolls

- Mix together the flours, yeast, sugar and salt. Stir in the peppers and 280 ml of warm water.
- Knead the mixture on a lightly oiled surface with your hands for 10 minutes or until smooth and elastic.
- Leave the dough to rest in a lightly oiled bowl, covered with oiled cling film, for 1–2 hours.
- Knead it for 2 more minutes then split it into 12 even pieces and shape into rolls
- Transfer the rolls to a greased baking tray and cover with oiled cling film. Leave to prove for 1 hour.
- Preheat the oven to 220⁰C (200⁰C fan) / 430F / gas 7 and slash the tops of the rolls with a sharp knife.
- Bake for 15–20 minutes or until the rolls sound hollow when you tap them underneath.
- Transfer to a wire rack and leave to cool.

PREPARATION TIME
2 HOURS 30 MINUTES
COOKING TIME 15–20 MINUTES

INGREDIENTS

350 g / 12 ½ oz / 2 ⅓ cups strong white bread flour, plus extra for dusting
50 g / 1 ¾ oz / ⅓ cup stoneground wholemeal flour
½ tsp easy blend dried yeast
1 tbsp caster (superfine) sugar
1 tsp fine sea salt
1 jar mixed roasted peppers in oil, drained

Roasted Pepper and Parmesan Rolls

560

- Five minutes before the end of cooking, sprinkle with Parmesan for a cheesy crust.

561

MAKES 12 # Cheese Scones

- Preheat the oven to 220°C (200°C fan) / 425F / gas 7 and line a baking tray with greaseproof paper.
- Rub the butter into the flour with your fingertips until the mixture resembles fine breadcrumbs then stir in the mustard powder and cayenne pepper.
- Add the milk and ¾ of the cheese and mix together into a pliable dough.
- Turn the dough out onto a floured work surface and flatten it into a rectangle, 2 cm / 1 in thick..
- Use a round pastry cutter to stamp out the scones then transfer them to the baking tray.
- Brush the scones with milk, sprinkle with the rest of the cheese and bake for 12–15 minutes or until golden brown and cooked through.
- Transfer the scones to a wire rack to cool a little before serving.

PREPARATION TIME 10 MINUTES
COOKING TIME 12–15 MINUTES

INGREDIENTS

75 g / 2 ½ oz / ⅓ cup butter, cubed
250 g / 9 oz / 1 ⅔ cups self-raising flour, plus extra for dusting
½ tsp mustard powder
¼ tsp cayenne pepper
150 ml / 5 ½ fl. oz / ⅔ cup milk, plus extra for brushing
100 g / 3 ½ oz / 1 cup Red Leicester cheese, grated

Cheese and Thyme Scones

562

- Add 2 tbsp of fresh thyme leaves to the mixture when you add the mustard powder.

563

SERVES 8

Mushroom and Prosciutto Loaf

PREPARATION TIME 20 MINUTES

COOKING TIME 55 MINUTES

INGREDIENTS

300 g / 10 ½ oz / 2 cups self-raising flour
2 tsp baking powder
250 g / 9 oz / 1 ¼ cups butter, softened
5 large eggs
200 g / 7 oz / 1 ⅓ cups button mushrooms, sliced
6 slices prosciutto, chopped

- Preheat the oven to 170ºC (150ºC fan) / 340F / gas 3 and line a large loaf tin with non-stick baking paper.
- Sieve the flour and baking powder into a mixing bowl and add the butter and eggs.
- Beat the mixture with an electric whisk for 4 minutes or until smooth and well whipped.
- Fold in the mushrooms and prosciutto then scrape the mixture into the loaf tin.
- Bake for 55 minutes or until a skewer inserted in the centre comes out clean.
- Transfer the cake to a wire rack and leave to cool completely before serving.

564

SERVES 8

Salmon, Dill and Goats' Cheese Loaf

PREPARATION TIME 15 MINUTES

COOKING TIME 30–35 MINUTES

INGREDIENTS

2 large eggs
120 ml / 4 fl. oz / ½ cup sunflower oil
180 ml / 6 fl. oz / ⅔ cup Greek yoghurt
110 g / 4 oz / ½ cup goats' cheese, cubed
110 g / 4 oz / ½ cup smoked salmon, chopped
2 tbsp dill, chopped
225 g / 8 oz / 1 ½ cups plain (all purpose) flour
2 tsp baking powder
½ tsp bicarbonate of (baking) soda
½ tsp salt

- Preheat the oven to 180ºC (160ºC fan) / 355F / gas 4 and line a loaf tin with greaseproof paper.
- Beat the eggs in a jug with the oil, yoghurt and goats' cheese until well mixed.
- Mix the salmon, dill, flour, raising agents and salt in a bowl, then pour in the egg mixture and stir just enough to combine.
- Scrape the mixture into the tin, then bake in the oven for 30–35 minutes.
- Test with a wooden toothpick, if it comes out clean, the cake is done.
- Transfer the loaf to a wire rack and leave to cool completely.

565

SERVES 8

Tuna and Cream Cheese Loaf Cake

- Preheat the oven to 180°C (160°C fan) / 355F / gas 4 and line a loaf tin with greaseproof paper.
- Beat the eggs in a jug with the oil, yoghurt and cream cheese until well mixed.
- Mix the tuna, flour, raising agents and salt in a bowl, then pour in the egg mixture and stir just enough to combine.
- Scrape the mixture into the tin, then bake in the oven for 30–35 minutes.
- Test with a wooden toothpick, if it comes out clean, the cake is done.
- Transfer the loaf to a wire rack and leave to cool completely.

PREPARATION TIME 20 MINUTES

COOKING TIME 30–35 MINUTES

INGREDIENTS

2 large eggs
120 ml / 4 fl. oz / ½ cup sunflower oil
180 ml / 6 fl. oz / ⅔ cup Greek yoghurt
3 tbsp cream cheese
300 g / 10 ½ oz /1 ½ cups canned tuna, drained
225 g / 8 oz / 1 ½ cups plain (all purpose) flour
2 tsp baking powder
½ tsp bicarbonate of (baking) soda
½ tsp salt

566

SERVES 8

Pine Nut and Herb Loaf

PREPARATION TIME 20 MINUTES

COOKING TIME 55 MINUTES

INGREDIENTS

300 g / 10 ½ oz / 2 cups self-raising flour
2 tsp baking powder
250 g / 9 oz / 1 ¼ cups butter, softened
5 large eggs
4 tbsp pine nuts
2 tbsp fresh thyme leaves
2 tbsp chives, chopped

- Preheat the oven to 170°C (150°C fan) / 340F / gas 3 and line a large loaf tin with non-stick baking paper.
- Sieve the flour and baking powder into a mixing bowl and add the butter and eggs.
- Beat the mixture with an electric whisk for 4 minutes or until smooth and well whipped.
- Fold in the pine nuts, thyme and chives then scrape the mixture into the loaf tin.
- Bake for 55 minutes or until a skewer inserted in the centre comes out clean.
- Transfer the cake to a wire rack and leave to cool completely before serving.

567

SERVES 10

Courgette and Beetroot Loaf

PREPARATION TIME 20 MINUTES

COOKING TIME 55 MINUTES

INGREDIENTS

300 g / 10 ½ oz / 2 cups self-raising flour
2 tsp baking powder
250 g / 9 oz / 1 ¼ cups butter, softened
5 large eggs
1 courgette (zucchini), quartered and sliced
2 tbsp thyme leaves
2 cooked beetroots, cubed

- Preheat the oven to 170°C (150°C fan) / 340F / gas 3 and line a loaf tin with non-stick baking paper.
- Sieve the flour and baking powder into a mixing bowl and add the butter and eggs.
- Beat the mixture with an electric whisk for 4 minutes or until smooth and well whipped.
- Fold in the courgette, thyme and beetroot then scrape the mixture into the loaf tin.
- Bake for 55 minutes or until a skewer inserted in the centre comes out clean.
- Transfer the cake to a wire rack and leave to cool completely before serving.

568

MAKES 12

Crab, Chilli and Lime Muffins

PREPARATION TIME 15 MINUTES

COOKING TIME 20–25 MINUTES

INGREDIENTS

2 large eggs
120 ml / 4 fl. oz / ½ cup sunflower oil
180 ml / 6 fl. oz / ¾ cup Greek yoghurt
2 tbsp Parmesan, finely grated
150 g / 5 ½ oz / ¾ cup fresh crab meat
1 red chilli (chili), finely chopped
1 lime, zest finely grated
1 tbsp coriander (cilantro) leaves, chopped
225 g / 8 oz / 1 ½ cups plain (all purpose) flour
2 tsp baking powder
½ tsp bicarbonate of (baking) soda
½ tsp salt

- Preheat the oven to 180°C (160°C fan) / 350F / gas 4 and oil a 12-hole silicone muffin mould.
- Beat the eggs in a jug with the oil, yoghurt, Parmesan, crab, chilli, lime and coriander until well mixed.
- Mix the flour, raising agents and salt in a bowl, then pour in the egg mixture and stir just enough to combine.
- Divide the mixture between the moulds, then bake in the oven for 20–25 minutes.
- Test with a wooden toothpick, if it comes out clean, the cakes are done.

Shrimp, Chilli and Lime Muffins
569

- Replace the crab meat with 150 g / 5 oz / 1 cup of peeled grey shrimp.

570

MAKES 12

Roquefort Mini Loaf Cakes

PREPARATION TIME 15 MINUTES

COOKING TIME 10–15 MINUTES

INGREDIENTS

2 large eggs
120 ml / 4 fl. oz / ½ cup sunflower oil
180 ml / 6 fl. oz / ¾ cup Greek yoghurt
150 g / 5 ½ oz / ⅔ cup Roquefort, cubed
225 g / 8 oz / 1 ½ cups plain (all purpose) flour
2 tsp baking powder
½ tsp bicarbonate of (baking) soda
½ tsp salt

- Preheat the oven to 180°C (160°C fan) / 350F / gas 4 and oil 12 mini loaf moulds.
- Beat the eggs in a jug with the oil, yoghurt and Roquefort until well mixed.
- Mix the flour, raising agents and salt in a bowl, then pour in the egg mixture and stir just enough to combine.
- Divide the mixture between the cases, then bake in the oven for 10–15 minutes.
- Test with a wooden toothpick, if it comes out clean, the cakes are done.

Bacon Mini Loaf Cakes
571

- Replace the Roquefort with 100 g / 3 ½ oz / ⅔ cup of smoked bacon lardons that have been fried in olive oil for 2 minutes.

Index

Index